Members of Rifaʻiya Order, Muslim New Year 1965

Saint and Sufi
in Modern Egypt

*An Essay in the Sociology
of Religion*

———◆———

MICHAEL GILSENAN

OXFORD
AT THE CLARENDON PRESS
1973

Oxford University Press, Ely House, London W. 1

GLASGOW NEW YORK TORONTO MELBOURNE WELLINGTON
CAPE TOWN IBADAN NAIROBI DAR ES SALAAM LUSAKA ADDIS ABABA
DELHI BOMBAY CALCUTTA MADRAS KARACHI LAHORE DACCA
KUALA LUMPUR SINGAPORE HONG KONG TOKYO

ISBN 0 19 8231814

© *Oxford University Press 1973*

*Printed in Great Britain
at the University Press, Oxford
by Vivian Ridler
Printer to the University*

ACKNOWLEDGEMENTS

THIS study was carried out in 1964–6 under the auspices of the Social Science Research Centre of the American University in Cairo. I should like to record the great debt I owe the Centre and its director, Dr. Laila al Hamamsy, and my thanks for all the facilities they made available. A year at St. Antony's College, Oxford, and a further year at the Centre for Middle Eastern Studies at Harvard University (under its acting director, Dr. Ted Lockard) gave me an opportunity to write up and then to rethink my material. Three months in 1968 on the Committee for the Study of New Nations at the University of Chicago provided an intellectual stimulus for which I am most grateful. Dr. Emrys Peters kindly made a detailed critique of an early draft of Chapter I. Dr. Bryan Wilson invited me to present my ideas to his seminar on the sociology of religion and was most helpful in his comments. Professor Ernest Gellner read the work in its doctoral thesis form and offered criticisms and suggestions that were as invaluable as was also his personal encouragement. My supervisor at Oxford, Professor Sir E. E. Evans-Pritchard patiently guided a student haltingly following in his footsteps in the sociological study of Sufi Orders. I owe special thanks to Mr. Albert Hourani who has been a constant source of wise counsel and scholarly criticism and has unstintingly given of his time. Elizabeth Stewart typed the work in thesis form and to her and Charles Stewart I owe a friend's particular gratitude. Miss Eleanor Kelly was kind enough to see the work through the agonies of the final typing stage for which I am most grateful. Finally, as is true of all anthropologists, my greatest debt is to those whose lives and beliefs I studied. Without the tolerance, humour, and generosity of Egyptians from every walk of life, and the particular help of Sheikh Ibrahim of the *Hamidiya Shadhiliya* and his followers, research would have been impossible. This book is only a small mark of gratitude for their kindness to a stranger.

MICHAEL GILSENAN

Manchester 1972

CONTENTS

INTRODUCTION

SUFISM (*tasawwuf*) is the term applied to the mystical life as it has developed within the general framework of Islam.[1] It has followed two main streams. The first, beginning in the early centuries after the Prophet Muhammad's death, is that of individuals who felt a call to the mystical or devotional life. The second, and our chief concern here, is the corporate pursuit of the 'way', the *tariqa* (pl. *turuq*), by groups of Muslims who came together in the Sufi Brotherhoods following one of the great Saints of medieval Islam.[2] Thus most of the Egyptian Orders claim spiritual descent from 'Abd el Qadir el Jilani (d. 1166) whose disciples began to gather around the end of the twelfth century, or Ahmad al Rifa'i (d. 1175), or Hassan al Shadhili (d. 1258) or finally Ahmad al Bedawi (d. 1276) whose tomb is still the centre of the most popular Saint's Day celebration in Egypt.

The beginnings of popular Sufism and of its wide geographical spread and diversity across the Middle East are thus temporally well defined. Let us note that at almost exactly the same period in Europe there was an equally significant upsurge of religious energy: 'For several centuries, until nearly the end of the eleventh century, the tendency had been to develop an ever greater degree of identity of purpose and organisation, and to delight in the unity of an achieved ideal. Then within little more than a hundred years all the main varieties of medieval religious organisation came into existence.'[3] These two relatively sudden flowerings of religious movements were generated in historical contexts that seem almost diametrically opposed. In Europe, the dominance of the great aristocratic Orders such as the Cistercians and the later spread of the Friars in the towns among the urban masses were part of an

[1] It is neither within the scope of this study nor my competence to give an account of the mystical tradition in Islam. I therefore limit myself throughout to the briefest discussion of the complex topics reviewed elsewhere in Western scholarship by R. A. Nicholson, Louis Massignon, and Fathers Anawati and Gardet (see bibliography).

[2] I have followed a simplified system of transliteration for Arabic words, omitting all dots and dashes.

[3] Southern, R. W., *Western Society and the Church in the Middle Ages*, Harmondsworth: Penguin Books, 1970, p. 215.

expansion of society in new political, economic, and social directions. In the Muslim World, on the other hand, though we know
relatively little of the specific circumstances of the Brotherhoods'
growth, it is clear that they arose in a period of retreat, instability,
and social dislocation. In part this was due to internal factors such
as the upsurge in importance of tribal groups (whether Kurdish,
Turkoman, or Arab) and the dynastic struggles of the twelfth and
thirteenth centuries; in part, also, to the external pressure of in-
vasions from the East (Baghdad was taken and sacked in 1258) and,
bridging the European and Islamic settings, to the advent of the
expanding West in the shape of the Crusaders.[1] There is some
evidence to suppose that in this context the Sufi Brotherhoods
answered a pressing need for guaranteeing the concentration of
large sections of the Muslim population at certain places and
seasons of the year convenient for military action. And it is reasonable to suggest that, in the urban centres which, generally speaking,
lacked a corporate municipal identity and a citizenry in the European sense, popular Sufism became a framework for associational
life within a common social, normative, and ritual order, at a time
when the very bases of this order were coming under increasingly
severe stress.[2]

The geographical and numerical expansion of the *turuq* has been
dramatic in scale. They exist wherever those who call themselves
Muslims exist—across the whole of the Near and Middle East,
through West and Central Africa, the Sudan, the Horn of Africa,
and the East African coast to India and into South-east Asia. The
Orders have been one of the main missionary channels of conversion
of non-Arab peoples to Islam. At the same time, as institutions of
cultural adaptation, they have provided a means of incorporating
local religious customs and beliefs into their eclectic fold with an
Islamic colouring, an adaptation which has often led to accusations
of permitting or encouraging non-Islamic practices by their
absorption of indigenous religious elements.

Despite the lack of detailed evidence still needed for so many
areas, a fairly clear picture does emerge from a wide variety of
societies over the more recent historical period. Talking of Egypt,

[1] It should be remembered that the main Crusader Orders adopted the
Cistercian Rule. Southern, op. cit., p. 257.

[2] On the question of urban life in medieval Islam the reader is referred to
Lapidus, I. M., *Muslim Cities in the Later Middle Ages*, Cambridge, Mass.:
Harvard University Press, 1967.

Heyworth-Dunne claims that by the eighteenth century few seemed able to call themselves Muslims without belonging to one or more of the Orders.[1] In West Africa, General Marty observed in 1917 that 'Les Noirs islamisés du Sénégal se classent d'eux-mêmes et sans exception, sous la bannière religieuse des Marabouts et ne comprennent l'Islam que sous la forme de l'affiliation à une "voie" mystique ou plus exactement sous la forme de l'obéissance à un Serigne. . . .'[2] I. M. Lewis says of the Horn of Africa that the hold of the *turuq* is such 'that the profession of faith is virtually synonymous with attachment to, if not formal membership of, an Order'.[3] While from a literary source we get this outburst in a description of village life in Egypt some seventy years ago: 'And the Sheikhs of the Orders! What about the Sheikhs of the Orders!!! They were many scattered around the regions of the country. The town was scarcely empty of them for a week. Their ways were all different and they split up the people among them and made them into factions.'[4]

Examples such as these could be multiplied. What needs to be stressed is that this wide dissemination of the Brotherhoods from China to Morocco and from Guinea to Indonesia is linked with a great variety of both form and function. Popular Sufism has demonstrated a considerable range and flexibility in its adaptation to societies differing profoundly both in social and political structure and in the wider cultural perspective. The classic study of a *tariqa* in a transhumant society, Evans-Pritchard's *Sanusi of Cyrenaica*, shows, for example, how the *Sanusiya* established themselves in the Bedouin society of the Western Desert of Egypt.[5] The Order fitted its own structure 'interstitially' to that of the tribes, setting up *zawiyas* on the boundaries of group territories, and often also on the major trade routes (this establishment of Sufi lodges along caravan routes has always been a significant factor in their growth throughout Africa and the Middle East). Coming from outside the social system and being therefore unattached to any particular interest or dominant lineage, they were able to operate

[1] Heyworth-Dunne, J., *Introduction to the History of Education in Modern Egypt*, London: Luzac & Co., 1938, p. 10.

[2] Marty, A., *Études sur L'Islam au Sénégal: les personnes*, Paris, 1917, p. 3.

[3] Lewis, I. M. (ed.), *Islam in Tropical Africa*, London: O.U.P., 1966, p. 9.

[4] Husain, Taha, *Al Ayyam*, Cairo, 1958.

[5] Evans-Pritchard, E. E., *The Sanusi of Cyrenaica*, London: O.U.P., 1949, *passim*.

over the normal divisions in the segmentary lineage structure. The lodges developed a multiplicity of spheres of activity. They were at once schools, caravanserai, commercial and social focal points, law courts, banks, storehouses, poor houses, burial grounds, and the source and channel of divine grace. In the very different setting of agricultural Senegal, on the other hand, the *Muridiya* Order administer whole villages centring on the Sheikh and the community of young disciples who for some of the year work in the fields and for the rest study and travel as missionaries. The holy city of Touba, the equivalent of the celebrated *Sanusi* 'university *zawiya*' of Jaghbub, serves as a place of pilgrimage, a centre for Quran studies and as residence for the *Khalifa* General of the Order, his collateral relatives and descendants, and the great marabouts. The *tariqa* pioneers sedentarization and land reclamation, and, in a country where the economy depends in large measure on the ground-nut crop, the *Muridiya* communities produce a little more than half of the total harvest according to Monteil.[1]

Both these cases demonstrate the former political importance of the Orders in the Muslim World. In segmentary lineage societies they cut across the ties of geography, kinship, and tribal affiliation, forming a framework for broader sets of social relations and political cohesion. They provided mediators and peacemakers in a system in which the feud was only one element in the constant tension born out of the need for security and the demands which ecology, the allocation of resources, and the political structure made of the constituent groups. They set up and became guardians of sanctuary areas, or traversed the uncertain line between the realm of central authority and the 'zone of dissidence' as was the case in Morocco.[2] By contrast, their importance in nineteenth-century Egypt and Turkey was often due as much to power at the Sultan's court as to their integral part in the daily life of the people.

There is one crucial implication that these random illustrations have, I hope, suggested, but which needs to be clearly stated. It is this: the term 'Sufi Order' is not in any useful sense a sociological classification. I mean by this that it does not denote a set of common defining characteristics which go to make up a distinct type of

---

[1] Monteil, Vincent, *L'Islam noir*, Paris: Éditions du Seuil, 1964; the present tense refers to the year of publication of Monteil's study.

[2] For a discussion of the historical developments in the role of the Orders in the modern period in Morocco and Algeria see Berque, Jacques, *French North Africa: The Maghreb between Two World Wars*, New York: Praeger, 1967.

social entity and mark it out as a special form of association with a characteristic pattern of social relations. On the contrary, in itself it conveys very little about important problems such as distribution of and accession to authority, or mode of entry, or content of membership of any group which designates itself a *tariqa*. Unlike the term 'sect', which through the writings of sociologists from Ernst Troeltsch down to Bryan Wilson has come to signify a particular complex of elements, 'Sufi Order' only indicates the notion of a fraternal organization founded on principles held to be Islamic, bound together by loyalty to a Sheikh or Guide (*murshid*) who is at the head of a pyramidal hierarchy of ranks, and is thought to be connected by a chain of grace or blessing and sometimes blood-kinship to a founding Saint. Of other key questions we can assume virtually nothing, and formal typologies developed in a sociological tradition centred in the study of Christianity are as likely to hinder as to help us.

What is subsumed under the rubric '*tariqa*' is a variety of religious groupings bearing a variety of social meanings and functions in a variety of social, economic, and political settings. The Brotherhoods became as multi-faceted as the worlds of which they were so integral and representative a part—now military, now pietistic; now devoted to scholarly and theological pursuits, now to ecstatics and the intoxication of the senses; now the province of the religious and social élite, now of the illiterate and deprived masses; dedicated to the highest mysteries of the few, and to the exoteric simplicities of the many. A Muslim scholar expresses this multifariousness in the image of a circle: 'The circumference is the Shari'ah (Holy Law) whose totality comprises the whole of the Muslim community. . . . The radii symbolize the *Turuq*. . . . Each radius is a path from the circumference to the centre. As the Sufis say there are as many paths to God as there are children of Adam. . . . Finally at the Centre there is the *Haqiqah* or Truth.'[1] This apt Sufi metaphor highlights the diversity and particularity of these 'paths' to the Centre. It is an indication of the flexibility and adaptability of the Orders that it is impossible to say that they are in some way inherently or essentially the product of, or more suited to, an urban or rural or desert environment; for they belong equally in all. In this sense, perhaps, they were the most socially

---

[1] Nasr, Seyyed Hussein, *The Ideals and Realities of Islam*, New York: Praeger, 1967, p. 122.

important demonstration of what it meant to speak of the Islamic community, the *umma*, and they gave it through the vast network of extra-local, extra-territorial ties, a social dimension lacking in the theological and constitutional theories of the legists.

In Egypt, the particular society with which this study is concerned, there are no doctrinal differences which set the members off from other Muslims, nor do any of the Orders claim a unique insight into the Revelation or the Sunna (the theory or practice consecrated either by the Prophet Muhammad's example or by the tradition of the Islamic community). Multiple membership is an extremely common phenomenon, though there is some indication that in parts of the country at different times association with a specific *tariqa* was linked with village, and even, in a looser way, with provincial social and political organization. In contrast to Evans-Pritchard's analysis of the *Sanusi*, then, the *turuq* of Egypt became an organic *part* of the structure of this sedentary stratified society rather than being in any sense 'outside' or 'interstitial' to it.

I shall examine and attempt to offer an explanation for the transformation of the position of the Orders in Egypt since the turn of the century. For it is quite clear that they have suffered a marked decline in what was once a centre of their activities, and have become quite marginal to the wider society. Much attention is rightly paid by sociologists to the rise of religious movements in the 'Third World'. The cargo cult and the 'native' African churches are dramatic and concentrated examples of the effects of the disruption of other cultures by the colonial experience. However, preoccupation with the problems of rapid large-scale change has turned the focus rather more on the way in which religious institutions emerge than on the equally fruitful question of why and how they decline and lose their social authenticity or relevance to wider social purposes. Yet this is the other side of the same analytical coin. When this entails, as it does in this case, the study of what is sometimes slightly despairingly called 'complex societies' by anthropologists, the uncertain line between sociology and history must at least be tentatively crossed if we are to deal at all satisfactorily with the types of social process with which we are continually confronted. I shall therefore try to relate the shift in the position and function of the *turuq*, and, indeed, of popular religious leadership in general, to the evolving structure of Egyptian society under colonial domination.

At the same time I shall describe the founding and fortunes of the only Order in modern Egypt which has succeeded, in however limited a way, in expanding its membership and activities. This organization, the *Hamidiya Shadhiliya*, was established in the first decades of this century and formally recognized in 1926. The founder, considered by his followers to be a Saint, died in 1939 and was succeeded by his son, the present Sheikh. At the time of my research in 1964-6 it was the most highly organized and active group in Egypt, and numbered somewhere between 12,000 and 16,000 members concentrated mostly in Cairo and the towns of the Nile delta.[1] Since some of the members who knew the Saint himself are still alive, it presents us with the opportunity of studying the dynamics of a religious movement at perhaps the most crucial period of its existence, in the years immediately following the leader's call. Though all the Orders are alike in their formal institutional structure, only the *Hamidiya Shadhiliya* stresses a comprehensive direction and control over its brothers. It is, therefore, something of a special case and its unusual features help to explain its modest growth and adaptation to change at a time when popular Sufism in general has undergone an eclipse in its social significance.

[1] According to the present Head of the High Sufi Council there are still some sixty of the Brotherhoods in existence, but the actual number of adherents in any real sense is only a very small percentage of the population. See Alwan, Muhammad Mahmud, *at-Tasawwuf al Islami*, Cairo, 1958.

I

SAINT AND FOUNDER

Religious Leadership

At the core of the religion of Islam is the once-for-all revelation of the Quran. It was delivered in the Arabic language in the form of verbal signs (*ayat*) which are held to be miraculous in nature and God-given. Secondly, it was conveyed through a human agent who was the 'seal of Prophecy', the last Prophet God would employ in his dealings with men. He is the final Prophet, preceded by others such as Moses and Christ but followed by none, for the final Revelation. A warner, a medium for what has been 'sent down' (*tanzil*), he is not a worker of miracles but the founder of a community, an *umma*, under the guidance and protection of an omnipotent, transcendent, historically acting God. The relations of members of this community to Allah are to be marked by absolute submission (the meaning of the word *Islam*), obedience, and thankfulness. At the same time Muslims are to strive to realize, through corporate action, the historical role of the community.

The profound tensions within Islam spring in part from the oppositions between God and Man, this world (*dunya*) and the hereafter (*akhira*) of the Quranic vision.[1] They derive also from the discrepancy between idealized Islamic history and its realities both in the relations of Muslim to Muslim and of the *umma* to those outside it. The Quranic opposition of believer and unbeliever is at the centre of a wider Islamic tension with the world which is not so much one of dichotomies of flesh and spirit, sin and redemption, temptation and deliverance, as of the outworkings of Muslim communal socio-political history, as distinct from the history of communities of the Dar el Harb (realm of warfare), and the rule of Holy Law. At periods of crisis and disruption in the internal and external life of the *umma* this tension has again and again exploded

---

[1] For a full treatment of this subject, see Izutsu, T., *The Structure of Ethical Terms in the Koran*, Tokyo: Keio Institute, 1959 and the same author's *God and Man in the Koran: Semantics of the Koranic Weltanschauung*, Tokyo: Keio Institute, 1964.

in one of the great religious movements of Islam, characteristically with a strong military and political dimension (the Wahhabis, the Mahdist movement of the Sudan, the Kharijites amongst many others). Such a period of crisis in the twelfth century sparked off the rise of the Sufi Orders, and such a period in modern times has brought about their decline, and the emergence of new forms of organization, whether specifically Muslim or otherwise.

The appearance of the *turuq* must also, of course, be linked to factors more strictly within the religious tradition as it had developed since the death of the Prophet. The guardians, transmitters, and, to a degree, creators of that tradition, were the learned men of religion, the *'ulema'*. Not a hierarchy of clergy mediating grace or access to the Divine, this élite of canon lawyers and religious scholars were *par excellence* the systematizers of Islam, the formulators of legal judgements and criteria for judgement, the legitimators of the holders of power (to whom a tradition of submission early developed), the preservers of the word of the Revelation and its exegetes, the teachers of religion and opponents of innovation. They were drawn in an open-ended way, and by a training which any Muslim might undertake, from all social strata, pursued every kind of occupation, and attained every degree of wealth. Though rarely capable of acting as an organized group, their many-sided competence, their permeation of all ranks of society, their vital functions in the establishment and maintenance of the legal and normative order, gave them enormous authority and social importance. This essentially conservative role, however, carried with it the dangers of dogmatic rigidity, slavish attention to the letter, and an inflexibility potentially fatal to the capacity of Islam to respond to the changing historical and existential demands of its adherents. The capacity constantly to recreate and renew the meaning of Islam in the world degenerated into a mere repetition of its forms. The response to this ossification on a spiritual, intellectual, emotional, and social level was Sufism and the Sufi Orders, mystical religion, and the organization of the popular Brotherhoods.

Much has rightly been made of the antagonism between the *'ulema'* and the Sufi Sheikhs and what each represents. It may be worth emphasizing, none the less, that this is not only an analytical opposition of two ideal types, legist and mystic, though such an analysis can certainly be justified. More significantly it reflects historical problems of the relations between the two, problems which were central at all levels from the philosophical to the social and throughout the different strata of Muslim societies for hundreds of years. On the one hand, Sufism presented the prophetic tradition with great theological difficulties which were never perhaps truly resolved. To the learning (*'ilm*) of the lawyers, it opposed gnosis or mystical understanding (*ma'rifa*); rather than the exoteric (*zahir*) it dwelt on the inner truth behind the outward symbol, the degrees of illumination that could only be attained through progressive initiation into the succeeding realms of the esoteric (*batin*), and the inward condition of a man's heart rather than his outward acts; and instead of the ethical and historical demands of the *umma* as traditionally conceived, it centred on the spiritual progress of the individual traveller on the path to God.

Most important perhaps for our concerns it produced a new order of religious specialists claiming a new order of knowledge and the capacity to mediate the relation between God and men. If the gate of Prophecy was shut, the path of Sainthood was open. The brothers became part of spiritual hierarchies culminating in a sheikh to whom they owed personal devotion and beyond whom was an invisible government of the Saints ruling the world. These forms of leadership and religious grouping were part of a most fundamental development within Islam and of lasting impact on the whole of Muslim society. Though we may now suggest that the Orders gave a vital energy to religion on the level of organized associational life just as Sufi thought did on the spiritual and intellectual plane, we can hardly wonder at the antagonism of the learned men.

The *'ulema'* were the products of a common training; they had clearly defined functions and social roles as the literate guardians of the tradition which was held to be the very ground of individuals' and whole societies' primordial identities; they ran the systems of the legal schools, courts, and education, and propagated and defended the Islamic ethic, cloaking public power in religious authority. They were accustomed to many other kinds of religious prestige attaching to persons—*mujahids* who fought in the Holy War (*jihad*), *hajjis* who made the pilgrimage, *sherifs* who were accepted as descendants of the Prophet himself,[1] and various holy

---

[1] With such descent as a banner of legitimacy, family dynasties have often dominated areas of the Muslim world such as North Africa and South Arabia.

men, wandering ascetics, writers of charms, and so on. But Sufism
in all its forms appeared to challenge the basis of their uniquely
authoritative position and to undermine the elaborate structure of
consensus, custom, and law they had so laboriously constructed.
Too often it has seemed to the *'ulema'* that the homogeneous institutional and moral universe of law and theology was being undermined by the personal authority of charismatic religious virtuosi,
credited with miraculous powers, who claimed to intercede with the
Divinity on behalf of their hierocratic, mystical associations.
Ecstatics and thaumaturgics made of the world a tangled magic
garden far different from the rational ordered proportions of that
assiduously cultivated by the legists.[1]

But it is of equal relevance to consider not only the opposition
between these two groups of religious specialists, but also the
historical conditions under which they were opposed, and those
conditions under which they tended on the contrary to come
together, so that in some circumstances in terms of personnel they
were even indistinguishable. A leading scholar of modern Egyptian
history has pointed out that the Azhar University of Cairo itself, a
bastion of orthodoxy, has from the sixteenth century been a centre
of Sufism and it appears quite clear that in succeeding centuries
there was a high level of overlapping between Sheikhs of the Orders
and the *'ulema'* and legal officers, for reasons we shall come to later
in this study.[2] It is, therefore, the process of the relationship, its
fluctuations over time, that need to be stressed.

The Sufi sheikh whose religious career we are to examine here
in some depth is important not so much for his personal qualities
as for the fact that he lived and founded a *tariqa* precisely at one
of the great crisis periods of Egyptian society. At a time when the
relations of popular Sufism, both with the religious élite and the
wider society, were being transformed, he attempted to organize
a new Brotherhood on a partly new organizational basis even as
the majority of people were turning in other directions. His life
and his Order will illustrate something of the nature of the crisis
and its impact on the social forms and meanings of Islam in Egypt,

---

[1] To adapt Weber's famous phrase, a *zauberung* (not an *entzauberung*) *der welt*.
[2] El Sayed, Afaf Loutfi, 'The role of the *"ulema"* in Egypt during the early
nineteenth century', in Holt, P. M. (ed.), *Political and Social Change in Modern
Egypt*, London: O.U.P., 1968, p. 267. The Azhar is the great mosque University
(founded A.D. 972) and the leading centre of Islamic education.

and of the redefinition of the area over which religious leaders could claim authority.

The Saint

Salama ibn Hassan Salama, the founding Sheikh of the *Hamidiya Shadhiliya*, was born in 1867 in Bulaq, one of the poorer quarters of Cairo.[1] His religious antecedents are exemplary. His family came originally from the Hijaz and he traced his descent back to Hussein ibn 'Ali, the Prophet's grandson and a figure highly revered by Muslims whether Sunni or Shi'a. More immediately he was related (his biographer does not specify in what way) to one Abu Taqiyya, whose mosque and tomb are in Minya. His grandfather, Hamid ar-Ridi, also has his tomb and mosque in Minya. Salama's paternal uncle, 'Abd ar-Rahman, lived the life of a *zahid* (ascetic) and another relative, Hagg Nasir, is buried in a tomb in Bulaq. Of his father we are told that he prayed a hundred *rak'a* (ritual prostrations) every night and made the pilgrimage to the Holy Cities of the Hijaz on foot.

Salama married twice. His first wife died after giving him four sons, one of whom died young, and two daughters, both of whom married members of the Order. His second marriage produced three sons; the eldest, Ibrahim, who was later to succeed his father as Head of the Order, another who died early, and the youngest, Hamid, a student at the Faculty of Commerce and now in business. The daughters, of whom there were four, all married members of the Order (p. 9). His love for his children was not of the ordinary kind. In the house they were his sons, in the meeting room (*maglis*) of the *tariqa*, brothers (*ikhwan*), and in the *tariqa* itself they ranked as postulants (*muridin*). There he was their teacher, as to any of the members. The sons themselves were not affected by the high prestige of their father (p. 205).

In very early childhood, at some time between the ages of seven and ten, he is said to have learnt the Quran by heart and the principles of mathematics, and at six he could write Persian. By nine years old he had written a pamphlet on ethics and morals, which is preserved in the library of the Order. Finding the teaching of the elementary school unsatisfactory he turned at this stage in his

---

[1] All page numbers are from Saif an-Nasr, *Sira al Hamidiya*, Cairo, 1956. The biography was completed sixteen years after Salama's death. Page numbers in square brackets refer to the present book.

intellectual and spiritual development to *'ulum at-tasawwuf* (the sciences of Islamic mysticism) for 'the satisfaction of the soul and the mind' (p. 11). At the same time his practical life began as a junior clerk in the office of the State domains (*maslahat al amlak*). He was thirteen. His rank was the lowest and his pay 175 piastres a month. He was eventually to rise to be 'head of his department',[1] a post he held while Sheikh of the *tariqa*. Kind, amiable, and devoted to his work, over which he took great care, Salama possessed all the virtues (p. 10). As departmental head he was an excellent supervisor of those under him, and treated all men of all religions and races in exactly the same way. Many Christians used to visit him, even after his retirement, to ask for his help and blessing (p. 11).

What Saif terms his *Jihad* (holy struggle) began, as with so many of the greatest figures of Islamic mysticism and religious thought, with ascetic practices, often of a very advanced and demanding nature. His sheikh—for he had by now followed the common path and joined one of the Sufi Orders (the *Fasiya Shadhiliya*)—devoted him to the *dhikr* (repetition of the names of God), to seclusion (*khalwa*), and to fasting until such time as '. . . his soul was pure and his sun shone forth, and his nature was refined' (p. 12).[2] For three hundred days in the year he fasted; each night he recited twelve thousand times the formula *la ilaha illa Allah* (there is no god but God); for six years he repeated as an individual *dhikr* the name Allah thirty thousand times in a night, and for two years he abstained from sexual intercourse, avoiding even the company of women. Finally, he prayed for the Prophet Muhammad, whom he always held in the highest reverence, for two hours each night. Such a discipline had a severe physical effect—piles, bleeding, and excessive thinness. He himself is quoted as saying that his parents and friends became extremely concerned and others mocked him (pp. 187–8). At last (though at what age we are not told) he came to see that effort of this kind was not sufficient and that truth might be sought within the individual soul without following so demanding a bodily ascetic regime. He then relaxed these practices, but never entirely gave them up, remaining a *zahid* until he died.

[1] (*Sic*); Saif does not give precise details of his position and function.
[2] Both the great Islamic modernist, Muhammad 'Abduh (b. 1849) and his more conservative disciple, Rashid Rida (b. 1865) belonged to Sufi Orders early in their careers. So, too, did the founder of the militant fundamentalist Muslim Brotherhood, Hassan al Banna.

Even from so cursory an outline of his life, certain obvious yet nevertheless important biographical themes emerge. We shall later return to these in some detail. Here it is sufficient to call particular attention to the current of asceticism, both in terms of rigorous practices of devotion entailing a degree of physical suffering, and as an inward form of spiritual self-discipline; to his fulfilling of the demands of worldly occupation and work; and to the lowly circumstances of his life, circumstances which he preserved even after rising to a position of relative financial security as head of a department. Saif tells us that he 'directed his spirit to heaven and only possessed of the vanities of the world (*hutam ad-dunya*) a humble house' (p. 135). He had a few acres of land but having no time to take care of them properly, a further illustration of his emphasis on the correct attendance to mundane affairs, sold them and paid the money into the funds of a benefit society of the employees of the department. All his salary went to the upkeep of the house and the *maglis*.

Yet he was always ready to help others by providing meals, and to assist his relatives and the poor. When he visited the house of a brother, which was an honour hotly competed for by the members, he only ate his normal amount and never burdened the host with furnishing more than was necessary—a piece of consideration of some significance in a culture in which provision for a guest, particularly so revered a personage, entails marked economic hardship in the offering of a meal of 'proper' size (i.e. far too much for normal consumption and a good deal of prestigious show in proportion to the importance of the visitor). If anyone was in need, the Sheikh took care that help was given; money was collected from the brothers and sent with a delegate so that the recipient would not feel indebted. He had always uppermost in his mind the convenience of the brothers, and put himself and his family to great trouble in order to visit them in the various towns and villages of the Delta particularly. Any difficulties they had, Salama shared with them, and a strong sense of his service to the members of the Order emerges from Saif's biography—a sense of the leader placing himself always at the disposal of his followers, without any thought for his personal comfort. Though he was their sheikh and *murshid* (religious guide) he often seems also to be their spiritual, not to say material, servant and helper. In return the Sheikh was the one to whom they looked in all circumstances for 'indeed he was everything' (p. 128); in him was happiness, content, fruitfulness, and life, and into their hearts he put mercy, love, and kindness. All were linked by the bond of love and it was a bond forged by Salama (p. 128).

Saif has scrupulously recorded many supplementary details of his personality and habits, of how he sat, walked, and ate, commenting on the model nature of his behaviour in all respects. Of his dress we learn that at work he wore European clothes, but outside the office he assumed the long garments associated with religious specialists, the *jubba* and *quftan*, and a green band (the colour of the *Shadhiliya*) round his tarbush (*fez*). His son, on the other hand, only wears such clothing on official occasions of the Order such as the *hadrah* and the *maglis*.

I was often told by older informants who had known the Sheikh personally that his appearance was captivating at the very first sight. His face, says Saif, showed the light in his heart and reflected the interior state so that no one could leave his presence unconvinced of his spiritual excellence and deep knowledge (p. 35). Before him the individual became like one who had committed a crime and now stood facing the *hakim* (judge); one's demeanour showed it—head hung, body trembling, voice diminished, gaze lowered, colour changed, tongue stuttering, mind lost, until 'if you were asked what half of two was you would not know' (p. 14). This state would remain even if you were remembering him in his absence. When he spoke the words went straight from heart to heart, so that years later after his death, members say they can recall every word and gesture he made in their presence. Saif pays tribute to his extraordinary spiritual power, saying that all fell under the love of this torrential, violent (*garif*—sweeping) personality; the proud, who deceived themselves in their self-esteem, fell into this deep sea and became brothers (pp. 52–3). For he was *gadhdhab*, a Sufi term explained by members as meaning one attractive to others in a mystical religious sense.

The Sheikh as teacher

This quality of captivating others informed his work as a teacher, traditionally the major element in the role of the Sufi Sheikh. Most of his formal instruction was carried out in the *maglis* of the Order. Texts of the Quran, of the Traditions of the Prophet and *hukm* (wise sayings) hung on the walls, together with a portrait of Salama

(p. 32). When he came in, all at once stood. No one either entered without his permission or sat without being chosen. No one spoke unless the Sheikh talked to him, and then only replied in a voice just above a whisper. Avoiding argument or bitterness, Salama would lead him, 'as one does a baby' (p. 39). In the *maglis* all differences of wealth, learning, strength, distinction, and considera- tion ceased. To all the hearts, minds, and spirits he imparted understanding (*'ilm*), courtesy grounded in religious humility (*adab*), and theological knowledge of the highest degree. Saif exalts his ability to awaken the feelings and open the hearts of the brothers present. If they were tired he would jest lightly with them until they felt restored. A member would sing a hymn or *qasida* (ode; poem) until one left the world of phantoms (*ashbah*—unreal appearances) and went to that of true essences (*arwah*—souls, spirits). In a 'spiritual unwinding' (*laffa ruhiya*) he led them from the shades of the earth to the light of the heavens (p. 33).

That this was so was in part due to the precision of his use of language. He weighed each word finely, and so placed it among the words of the sentence that its full meaning emerged and the exact sense of what he wanted to say lodged itself in the heart (p. 81). It should be pointed out that this goes further than merely saying that Salama had a good command of language and expression. An ability in the eloquent use of Arabic considered as great as that described by Saif and members of the Order *in itself* indicates to the brothers a God-given gift rather than simply a highly developed individual capacity. Manipulation of the language reaching such a degree of excellence immediately suggests a mystical link with the Divine from whom the Revelation of the Quran came in Arabic. More generally, it is also of course true, that where the dominant mode of transmission is oral, and where particularly this is combined with the existence of sacred texts accessible in the nature of the case only to the religious élite, a certain 'power' is accredited to those who can understand the mysteries and transmit such understanding at whatever level to the people. The word has power which it bestows on those who have knowledge of it. We shall see that this quality of Salama's was in fact taken as a sign of his special relation to God.

His teachings

A full consideration of the doctrines and social ethic of the Order will be undertaken elsewhere. It will serve our purposes here, however, to draw attention to certain salient features of Salama's teachings which were to be major themes in the 'ethical charter' of the *Hamidiya Shadhiliya*.

What Saif calls the subject-matter of the *maglis* was dealt with by the Sheikh at three levels. Broadly speaking he was concerned with *'ulum al haqiqa wa 'ulum ash-Shari'a*—the sciences of the Truth and of the Holy Law. He recognized, as all the Orders do, that not every man is of such a level of education and spiritual advancement as to be able fully to comprehend the subtleties of mystical instruction. With the mass then, he was chiefly concerned with the laws of religion and the Holy Law, with explanation of the prayers and of the duties of Islam and so forth. With those of the 'middle stage' he elucidated the doctrines of, and distinctions between, the four orthodox schools of canon law, Hanbali, Hanafi, Maliki, and Shafe'i (p. 40). Finally, with the *'ulema'* and those of a comparable degree of understanding, he turned to the subject of 'the purifying of the heart, the cleansing of the soul and the rejection of worldly passions'. In his *tafsir* (explanation) and eloquence he was, Saif assures us, without peer. He asked his pupils questions that in themselves illuminated, and then clarified, the issues, and swept away ignorance (p. 45). His learning brought a light like the sun into the hearts of men.

He regarded Sufism itself as a science or branch of knowledge whereby one comes to know how to purify the soul from blameworthy characteristics. Its main concern is with the 'deeds of the hearts in the most important direction'. Its fruit is coming to eternal happiness and spiritual success (*fawz*) (p. 19), though he emphasized that one should love God because He is God and not out of fear of Hell or eagerness for Heaven (p. 181). Its excellence (*fadl*) lies in that it is the highest of the branches of knowledge since it is connected with coming to God (p. 19). Slightly changing the metaphor, he referred to it as the fruit on the branch of the other sciences. It leads to praiseworthy characteristics and morality.

Of the world he taught that the nearer one is to this, the farther one is from the next (*al-akhira*). He encouraged the brothers to work, and the most hateful thing to him was the idle man who would not go out and seek for his daily bread, but rather lived as a burden on other people. One should use the ways of the world as a means and not as an end in themselves. For the world was only created for man to pass through 'lightly' (*khafifan*—softly). He therefore always took the simplest way (p. 137). The intelligent man is one who leaves the world, though it is made of gold, and turns to *al akhira* even though it is made of clay. He would give examples of the unimportance of the world and greatly disliked any wealthy member of the Order who did not make use of his income for the good of all (p. 138). Salama would often quote a story concerning 'Ali ibn Abi Talib, the Prophet's son-in-law and fourth orthodox Caliph, which ends: 'Verily God has demanded of the people of justice that they should put themselves with the weak so that the poor will not be upset by their poverty.' The Sheikh's maxim was 'do not worship the world and do not neglect it; take only what is useful and leave the rest to whoever wants it' (p. 139).

He particularly extolled the importance of love in all one's dealings. Not only of love of brother for brother but of every brother for God and the perpetual lodgings of the *mahbub*—the Loved One, in the heart of the *muhibb*—lover, who is under His command. All things become clear in the love of Allah and it is this love which is the root of all labour and work in the world (pp. 181–3). To explain this to me (as a Christian outsider) informants have sometimes linked his name with that of Christ in trying to emphasize the primary significance which Salama attached to this principle. He followed the way of the *Shadhiliya* because it is based on *al mahabba* (love) and this is also true of Christianity. It was the Sheikh who brought back charity and piety after it had decayed since the time of Hassan ash-Shadhili (p. 22).

He was especially devoted to the Prophet and had, in Saif's words, 'true *ma'rifa* [properly gnosis in the Sufi sense, but here perhaps rather "perfect understanding"] in his knowledge of him' (p. 194). No religious occasion of remembrance passed without his being the first to greet it and summon the brothers to its observance. Saif emphasizes how much Salama mixed himself completely in the heart, feelings, and spirit of Muhammad. His devotion, while probably hovering on the borderline of orthodoxy rigorously interpreted, is an interesting illustration of a tendency in his teachings (and in popular Sufism in general) which counterbalances the instruction on the formal and doctrinal aspects of Islam. He paid great attention to the 'personalizing' aspects of religion; not only to the Messenger of Allah but also to those figures who are believed to have mediated between the Divine and the World, the *awliya'* or Friends of God, the Saints. He considered them part of his spiritual family, celebrated their *mulids*, and with his sons filled the mosques with *dhikr* for them (pp. 210–11). These practices have continued since his death, and particular care is given to those *dhikr* for Salama himself. For to the brothers of the *Hamidiya Shadhiliya* he also is a Saint.

The Miracles of the Saint

From his biography thus far certain key features are already beginning to emerge. His family is devoted to religion, its duties and meritorious ritual acts, a devotion which his own early asceticism continues. Descent is traced back with pious inevitability to the Prophet. His conduct is exemplary in matters small and great, in his behaviour towards his own kin and towards the brothers to whom he is a humble and infinitely concerned 'servant' (*khadim*). He is a renewer of piety in what is typically seen as a time of its decline. Above all he is a learned teacher, though formally little schooled, and has a command of those 'signs' which have not yet lost their sacred power for this culture. These features, all enthusiastically endorsed and witnessed to by members who knew him, give us a crude outline of what expectations men had of those who sought sacred status. The fact that they would be claimed in almost the same words for almost any such person in no way diminishes the truth of this particular reference. It does, however, show the force and continuity of this specific cultural model around the thematic core of which cluster further necessary attributes of saintly authority.

The word normally translated by 'saint' is the Arabic term, *wali*, derived from a verb root carrying connotations of nearness and protection. The verse of the Quran most commonly cited on this subject, 'Verily no fear shall come upon the friends of Allah, neither shall they grieve' (Quran, x. 63), provides the necessary support for twin streams of belief about the Saint; that developed by the theologians and some of the great mystics, and that enshrined in popular practices and notions. It is generally accepted that the Saint is one who is '*'arif bi''llah*', one who 'knows God', a phrase specifically used by Saif of Salama. Such individuals, some of them invisible, are in a hierarchy which governs the universe. They are headed by one known as *qutb az-Zaman*, the Axis of the Age, again a title used of him by his followers.

The most important factor to the mass of believers, however, is that the Saint can perform miracles, or what might better be called 'grace acts' (*karamat*). In view of the presence of the Azhar University in Cairo and the somewhat antipathetic attitude of the Government towards popular religious manifestations, the Order is and has to be carefully orthodox in its published writings on the subject. Saif explains at some length in his biography that man is only the agent, the means of the actions, and does not bring them about by his own power. Such deeds are 'honours' from God bestowed upon the individual. Being thus 'honoured' by God may manifest itself in many ways. One must be *salih*, a righteous man; perhaps an *'alim* (learned man of religion), clothed in the suit of knowledge and the scarf of understanding; or a charitable man honoured with riches (p. 221), or a just ruler with power, or a teacher, doctor, or engineer honoured with occupation. Alternatively, the individual may be one of those set on the spiritual way, the *salikin*; a knower directed to the heart of things and secrets. Furthermore, the true *wali* does not take the demonstration of *karamat* as an end but goes beyond these first steps which may even, in so far as they distract and amaze, hinder his completion.

What concerns us more, however, is not so much the doctrine of what constitutes *karamat* as the types of action and event which are considered miracles, those who accept them, and what part these irruptions of the Divine are thought to play in worldly affairs and chains of causation.

The more educated members of the Order tend to cite 'the plain unvarnished facts' as *karamat* without invoking any dramatic disruption of the normal. These centre on great abilities of the Sheikh rather than specific actions he performed. The following are representative:

I (a) Saif says that Salama had two everlasting *karamat*:

   (i) Though none of his family were Sheikhs (i.e. men of religious learning) he memorized the Quran at six years old, which demonstrates his capacities and is a sign of God saving him for the world.

   (ii) Despite the fact that he was not trained at the Azhar yet the great and the learned came to him for knowledge and found everything in his writings.

   (b) From an informant who had known the Sheikh: Although possessing little formal education, he had gathered all hearts together from every quarter and area of the country and had become celebrated in all places.

II An informant who knew the Sheikh and is close to his successor Ibrahim (he is the director of a small commercial company) described to me how he could remember quite literally each word and gesture that Salama had ever spoken or made to him during the five years that he had known him and that this was an obvious *karama*.

Examples of this kind are numerous and current throughout all levels of the Order, though chiefly cited by the literate and educated. They are held to be proof of the Sheikh's special place in God's favour. There are others, however, which are of a more obviously remarkable nature and which are often, though by no means exclusively, quoted by the less sophisticated. Many of these accounts, as far as I could tell, were of events held to have occurred after the Sheikh's death.

I now give examples to illustrate certain major themes in the *karamat* of Salama. The first two groups, III and IV, might loosely be classified under the heading of the 'Confounding of the Opposition', though each deals with a distinct type of opposition. (All narrations are from different informants.)

III (*a*) Some men of the Azhar went to visit Salama and he said: 'Is it not possible for a small and insignificant man like me to ask that these walls be struck down? Is it not possible that God will grant it?' As he said these words the whole house shook violently and they were so flabbergasted that they got up and left. (Illiterate factory-worker.)

(*b*) One day three men who were teachers of philosophy in Cairo University came to a *hadrah* in a mosque and saw Salama. They asked the informant whether he was a learned man, and other related questions. The member gave them the date and time of the *maglis* (meeting) and on that day the Sheikh, who knew nothing of them, said: 'Isn't someone coming?' The member, who had forgotten about the three teachers of philosophy, replied 'No', as he could not think to what the Sheikh was referring. Then the Sheikh said: 'I thought someone was coming' and he remembered and said 'Yes'. The teachers duly arrived and asked forty-four highly difficult questions demanding great theological and philosophical understanding, and he answered them all. This shows (said the informant) that he was a great *wali*—that means he was a great teacher. (Literate worker.)

(*c*) Some of the '*ulema*' came to him and he was able to provide answers to extremely difficult questions. Then he put a question to them and the Sheikh al Islam[1] took three months trying to frame a reply and then he was still unable to give one. (Business man.)

(*d*) Though not a product or member of al Azhar, the Sheikh had put certain questions on *tawhid* (the doctrine of the Absolute Unity of God) to the most important *'ulema'* and they had sent it back saying that only the one who asked the question was capable of answering it. (Lawyer in the legal section of a Government department.)

Such accounts of Sheikh Salama demonstrating his learning and power at the expense of the guardians of the orthodox tradition are common. In the context which I attempted to sketch out at the beginning of this chapter the meaning of these stories will be apparent. For reasons to be examined later, the modern period in Egypt has been one of a change from symbiotic relations between Sufi Sheikhs and *'ulema'* to hostility and the denunciation of the *turuq* as deviant. Previously the learned men had attempted accommodation to, or quasi-absorption of, the organized secondary religion of the masses. Often they had utilized the framework of the *tariqa* to bolster the personal authority and influence of a learned family over time through the monopoly of Sheikhly office, other means of ensuring such continuity being highly uncertain and limited given the capriciousness of Mamluke government. But as the Orders declined in size, range, and influence the *'ulema'* have denigrated them as a perversion of true Islam in the eyes of Muslims and of non-believers.

The legists had already in Salama's lifetime begun to redefine 'proper' religious behaviour and to reassert their dominance. Whether as traditionalists, or as reformers, they attacked the Brotherhoods' wrapping of folk-belief and magical practice in the mantle of the Faith. It is notable, therefore, that while Salama is shown triumphing over them, *the battle is on their own ground*; he is portrayed as more learned than the learned in matters of orthodox theology, not in the mysteries of esoteric Sufism or the display of wonder-working. Implicitly it is their set of standards which is accepted as the arena for the debate. As the Orders gradually became restricted to the lower strata in a society increasingly internally differentiated and urbanized, so they have had to suit the form and content of their activities and teachings to the demands made by the State and pressures exerted by the *'ulema'*. As opposition grew between the two groups, the Saint, who to all save his

[1] The Rector of al Azhar University.

followers spent his life as merely an obscure and poorly educated clerk in a government office, conformed to the sober scripturalism of the doctors of religion. In recounting his defeat of them, the stories acknowledge his subordination none the less to their judgement of what is truly Islamic.

Group IV also concerns the discomfiture of the opposition, but in this case of a very different nature.

IV (*a*) The Sheikh's superior in the Ministry did not like his followers coming there, and complained to Salama about it. As he (the superior) was going down the steps, he bent to tie up his shoelace and could not straighten up. Doctors could not help and his wife sent for Salama who prayed for him. The man was cured. After that he arranged a special room for the brothers. (Clerk in a legal office.)

(*b*) The director of the Sheikh's office, an Englishman named Mr. Antony (in all probability the man referred to in IV (*a*) above) came along and found some of the brothers waiting on benches outside the office and demanded to know who they were. He was told that they were followers of the Sheikh. 'What Sheikh?', he asked. 'Sheikh Salama', came the reply. 'Who the devil is he? Get rid of them.' So the brothers were sent home. On hearing of this Salama was angry and left the office saying that if the director sent any of the brothers away it was the same as sending him off. Mr. Antony then sent for him and on being told that he was gone, asked for the two account books to be brought. Both were found to be completely blank, though all expenditure and income and capital etc. had been entered in them before. The director then sent for Salama who said that if the director wished to see him he would have to come to his house. Eventually the Englishman came and Salama soundly berated him. When the former complained about it, Salama said that this was his house and he would speak as he wished. The director apologized and the Sheikh then said the opening *sura* (chapter) of the Quran (the *fatiha*) over the books and when they were opened there were all the accounts. (An ex-engineer of low government position; one of the senior members in age.)

We notice subsidiary motifs in these *karamat* which become dominant in other stories. There is first *the insight into secret things and God's purposes*, about which the Sheikh could have had no way of knowing without Divine Grace, since they are a mystery known only to God. These events occur before his death and his physical presence is involved. After death, he is liable to be heard or seen in a dream under virtually any circumstances.

V (*a*) Salama came to the informant's house one day to take tea and the informant's sister had asked to be allowed to meet the Sheikh in order to kiss his hand. Salama agreed and the girl duly had her wish. The Sheikh then said that she would change her name. That night as she was asleep she saw Salama in a dream and he told her that in future she would be called Fatima after the daughter of the Prophet; to her parents she would still answer to her original name but to her brother and to himself she would be Fatima from then on. The next time he came to the house he immediately greeted the girl by that name. (Informant as above.)

(*b*) One of Salama's servants was short of money and needed five pounds urgently. Salama never carried around money in the pockets of his *quftan*, and in any case was not a person who was likely to have any about him. The servant was sitting near him in the mosque one day and mentioned his need to a companion out of Salama's hearing. The Sheikh suddenly said words to the effect: 'Go and see if there is any money in the pocket of my *quftan* and if there is take five pounds.' The man was astonished as he knew there was nothing there, but all the same he went out, put his hand in the right-hand pocket and drew out five new pound notes. No one knew from where they had come. He went to thank the Sheikh but the latter cut him short, saying abruptly: 'Not one word, just go.' (Brother of the previous informant, retired minor government official.)

Perhaps the most important text concerns, among many other ideas, a striking example of this notion of the knowledge of secret things and I therefore quote a full account of it here. It includes the crediting of *karamat* to Sheikh Ibrahim, Salama's son, and to this and other points I shall return later. The incident was retold with an Egyptian wealth of expressive gesture and enthusiasm, and interrupted by a constant stream of exclamations of wonder and pious maxims from the hearers. I give it verbatim from field notes since the minor details are of some interpretative significance as we shall see.

V (*c*) The informant, let us call him Ahmed, began by saying that Sheikh Ibrahim had made an astounding *karama* on the day of the trip to Kafr ash-Sheikh (an industrial town in the Delta; there are several *zawiyas* of the *Hamidiya Shadhiliya* located there and a group of about two hundred brothers from Cairo were going to visit and hold a *hadrah* with the members from that region). Ahmed had made a private arrangement with a friend (a senior member in the Order) to go to Kafr at ten in the morning in order to avoid the crowd and to arrive early. They were to meet and take a Pullman bus. This was agreed on

Monday. On the Tuesday the Sheikh (Ibrahim) was ill and so could not attend the *hadrah* held, as was customary, in the mosque of Hussein in Cairo. On Wednesday he was also indisposed, so he knew nothing of the arrangement.

On Wednesday night, Ahmed went to the *maglis* and met the secretary of the Order and while he was sitting with him someone came in and said that he had heard that Ahmed's friend and another senior member had rung up the Sheikh's confidential secretary and would now go to Kafr in his car, and not by bus as they had planned. This irritated Ahmed very much, and he said that in that case he would not go on the trip at all, and he went home in high dudgeon. He stayed awake till about five in the morning not even closing his eyes and thinking all the time about the visit and whether to go, and the fact that if he did not the Sheikh would be angry and ask after him and why he had not come. (He has been a member of the Order since the time of Salama whose neighbour he was.) Then he had a *ru'ya* (truthful vision) of Sheikh Salama and Sheikh Ibrahim standing together and Salama said: 'Do not upset yourself Ahmed', and Ibrahim said: 'I know what the trouble is.' So he turned over and went straight to sleep.

The next day he got up and set off to the bus station where he found a new Pullman coach *with no one in it and extremely clean and very fast* (his emphasis). He got in and sat down in great comfort alone near the driver. About ten of the brothers came, too, and they got to Kafr early.

On arrival he was met by members from the area who gave him lunch and served tea. He was then shown to a room for himself to lie down, with a bathroom just near and everything spotlessly clean. The others did not arrive till five or so in the afternoon, feeling very tired. The *hadrah* began an hour or two later and did not end till about eleven. There was a huge crowd and the place was absolutely packed out with people. After that they held a meeting in one of the *zawiyas* with all the brothers standing outside. The latter then said that they wanted to make the ritual hand kiss with the Sheikh. Ahmed's friend stood up and said that it had been a long day and the Sheikh would be tired out. But they very much wanted to and so the Sheikh overruled the friend and made the hand kiss with each one which took until 3.15 in the morning. When it came to Ahmed's turn, the Sheikh gripped him hard by the arm and said: 'How did you come here?' He replied, 'In a Pullman'. Then the Sheikh turned to the friend and the other senior member and said in a very loud voice so that everyone could hear: 'What sort of people are you? Where is my secretary?' The latter came in and the Sheikh ordered him to make room for Ahmed in his car on the way back. After this they all left.

Just after they had departed a man, who was a relative of the family in whose house the *maglis* had been held, died suddenly.

My informant then sat back immensely gratified with his narration and its impact on his audience, but leaving me somewhat puzzled as to the exact significance of the last and obviously critical piece of news. The others in the audience (about five) appeared at once to see the point, and on being asked for an explanation patiently told me that if the man had died while all the celebrations were in progress there would have been a great disturbance, and the whole occasion would have been ruined. As it was, the *karama* lay in the fact that the Sheikh had seen that God's hidden purpose was to end this man's life and so had left just before the event.

A second motif which recurs time and time again is that of 'help given in distress' (*nagda*), or the defence and assistance of a brother by the Saint. Members speak of such occurrences as *fuq al'aql* (literally, above the intelligence; hence 'beyond comprehension by reason') and *fuq al bashariya* ('above human nature'). Some stories are concerned with quite dramatic intervention. One man in a small rural village was snatched away from the path of a train which he had not seen racing down on him. Another fell off one of the main bridges across the Nile in Cairo and was then pulled out of the water, and the Saint's voice said: 'You must take better care next time.' One or two of the more sophisticated members expressed a certain cautious reserve when questioned about such *karamat*, but allowed that the narrators were all members of the Order and therefore their word was obviously to be accepted. They were none the less apparently sceptical and never produced such examples themselves. Other accounts of a less startling and somewhat different type are, however, generally retold; members say how they were prevented by what at first seemed to be mere chance, or some mistake, from carrying out a course of action that would, as it later turned out, have been disastrous—missing a train which crashed, or a taxi which fell into a canal, and so forth.

The three further examples below are useful in so much as they illustrate Salama's help in the minor rather than the major critical circumstances. The first answers a direct prayer for assistance.

VI (*a*) The informant was one day walking to his village with his small brother. He had only three piastres in his pocket and no other money. It was quite a distance, and as his brother was only about five years old he wanted to take a taxi. This would cost six piastres. The informant prayed to Salama and then heard a loud voice saying: 'Abdulla, take the five piastres from your pocket.' He was amazed and looked round. The road was deserted. Then he put his hand in his top pocket and took out a new five-piastre note. So he got a taxi for his little brother and the latter said after getting into the cab, 'Give the driver the six piastres and give me the two left over.' Abdulla asked: 'How did you know?' His brother replied: 'Sidi Salama told me.' (The informant is a young bank clerk, a graduate of the Faculty of Commerce of Cairo University, with a limited knowledge of English and French. Salama died before he was born. He has belonged to the Order for about ten years.)

(*b*) One of the brothers had been going to Tanta and was waiting by a bridge for a taxi. He waited for a long time without getting one and was even bumped into by a car. So he got very flustered and then had a *ru'ya* of Salama saying to him: 'Look, here comes a car for you', and there was a cab coming over the bridge; so he got in and eventually arrived in Tanta. Then he went into the mosque and prayed, and when he was coming out he remembered that in his confusion he had left his travelling bag behind at the bridge in Cairo. *Just then a man walked up with the bag and gave it to him* (narrator's emphasis). The man said that he also had been waiting there to go to Tanta and had seen the bag and brought it with him, knowing to whom it belonged.

(*c*) One day the informant had met a dozen or so members of the *Hamidiya Shadhiliya* from his village when he was in Mehall al Kubra (an industrial town in the Delta). It was pouring with rain and they were sheltering in a stationer's shop. He himself had gone to buy things for school. The brothers could not possibly walk home in the rain, and none of them had any transport. So he had to invite them for the night to the flat he had rented in Mehall al Kubra for the duration of his studies there (the flat was extremely cheap, around one and a half pounds a week). This naturally involved him in the expense of buying food for them. The next day, as he was looking through his books, a pound note dropped out of his physics book. This absolutely amazed him and he thought that one of his guests must have put it there but knew this was unlikely for none of them had any money. None the less he decided to ask them. They all said they were as amazed as himself. Then he heard the voice of Salama saying: 'That is to pay for the dinner of the brothers.' (Informant as VI (*a*) above.)

There are finally various stories with no particular theme save that they link Salama with the 'realm of the supernatural'. Some of the brothers express tentative doubts about them, but the first incident in fact features one of the senior *khulafa'* of the Order and a man of a high reputation for probity. Both he and his two brothers have been members for years and they were all close to the Saint.

VII (*a*) A young boy of about twelve, Hagg ʿAbd ar-Rahman (the senior *khalifa* referred to above) was going late at night to see Salama. It was very dark and being rather afraid he recited the *fatiha* as he went along. Suddenly he met a man looking like a peasant (i.e. rough and strong), dark-complexioned, and wearing a short gallabiya. He talked to the boy and told him things that he (ʿAbd ar-Rahman) had no way of knowing. When ʿAbd ar-Rahman asked his name the man gave it and then went away. The boy went to Salama and told him and the Sheikh said that it was one of the *awliyaʾ* and a companion of the famous Saint buried in Alexandria, Abuʾl Abbas. He warned ʿAbd ar-Rahman not to tell anyone before him should it happen again.

(*b*) One of the members told a story of 'one of the Sultans of Egypt', he did not know which, appearing and greeting the Sheikh. (This was commented on with open scepticism by the outspoken brother of Hagg ʿAbd ar-Rahman though others present said nothing.)

We have seen that the *karamat* cluster round a small number of themes and that one is usually dominant, though others may be present in a secondary position. Principally these themes are:

(A) *The Sheikh's learning* (I and II, pp. 21–2 above), which was extraordinary and could not be accounted for by any reference to his family or intellectual training but could only be attributed to Divine grace. He also had the capacity to transmit his knowledge to others of theoretically far greater education and intellectual standing. What he *was*, rather than what he *did* is primary here.

(B) *The trial successfully undergone and the confounding of the opposition* (III and IV, pp. 22–4 above). The significance of his routing of the *ʿulema*' has already been touched upon. Members have often told me of these *karamat* specifically against the sheikhs of al Ahzar—a kind of 'attack is the best form of defence' reaction and also as part of the justi-fication of the superiority of Salama strictly within the bounds of orthodoxy. Beyond that, to *ʿilm* (knowledge) which they, or some of them possess, he adds *maʿrifa* (gnosis) and shows himself as the complete *murshid* (spiritual guide). IV(*a*) and (*b*), which also contain the defence-of-the-brothers theme, reveal how his power could be effectively demon-strated to one over him in worldly terms, a member of the colonial nation and a non-Muslim besides. An implicit attack on the Sheikh brings its own response; in the one case directly on to the offender and in the other by a public proof of his special power.

(C) *Understanding of the Hidden* (V(*a*)–(*c*), pp. 25–6 above). This involves the Sheikh's insight into things to come (V(*a*)) as well as into present circumstances (V(*b*)). Leaving for the moment text V(*c*), these stories illustrate what I was often told: that Salama sees (present tense used) everything and understands everything. He knows God's purposes, what men are thinking, and what is troubling them, whether spiritually, intellectually, or materially. This insight is allied, where necessary or fitting, to the power to ameliorate their difficulties.

Informants tell of how his advice based on this superior understanding was always correct, even though it might at first have seemed, if not actually wrong, at least very puzzling. As an example, the present Sheikh's private secretary (informant for text II) who knew Salama for five years, told me how the Saint had sent him a letter giving his approval for his marriage even though he (Salama) had never seen either his intended bride or her family. The marriage was not initially at all successful, but the Sheikh always refused to allow him to divorce his wife. Only now, twenty-five years later, had he come to realize how much he owed to her and all that she had meant in his life. Salama had known this and what was to come at the beginning.

The members feel that those events in life that are part of the inscrutable purposes of the Almighty and therefore by definition can only be accepted without comprehension by ordinary mortals are known to Salama; at a different level too, that those things which for some reason or other they keep secret from even friends and family, are also seen by the Saint and somehow taken care of where he sees fit.

(D) *Assistance, and help given in distress* (p. 27 and VI(*a*)–(*c*), pp. 27–8 above). Some of these, as we have seen, were of a particularly striking nature. Such stories cause a certain hesitation in the more educated of the Order; even embarrassment before the questioning observer, who might well be expected to regard such narrations as fictitious and therefore discreditable both to those brothers who made and to those who accepted them. They appeared only capable of making a half-willing suspension of disbelief. The vast mass of members, however, do accept these *karamat* as perfectly accurate accounts of actual occurrences.

The grace acts sometimes occur in response to direct appeals in prayer to the Saint but more often by his uncalled-for intervention in the everyday world.

(E) Finally, the two texts VII(*a*) and (*b*) (p. 29 above), presented instances showing Salama's *connection with the realm of the supernatural*; they otherwise have no direct relevance to the brothers. They are, of course, proofs of his Sainthood just as are all the *karamat*.

Let us now return to what I described as the most important of the texts V(*c*) (pp. 25–6 above). It was referred to in those terms chiefly because of the clear light it throws on the notions of causation which are implicit in the brothers' discussions of Salama's *karamat*. It also contains various levels of action by the Saint and by his successor—(1) Ahmed has a vision of both of them in which they demonstrate their knowledge of his predicament and reassure him; (2) he catches a bus of quite outstanding speed and cleanliness, which neither he nor his hearers, who uttered innumerable phrases of praise of the Sheikh, were in any doubt was due to Salama and Ibrahim (help in distress); (3) absolutely everything on the journey turns out perfectly for him; those who let him down are publicly reprimanded and he is accorded special treatment in recompense for their behaviour; (4) lastly, the Sheikh Ibrahim sees that God wished to end the life of a relative of the hosts (*rubbuna kan 'ayiz yimawwituh*) and so left before this could happen and ruin the occasion. This last is the most startling of all the *karamat* involving the knowledge of hidden things. As has been already pointed out, however, it was immediately obvious to all the members of the audience, except myself, that this was what had happened. They needed no explanation from Ahmed.

We note first of what a mundane matter the Saint's intervention may be. (See also V(*b*) and VI(*a*)–(*c*).) No event is so apparently insignificant that divine grace manifested in the person of Salama may not work in it. The *karamat* may as easily lie in the catching of a fast bus as in the dramatic snatching from the waters of the Nile; in the provision of five piastres as in the rescue from the path of a train; in the most trivial circumstance as in the direst emergency. There is no occasion in which the Saint may not act. When he does not, and misfortune befalls, that is Allah the Merciful in His mysterious Wisdom, the *dunya* (the world), or alternatively some evil or failing in the individual. When he does, it is yet another example of his position as a *wali* of God and adds further lustre to his reputation, and thus to his devoted followers whom it confirms in their devotion to him and to the Order which he founded. As always, the system is self-sealing.

This range in the *karamat* from the mundane to the exceptional leads to what to us is a paradox. Since the Saint may act at any time and in any set of events, though his intervention is always extraordinary it is at the same time part of the scheme of things. It is of the fabric of life that Salama should do so, while each new manifestation also arouses great delight and awe in the brothers. There is no idea here of the separation of a Sacred and a Profane, and the use of these two categories would neither reflect the ways of thinking of the members nor be analytically useful. It is expected that the everyday world will be shaped or interrupted by the action of the *wali*, who may frequently appear in person in a vision, or whose voice may be heard on these occasions. He thus gives a guarantee of his continued presence and his hand in the particular circumstance.

We are therefore concerned not only with events which are 'uncanny' in any immediate sense; events in which the elaboration of some mystical explanation would seem as natural since no other construction can possibly be put on them and they cannot be conceptualized in terms of ordinary or available notions of causation. For to a non-member of comparable social background and education many occurrences regarded as *karamat* (excluding of course those where the Saint appears—which he does only to members) would give rise to no particular comment or attention but would be accepted as chance (the bus), coincidence (the suitcase), or even mere forgetfulness (the pound note). One might speculate, though it would be no more than speculation, that the death of the relative after the Sheikh had left would not call forth the idea that he had foreseen it to one who did not belong to the *Hamidiya Shadhiliya*; further, that had it occurred to another Order, such a claim would not have been made for the head of the Order involved. It is rather that the mystical explanation is preferred over the alternative. The mind leaps to the idea of Salama (or his son) and the event is ascribed *directly* to him as agent of the Prime Causer. The 'miracle' is in the eye of the believer.

This disposition to supply the notion of saintly intervention and to give a new structure and articulation to situations—whether they are or are not open to other modes of explanation—depends of course on the initial acknowledgement of his status as *wali*. From that all follows. But at the same time also as one member, Sheikh Ibrahim's private secretary, put it: 'Men came to him because he made *karamat*. He did not perform them in order to attract people to the *tariqa* but it was because of this men gathered to him.' The *karamat* thus play a key part in both the establishment and maintenance of his special status and of the organization based upon it.

For here is a Saint who specifically watches over his followers who have many tales to relate of his assistance, a Saint whom many men have known, whose life is described in detail in a biography by one of his officials and whose photograph is the most treasured article in any member's pocket-book. Visions of him are seen and his voice is heard with heartening regularity and as part of the normal course of events. Most members have either been the direct beneficiaries of the *karama* that God bestowed on him or will eagerly tell of friends who were.

His acts are perhaps the major topic of conversation among the brothers when they gather for meetings after special occasions, or when they sit together in the coffee shops after the *hadrahs*. Ahmed's narrative was typical of what goes on at such informal gatherings. Here was a man who had known Salama intimately for years, who could cite countless examples of his sanctity, recounting in a powerfully dramatic way yet another demonstration of his all-present care. The sense of immediacy impinges strongly on the audience who might be said to participate vicariously in the *karama*. It renews the faithful and draws perhaps the uncommitted into the fold of the *Hamidiya Shadhiliya*. But behind this lies the fundamental point that the Saint and his *karamat* are what they are to the brothers *because they are part of a wider universe of explanation*. They belong to a deeper 'reservoir of significance' by means of which the world is not so much comprehended as apprehended.[1] The Saint is only one strand in the subtly interwoven threads of a moral and interpretational order. His power, and therefore Allah's, is demonstrated and evoked in certain complexes of events or recurrent contexts with certain dominant thematic motifs. He is a means that a mysterious, transcendent, predestinating God is assumed to use in the regulation of all things. In this aspect Salama is a symbol of an ever-continuing process of divine control and grace in the world, just as his spiritual descent line of Sheikhly office and his presumed genealogical link to the Prophet's grandson are signs of historical continuity and legitimacy. But he is only one sign or mode of God's power on earth related to many others in different ways.

The notion of *baraka*, so closely associated with saintliness, must be viewed in the same way. So often treated as though it were a separate social fact examples of which can be catalogued to illustrate the wide range of acts and objects thought to transmit it, *baraka* must be understood rather as part of the whole complex of

[1] Luckmann, Thomas, *The Invisible Religion*, New York: The Macmillan Company, 1967, p. 52.

forces, thought in an ultimate sense to constitute as well as to govern the world. There are maleficent powers to be warded off by the saints, by amulets, talismen, verses of the Quran, the virtuous life, and trust in God. And where the balance turns against you there is the final radical explanation of the mystery of God's will. All these elements are 'givens', accepted principles of the universe of meaning. I shall argue that this set of meanings has been disrupted for many as a result of the pattern of changes in Egyptian society. Yet for many others it remains at root still intact.

These latter are predominantly drawn from the same social stratum as that from which Salama himself sprang, the largely uneducated urban lower classes. Born fifteen years before the British occupation of 1882, he became a minor cog in the State bureaucracy under foreign rule. Egypt was changing, but not in ways which gave new power over their life circumstances to these lower levels. The national political system was in a state of upheaval, and bewildering shifts were occurring in the economic and social spheres. But the urban mass remained, as before, subject to structural forces in the society beyond their control, and largely, no doubt, beyond their comprehension. Traditional values enshrined in popular religion had been challenged and even apparently swept aside. Everyday life, objectively uncertain and structurally determined, could and can at least be given meaning by the sanctified dream-vision, the hope of miracle, the flow of blessing, the saintly intervention, the sureness of another world. Here all the forms of folk Sufism could be reduced to a mystifying idiom in which the real restrictions and frustrations of the life of these strata might be expressed, and for some transcended.

Significantly, as I have remarked above (p. 21), the further up the scale of occupation, education, and financial standing a member is, the more likely it is that he will see the *karamat* and the Saint himself through eyes that perceive learning and qualities of character where others dream dreams and hear voices. Those of this group will tend to emphasize the sober doctrinal nature of the Order, the rationalization of its organization (in which they are frequently officers), and the Sheikh's orthodoxy and capacities as a teacher. They look for different signs of grace, and regard with a certain patient but slightly embarrassed indulgence, the enthusiasm and eager witness to saintly action of the mass of the brothers, recognizing that if the Order is to remain numerically strong, then proclamations of *karamat* and the inexhaustible flow of Salama's powers are essential. Saif's hagiography is a good example of this pious presentation of their image of Salama's sanctity. The same restraint and control govern their ritual behaviour. This emphasis plays an important role in that it opens a way for recruitment of individuals drawn from classes above the vast mass of the urban poor. The Order is flexible in its presentation of itself and in its message. The Saint practised extreme asceticism, but later modified it; he made *karamat*, but what men recognize as *karamat* embraces a wide range of action and interpretation, and he stressed that such grace acts were not the essence of his mission, and could even be a distraction; he offered the drama of saintly intervention in the everyday world, and the quiet contemplation of Quranic exegesis. Men can make what they wish of his *baraka*, and they do so after the pattern of elective affinities which the study of his miracles reveals. It is a pattern which Salama's career also yields, moving as it does from self-mortificatory ecstatics to the bureaucratic planning of the *tariqa* organization.

The Foundation of the Order by Salama

Detail of the early years of the *Hamidiya Shadhiliya* is scanty, and we can only provide a short examination of the means adopted by Salama to establish his own *tariqa*. Saif devotes very little space to it in his book and none of the original members are still living. There is just enough material to allow us to piece together an outline of the process.

The cardinal point is that it is said that the Sheikh did not go out into the world seeking to found a *tariqa*, but was under the *order* of God to do so. In other words he began his mission not of his own free will and decision at all, but on a Divine command sent in a *ru'ya sadiqa*. This 'truth vision' is held to be from God, and it is not uncommon for the foundation of a brotherhood to arise out of such a *ru'ya*.[1] An obligation is laid upon the charismatic figure by the source of Grace and is not claimed by himself for himself. His role is humbly to obey the direction of the God whose

---

[1] Lings, Martin, *A Moslem Saint of the Twentieth Century*, London: Allen & Unwin, 1961, pp. 63–6.

See also the tradition of the Prophet: 'Visions are from God, and dreams are from Satan.' Bukhari, *Kitab al Hiyal*, Bab at-Ta'bir.

purpose he merely fulfils. His vision is the legitimization as leader of the new Order, and is either accepted as such by others, or rejected, depending on factors to be considered below. Other individuals, though this did not happen in the case of Salama as far as I was able to discover, may even have confirmatory visions, thus witnessing to the inescapable nature of the leader's assumption of his position.[1] It is possible that such confirmatory visions are more likely to occur where, as in the example of the Sheikh al-'Alawi given by Martin Lings, there is considerable dispute and rivalry over the question.[2] This tension does not appear to have existed at the time of Salama's establishment of the *Hamidiya Shadhiliya* (if any strain did exist between him and the branch of the *Shadhiliya* of which he was originally a member, there is no record of it. Given the general decline and amorphous character of the Egyptian Orders I think it most unlikely). This probably reflects a somewhat moribund state of the branch of the *Shadhiliya* to which he belonged. Succession to Salama, on the other hand, involved a serious crisis.

In his vision, then, the Sheikh is said to have been instructed to follow the path of the Saints and to form an Order. He heard a *hatif* (an invisible caller or voice) which commanded him in his innermost essence (*sirr*). He followed the *Shadhili* way because they regarded the Sheikh al Junaid[3] as the *Sheikh at-Ta'ifa*, Sheikh of the *Sufiya* and he (Junaid) had become a *Shadhili*. 'They say that "our beginning is the end of all others" for all go back to him' (Sheikh Ibrahim's private secretary).

Salama's reputation spread, and he became, Saif tells us, 'the cynosure of all eyes' (p. 30). Members say that God made many followers round him and that men journeyed to see him from all over the country. In 1926–7 (A.H. 1345, by which time he was sixty years old) the Supreme Sufi Council under the direction of the Sheikh al Bekri, then head of all the Orders, decided to recognize the *Sigada* (here in the sense of independent organization as a *tariqa*) of the *Hamidiya Shadhiliya*.

A significant fact about the foundation is the strong proselytizing sense which seems to have been characteristic of Salama after the

---

[1] Lings. op. cit., pp. 64–6.   [2] Ibid., p. 63.
[3] Died A.D. 910. One of the leading orthodox exponents of Sufism and held in the highest esteem. See *Shorter Encyclopedia of Islam*, Leiden: E. J. Brill, 1953, p. 93.

vision, and which the Order has maintained since his death. This complements the idea of the Sheikh as the passive vessel of Divine Grace to whom men come of their own volition without his seeking them out.[1] The classic pattern, to which Weber and later Troeltsch drew attention, of disciples gathering round the master in a small group and all in personal contact with him (as is claimed, for example, by Lings of Sheikh al-'Alawi) holds true of Salama, but we need to bear in mind that he very early thought of this first group as a recruiting élite to go out and draw members into the new *tariqa*.

His mission had, from the beginning, a particular character which Saif explains in a key passage in his biography. It was, he says, in two parts: first, God 'drew aside for him the veil of contingent causes so that he might go down into this world and mix in the ranks of the people to help them with their troubles, and treat their sicknesses, and make straight their deviations (from the proper path), and take them by the hand to the heaven of perfection' (p. 149). God raised him to the lofty rank of *wali* and singled him out particularly for the people. So the voice of the *Hamidiya Shadhiliya* became loud enough to be heard by those who had (before) failed to hear and its light covered all others. The second part of his mission was his knowledge that he was worthy of the place to which he had been raised and that other leadership (the sheikhs of al Azhar and the leaders of the various *turuq*) did not wish to call to the way of God those they felt not worthy of it or those they thought were unable to proceed in the way and lacked the patience to do so (p. 150). Such men had held back from the mass and were satisfied with the élite. But God did not want others to be lost without a shepherd and so moved the heart of Salama for them that he devoted all his efforts to helping them until their stubbornness passed and they entered into obedience to Allah (p. 151).

There is considerable stress here on the Sheikh's attracting to himself the humble and those who were ignored or held in contempt by other religious leaders, and on the reforming characteristics of his efforts. We are told that he drew even thieves from their trade (p. 180). A great part of his overt appeal was to those 'without a shepherd'; to those whom he felt were untouched or unaccommodated by the existing religious institutions. We find a further attack on the Azharis of the kind which has been discussed

[1] We remember that he was referred to as *gadhdhab*, possessed of a quality of spiritual magnetism. See above, p. 16.

above, and on the heads of the other Orders. The Sheikh apparently felt, as his followers still feel today, that the other brotherhoods had failed to adapt to the times and that their leaders were ineffectual and ignored the broad mass of the people.

Salama certainly possessed a keen sense of the problems and demands involved in the setting up and maintenance of a religious organization. He devised the *Qanun* (Laws, see Appendix for full translation) of the *Hamidiya Shadhiliya* for the comprehensive regulation of the Order. So early and rigorous a rationalization of the new organization is extremely unusual. It is particularly so in a movement which depends on a charismatic religious personality for its establishment. Even though a model of organization lay close at hand in the traditional structure of a *tariqa*, the actual laying down of an elaborate quasi-bureaucratic charter for the Order is extremely rare, if not indeed unprecedented. Salama thus attempted to fix permanently the structure of the *Hamidiya Shadhiliya*. The laws are the personally written instructions of the Saint and founder and as such are of unquestioned authority. This argues a fervent desire to ensure as far as lay in his power a continuity in all respects of the Order over time and a provision against the inbuilt elements of fission in such groups.

It must be noted here that the rationalization was specifically presented as being due to organizational necessity rather than to any doctrine of spiritual inequality with its corollary of varying degrees of fitness for the positions set up within the Order. Though the *khulafa'* and *nuqaba'* have in fact, as we shall see, a considerable degree of power in the *Hamidiya Shadhiliya*, they are still *in the terms of the official model of the Order* merely organizers, *munazzimin*, there simply to ensure the efficient running of the group. Saif says that such posts were established 'as the organisation of the different groups made it necessary' (p. 30). A degree of ambiguity therefore surrounds these points in the structure. Salama's message was to the poor, preaching the love of all for all in brotherhood under Allah and the equality of all. The officials have had to be theoretically accommodated to this basic ethic.

At the same time, the Sheikh was extremely careful, not to say scrupulous, in his choice of the first members; and in a way which indicates that he was from the beginning intent on setting up the *Hamidiya Shadhiliya* on a firm basis. Despite the stress on the mission to the neglected and the implications that, in contrast to other religious groups, all were to be accepted as worthy, only a few initially were chosen. Saif explains that his way was very particular. When anyone came to him he would delay the would-be member's entry into the Order for days or even months, giving him no encouragement or help. During all this period Salama would watch until he was sure of the man's sincerity, the truthfulness of his coming, and the strength of his endurance, then he would lead him step by step until the *murid* felt the Order to be part of his very being and his heart, would know that he was responsible before his Sheikh and Allah (p. 60), and would be filled with total love and reverence for the Sheikh.

Entry into the Order was thus the result of thorough testing of the initiate by the Saint. Not all were fitted for membership. For though he explicitly aimed at a particular type of member, Salama seems to have been acutely aware of the need to provide the Order with a 'hard core', personally utterly devoted to him and in whom he would have absolute trust. He may well have been partly inspired in this by the structural looseness and attenuation of the other *turuq*. In this process of 'ordeal', some were discouraged, and being so, failed the examination to which the Sheikh had put them. In this way, he very early attempted to establish the organization of the *Hamidiya Shadhiliya* on rational lines (in the Weberian sense). The testing so piously described by Saif enabled Salama to sum up the character, dedication, and social position of each of these crucial first members of his staff, and to judge them for the roles of organizers and deputies in the fledgling Order. The setting up in full detail of the means of control, administration, and regulation within the brotherhood, often a long process of development in religious groups, was closely integrated here in its inception. Just how thorough was this procedure can be seen by a glance at the *Qanun*.

Those men that he accepted were to be the teaching and recruiting élite of the *Hamidiya Shadhiliya*. In their hands would lie the responsibility for the spread of the Order throughout the country. They would draw others to the way of the Sheikh and the whole future of the *tariqa* thus depended on them. Members of this élite were sent out to establish *zawiyas* in various areas of Cairo, Alexandria, Beni Suef, the Faiyyum oasis, Giza, Tanta, Mansura, Manufia, Desuq, Isna, Asyut, and Minya (p. 31). The Sheikh travelled extensively around these new centres, putting himself into personal contact with the *muridin* attracted to his way by his deputies. Indeed it was on one of these journeys that he contracted his last illness.

The strict policy of testing was later relaxed when its purpose had been fulfilled and the requirements of the organization changed from the qualitative to the quantitative level. Rather than wait for men to come to him, we are told that he went out and actively recruited. When a *hadrah* was held, he would afterwards greet those present individually with the hand-kiss (*musafaha*) and accept them into the brotherhood by administering the oath (*'ahd*) *on the spot* if they so wished. He no longer bothered to investigate those who came asking to be *muridin*; it was enough that the person should ask, and he would be welcome to membership of the Order *without any question whatever* (Saif, p. 147, my emphasis). This change-over is reported to have taken place around 1930. The Sheikh thus spent the greater part of his mission, from its very early beginnings in 1909 for the next twenty-one years, chiefly in training his *munazzimin*. Only at the end did he open the Order to all.

Salama's religious career thus falls into three stages. The first is the crystallization of the idea of his mission and his preparation for it. Extremes of asceticism and self-mortification, long fasts, sexual abstinence, and seclusion were combined with a daunting series of private recitations of the names of God. He 'put on the mantle of holiness', cloaked himself in the external attributes of sanctity and, as he later appears to have realized, concentrated at first on the outer signs, the external (the *zahir*) rather than the inner self (the *batin*). His whole life was regulated by ritual standards prior to the claiming of Sheikhly status which would legitimize his demands on his followers. This stage represents an absorption of his identity into a culturally given paradigm, into a tradition of ritual and symbolic behaviour; it is an evocation of a set of meanings and powers he also will embody. He made himself a condensation of a whole tradition in a specific mode of being. In his re-creation of the role of Sufi sheikh and founder of an Order, Salama asserted its unchanged significance and authority. He defended the social authenticity of the tradition and its continued capacity to 'make sense' of the world in the face of those dislocations between them which he partly recognized.

The second stage was the prolonged process of initiating the movement and training the core group of administrators, recruiters, and teachers. At the same time he set in train the routinization and codification of Sheikhly charisma in the Rule of the *Hamidiya Shadhiliya*. This understanding of the need to centralize the Order for effective administration and growth is one aspect of Salama's grasp of the objective realities of social change in Egypt. Obviously he thought that the time was ripe for the establishment of a new *tariqa* that would avoid the diffuseness and cross-cutting ties of multiple membership of the other Orders, and he attempted to build up a considerable following for his divinely commanded mission. He had noted the shift in relations with the '*ulema*' and the State and sought to outflank damaging attacks on his orthodoxy by insistence on the Holy Law as the basis of the brotherhood. Furthermore, and this brings us to the final stage, he had selected the strata from which he would recruit on a completely open basis, and was now prepared to delegate his authority to the chosen deputies so severely examined. He lived through a vital period of modern Egyptian history and in some respects was clearly able to map out a strategy for his Order; witness his pattern of leadership, the defence against possibly harmful charges by the authoritative élite, the carefully constructed organizational skeleton, the identification of the pool of potential membership. Yet the *Hamidiya Shadhiliya*, though having a distinctive character, has always had only a fairly restricted following, not more than a humble group on the margins of Egyptian social life. What were the limitations of Salama's vision and leadership?

Saint and Society

Sheikh Salama came from a humble family and in part escaped the restrictions of his social situation by seeking religious status, a common enough avenue for men of his class throughout Muslim history. More than this, however, he was possessed of a profound sense of a mission, and his life is essentially the story of the attempt to answer fully to the missionary imperative. Here two factors at once become relevant. The first is the theme of the bearer of holiness as a model for existence, the greatest example of which in Islam is the Prophet Muhammad himself. Being a '*sunni*' (usually translated as orthodox) Muslim means in fact following the Sunna or path of Muhammad as contained in the canonical traditions,

traditions which cover virtually every aspect of life. Though it is true that there has always been an emphasis in the *turuq* on successive stages of esoteric understanding for the élite, this other exemplary theme has been of considerable importance. The second factor is that in the Muslim world the enactment of such a mission was generally encompassed within the institution of the Sufi *tariqa*, and that the would-be religious leader had (in Salama's early years) this given form of action and virtually no other before him. It was still an integral element of the life of Egyptians in the widest sense. Any new religious movement almost automatically took on its shape, though naturally the content of the call might differ.

The Orders had emerged originally in a period of radical change as a challenge to orthodoxy and a redirection of popular associational religion. They had evolved in Egypt towards a more symbiotic relationship with the legists and in the process had been incorporated as a vital part of the meaning of being a Muslim. Through their vast range of variation and flexibility in doctrine and practice they served to canalize, absorb, and turn into socially legitimate channels the always potentially disrupting charismatic impulse that might manifest itself in areas of strain or anomy. The Brotherhoods counterpoised learning with illumination, exegesis with communion, law with intercession.

The role of the Saints was central to this framework of a cognitive, moral, and social order. They redefined and re-ordered the lifeworld of their followers, requiring of them not only devotion but prescribed patterns of behaviour. The nexus of their virtuoso religiosity and the religiosity of the mass was established in the *tariqa*.[1] For their adherents, and in a more diffuse way for those who accepted their sanctity but did not lay themselves under particular allegiance to them, they reorganized the system of status, not in the world's standards, but on the basis of spiritual worth. It is the potential of this devaluation of the world to be transformed into a call for the *reshaping* of the world on the divine paradigm which made them such ambiguous figures in the eyes of the official religious authority and of the State. The implicit challenge was constant even where the elements of ecstasy and the displacement

---

[1] See Max Weber, 'The Social Psychology of the World Religions', in *From Max Weber*, trans., ed., and with introduction by Gerth and Mills, London: O.U.P., 1958, p. 287. The use of 'mass' here is also Weber's and refers to those he calls the 'religiously unmusical' and not to the lower social strata.

of hope from this world to the next dominated a given grouping. Mystification and violent political action might as easily combine in popular Sufism as in any other form. One could not predict what plants might grow in the magic garden.

I have emphasized the sense in which the Saint is a symbolic representation of a total order of things. The authority he claims for this imperative role depends on individuals' acceptance of his special link with God and their recognition of certain acts and signs as demonstrations of that connection. He must fulfil certain expectations in patterns of behaviour and articulate an authentic call before charisma will, as it were, be granted to him by others. Once it is and the following gathers round him, his authority and judgement are placed above dispute. He is teacher, spiritual guide, councillor; his power is held to deliver men from danger and to guard them against misfortune. The Saint *arbitrates* between men by virtue of their belief that he *mediates* between them and Allah. For he embodies the final 'criteria of reality' through his position as one connected with the Power which revealed these criteria. His miracles prove the connection. As one of the spiritual élite he has unique comprehension of God's inscrutable ways. Linking men with their concepts of the Divine plan he restates it and guarantees its mysterious outworkings. From him they can obtain *baraka* and through him they intercede for assistance in mundane affairs.

This is not to say that he is necessarily to be depended on to the exclusion of individual striving in worldly matters. Salama demanded a strict attention to the tasks and duties which are each man's lot in the occupation he undertakes, and more than fulfilled this teaching in his own life. The cry for *madad* (help) is not to serve as a substitute for action in the face of problems which may be resolved by the individual's efforts. The world must not be turned from in passivity; he offers no retreat from circumstance but exhorts men to the proper accomplishment of their duties in work. Though the standards prevailing beyond the Order may not be identical with those within it, and the granting of status is founded on different criteria altogether, this does not absolve members from their due labours. At the same time, work is not a virtue to be pursued for its inherent goodness or because it is the basis of an ethic; it is not by works that Muslims achieve salvation or demonstrate spiritual worth and distinction. For those capable of it the higher reaches of mystical illumination are to be sought through spiritual discipline and concentration, pre-eminently in the *dhikr*. For the mass there is no seeking after a rational mastery of the world but simply a fulfilling of its functional requirements, no more and no less. This together with the prescribed duties of religion and those of the *tariqa* suffice them.

There is a further aspect of the Saint's role which should be noted. That is that his death, though in our example organization-ally critical, in another sense is almost incidental. The physical removal of the individual figure from the scene makes little difference to his performance of his role. Indeed he is not even physically removed in so far as his shrine serves as a centre of con-centration of his power and the blessing he bestowed during life. Death may actually increase the power attributed to him, and in many cases he may not be regarded quite as a Saint proper during his lifetime. The range of miracles credited to him becomes even wider after his demise, and a freer rein is given to the attribution of miraculous intervention to him. However, it must be reasserted that the continuation of his reputation, its growth or diminution, and the ensuring of the viability of the organization founded by him are crucially affected by other external and internal factors. This particularly involves the transmission of authority, and processes of maintenance and control within the *tariqa*; the nature and function of its teachings and the activities demanded of the committed; the relation of these to the wider social situation; and finally the continued relevance of the ethic and ideology of the group to what Karl Mannheim has called the collective purposes of the time.

This brings us back to the limitations on Salama's understanding of changes in the fabric of his society. Essentially he worked and thought within the traditional framework of religious and social movements in Egypt. He came from the urban poor and relied for the generality of his members upon them. We might suggest that this stratum, being most structurally determined in its range of social possibilities, most subject to forces that appear to act upon it from without, and highly restricted in its control of its own future, is most attached to a traditional world of (in this case) fatalism, God's will, and the hope of *baraka*. It may furnish a mob, but it is unlikely to be the backbone of sustained radical social movements because of the major obstacles to any transcendence of its social situation in either consciousness or practice. Salama succeeded in identifying the weaknesses of the *turuq* as they were at the end of the last century. In ways to which I have already pointed he was capable of developing a coherent strategy for his mission. But the mission itself, his response to the historical crisis, was in essence backward-looking and the product of his social milieu. It was an attempt to preserve the viability of the old forms and meanings and to assert old continuities when all around him they were being ruptured. It was, in short, an effort to stem the tide.

What resulted was a basically quietist, modest group of the pious, accommodating and conciliatory towards the *'ulema'*, fortified by brotherhood and by the Saint's protection against the trials of the world. The story of the humiliation of the English superior (IV(*a*) and (*b*), p. 24, above) shows at least a naïve understanding of the implications of the British occupation and the various currents of the nationalist movements. But there is no evidence that the Sheikh made any effort to associate the *Hamidiya Shadhiliya* with these movements. By background, education, and outlook he was unable to grasp the way in which the very definition of politics in Egypt was being transformed. New leadership from the liberal middle classes was founding mass parties such as the Wafd; Islamic modernism emerged under the influence of Jamal ad-Din al Afghani and Sheikh Muhammad 'Abduh; figures of the stature of Mustafa Kamil and Saad Zaghlul mobilized the people against foreign rule. In the last decade of Salama's life Hassan al Banna forged the Muslim Brethren out of the urban petite bourgeoisie, and made of them the most significant religio-political movement in modern Egyptian history. The heads of the Sufi Orders no longer had an arena for public action, and were pre-empted by the élite of politicians, landowners, lawyers, and journalists from asserting their leadership in the wider social context.

This shift in the nature and bounds of the political realm had a most important implication for the basis of authority on which the *turuq* had once relied. For the whole notion of *baraka* and indeed of *wilaya* is bound up, not with vague ideas of other-worldly holiness, but with the capacity for significant action in the world. The presumed vertical link between a man and God must be demonstrated in the horizontal links he may make in relations between men. The two are inextricably interconnected. *Baraka* and *wilaya* must be worked out in the field of mundane circumstances through acts held to manifest a power that the individual derives from God.

Religious authority has to be won, and once gained must be continually renewed and recharged.

Now in the traditional system the opportunities for doing so were ever-present and institutionalized in the positions of the *'ulema'* and the Heads of the Orders who were structurally cast as mediators between high and low, rulers and ruled, and between those at the same level of society. But it is precisely this crucial function of which they have been deprived. The idiom, the nature of power and authority were changed and taken over by other agencies with other means and aims. Other groups take account of the demands of the changing situation, and in the thirties we see in addition to the parties the dramatic flowering of mutual-benefit societies, co-operatives, and religious groups that put associational life on a different basis at many levels of the society.

Sufi Sheikhs' capacity to order relations between men declined. They found themselves increasingly identified merely with one aspect of Islam, and that an aspect under constant attack. From their shrines the Saints might continue to play a vital part in popular religion both in the mass pilgrimage and the private prayer. Secure in posthumous reverence they maintained their individual reputations for blessing and help. But the situational possibilities for *new* sainthood to be claimed or acclaimed by large numbers of Egyptians grew ever more restricted. It took nearly twenty years of intense activity by Salama before his group was officially recognized by the Sufi Council, yet he had aimed at what was still by far the majority sector of the urban population which might well have been expected to respond most actively to what the *Hamidiya Shadhiliya* represented. That it did so only in very limited numbers suggests that even the most traditional stratum found Salama's attempted revitalization of a *tariqa* inadequate, and more generally, that his mission no longer answered to the problems and purposes of Egyptian society.

II

SAINT'S DAY

THE *mulid* is technically the celebration of the day of the birth
or death of a Saint. I say technically because in fact a *wali* may
have several such days devoted to him during the year and
each celebration continues for three or four days with a final 'big
night' at which festivities reach a climax. It would in general be
true to say that in Egypt, at least, a Saint without a *mulid* is as incon-
ceivable as a Saint without miracles, though the latter are of course
a precondition rather than a necessary adjunct to his position. As
an integral element in the social pattern of sanctity the lapsing of
a *mulid* with the implied withdrawal of recognition of his active role
in human affairs indicates that the social function and identity of
the *wali* are at an end.

These festivals fall into four main categories:

(*a*) The large public occasions such as the *mulids* of the Prophet,
of Hussein, and of Seyyida Zeynab.

(*b*) Equally public, those ceremonies which were originally
associated with the Saint of a particular *tariqa* but which are now
'common property' and participated in by all. The best examples
here are the famous *mulid* of Ahmad al Bedawi in Tanta and of
Ibrahim al Desuqi in the town of Desuq.

(*c*) Those of Saints and founders of *tariqas* which have not taken
on a mass character but remain primarily celebrations of the Order
concerned, with peripheral public activity principally involving
people of the area in which the tomb of the Saint is situated. Our
major example and the substance of this chapter is the *mulid* of the
Hamidiya Shadhiliya held for Sheikh Salama.

(*d*) Those associated mainly with particular ascriptive social
groupings based on structural relations of kinship, politics, and so
forth. We may cite those connected with lineage segments among
the Bedu[1] and with families who hold a *mulid* for a Saint as a

---

[1] Peters, E., 'The Proliferation of Segments in the Lineage of the Beduin in
Cyrenaica', *Journal of the Royal Anthropological Society*, vol. 90, Part 1,
pp. 29–53. Ernest Gellner has pointed out to me that the tribal Saint's days in

'private' festival which honours, not only the *wali*, but also them-selves. A good deal of conspicuous consumption as well as the acquisition of religious merit, is attached to the latter kind of group endeavour. Here the range of persons attending and their social relations with each other are critical and often of local-level political importance. Such occasions give an opportunity for establishing, renewing, realigning, or severing social ties before an audience of significant others. Groups may publicly define their interrelations within the framework of the spectacle of the day of the Saint, part of whose religious constituency they claim to be.

The first two categories above retain their importance to the present time and there seems to be little diminution in their popu-larity. They have a very strong element of the medieval fair and people from all over the country, particularly from the Delta and Lower Egypt, attend. Writing of the decade before the Second World War, McPherson records a marked hostility on the part of the government to the *mulids* in general. The agencies of political authority have, however, long recognized the wisdom of association with, rather than opposition to, those in categories (*a*) and (*b*) which are among the greatest communal religious festivals in the country. Official estimates of the attendance at the 1964 Tanta *mulid* for example were one and a quarter million people and there may well have been even greater numbers. If it is generally true, as Berque asserts of Sirs al Layyan, that village participation has diminished, the reduction has certainly not had any dramatic effect.[1]

I did not collect data on the economic function of these occasions but there is no doubt even now of their considerable importance in this respect.[2] Both Tanta and Desuq are large market towns, and the major *mulids* both fall just after the cotton harvest in the Delta in the late summer (October). Significantly too, they are fixed by the Coptic calendar which means that the date remains the same from year to year, rather than moving backward annually by some ten

Central Morocco are generally not 'private' but *inter*-tribal (private communica-tion).

[1] Berque, J., *Histoire sociale d'un village égyptien au XXème siècle*, Paris: Mouton, 1957, pp. 38–41.

[2] This will by now be less significantly related to distribution of goods and products. The *mulids* form a kind of circuit which supports a whole caravan of itinerant tinkers, sweet-sellers, and petty tradesmen who move from one to the other in rotation. A great deal of research on the *mulid* as a matrix of economic and social relations needs to be carried out.

days as must those which follow the Muslim lunar calendar. As so often with festivals everywhere they are held at a time of plenty. The social importance of Ahmad al Bedawi surely grew as much from strategic location as from other factors. It might be suggested indeed that he is only the most striking example of reputation for holiness and the developing cult growing up as a function of a particular combination of social interests and a structure of economic and political relations.

In the case of the Tanta *mulid*, the part played by the 'founding' *tariqa*, the *Ahmadiya*, is now almost peripheral. It no longer constitutes the organizational framework for the gathering, but has become merely one of the many groups who are represented there, perhaps retaining a shadow of its former pre-eminence because of its illustrious founder. The final *zeffa* (procession), called by McPherson the 'clou' of the entire festival, is notable more for the fixed bayonets of the parading government troops than for the attention paid to the *khalifa* as he rides in the rear with a small group of followers. In the year that I visited Tanta the somewhat pathetic group of *Ahmadiya*, quite upstaged by the military band, had to endure the further indignity of a barrage of stage whispers as to their respected Sheikh's condition. He seemed somewhat dissociated from the occasion, having to be supported on his horse, and some members of the highly entertained crowd unworthily suggested that wine other than that of Paradise had passed his aged lips. His young retinue were quite unable to deal with this irreverence and were put sadly out of countenance.

The main and last night of the *mulid* is climaxed by a firework display put on by the government in the open area outside the town centre in which the Saint's mosque stands. Though the various *turuq* have tents here for members, the scene was dominated in 1964 by the marquees set up by the Arab Socialist Union and by the large firework set piece of President Nasser. On the way to the display ground there were innumerable coffee tents crowded with people, and fair stalls and dimly lit booths offering everything from the wall of death and trials of strength to singers, the painted advertisements for whom had as little to do with religion as with art. Hundreds of thousands of people elbowed, charged, and struggled their way up the narrow road from mosque to fireworks. Children were trampled and barely rescued, students snake-danced their way through the infinitely good-tempered chaos effectively blocked only by formidable black-swathed peasant women carrying huge bundles and screaming out for their lost offspring; men hurled themselves across the flood to reach the lavish spectacles promised by huge posters of incredibly-endowed belly dancers announced as producing pleasure that even the infinitely resourceful Arabic language could scarcely describe. The white haloes of spirit lamps illuminated patches of dusty earth where families who had travelled many miles for this great night stretched out exhausted on the ground. The President's face spluttered and flamed like some fiery icon above Egypt *en fête*.

If the part of the *turuq* in the *mulids* of these categories has declined notably, however, the veneration paid to the Saint has not. The visiting of his tomb, the *ziyara*, is an essential element for virtually all who attend. People crowd into a tiny room to circumambulate the shrine, pressing themselves against the outer brass railings, kissing it and rubbing their clothes and hands over it, and then making a washing motion of the hands over their bodies to transfer the *baraka*. This is, *par excellence*, the propitious time at which to do so; in the popular phrase, '*khud al baraka min al mulid*' ('take the *baraka* from the *mulid*').

People do so vocally and with feeling. There is almost as much noise as at the fireworks, and anyone who has absorbed Victorian notions of reverent behaviour as being synonymous with whispers and quiet decorum soon has his assumptions disrespectfully shattered. As far as the Saint is concerned reverence can be demonstrated as well by shouting as by muttered prayer. Attendants roar and push the struggling mass round the shrine, using bamboo canes on those who cling too long to holiness. Those who leave must do so through those clamouring to enter. Huddled in a corner, chewing on a sweetmeat dangerously thrown over ecstatic faces by a mosque servant, the anthropologist has time to reflect on the wreckage of his own fixed ideas about proper expressions of piety.

The *fatiha* is recited which brings blessing on both the *wali* and the reciter. A *nadhr*, or conditional promise, is made: 'If you do such and such a thing then I will do . . .' etc. As Durrell has aptly observed, on these occasions 'prayer is a form of bargaining: you will see at once that the psychological attitude to the Saint is one of rough familiarity'.[1] Though one prays to him, seeks blessing

---

[1] Durrell, L., *Prospero's Cell*, London: Faber (paperback), 1962, p. 32.

from his shrine, pleads to him for freedom from sickness for a child, for life for a relative, and for fertility, such actions are often performed on almost a 'man to man' basis and tone. You will do this, but he must keep his share of what is, in effect, looked on as a contract. One man came into the small room containing Bedawi's tomb, and having recited the *fatiha*, shouted out: 'Ya Ahmad! Ya Bedawi! Ya Sheikh al 'Arab!' much as he would have done to someone across the street, and his manner provoked no comment or response from anyone. We shall need to return to this point later, but it should be borne in mind here since it is of considerable significance.

Finally, it should be remarked that such *mulids* are an important element in the social life of the great proportion of the entire population of Egypt, both male *and female*. Together with the feast of sacrifice and that at the end of the holy fasting month of Ramadan they make up the high points of communal life; the periods of concentrated religious activity centred round the *walis* who play so vital a role in the cosmological and ideological systems of the people. Groups travel together from their various villages to participate in the days of the *mulid* and secure blessing from its saint. Women come as well, and as many of them press about the tomb as men, ululating the shrill cries of celebration (*zagharit*). They often bring their babies to be 'washed' in the *baraka* of the shrine. Children are thus accustomed to be taken to the *wali* from the earliest age by either their parents or siblings. It is at the *mulid* that vast numbers of small boys are circumcised, their screams drowned by a blaring drum and trombone. The child is taught reverence for the Saint, of the multitude of the *karamat*, and the rewards to be looked for from the occasion. These visits are therefore an integral part of growing up in many families in Egypt.

The *mulids* of category (*d*) are outside the main concern of this chapter. It is sufficient to point out that they serve a very different primary function from those in (*a*) and (*b*). In the Western Desert, the pilgrimage to the tomb of a saint culminating in a sacrificial meal takes place annually. Peters explains how it is well known which tribal sections should gather at which shrine.[1] Failure to attend the *mulid* on the part of a group which has always previously been present is taken, and intended, as an expression of lineage

[1] Peters, E., op. cit., and 'The Sociology of the Beduin of Cyrenaica', unpublished D. Phil. thesis, Oxford University, 1951, particularly pp. 63–7.

segmentation and the claiming of social distinctiveness by a new section. Here the festival serves as a proclamation of fission, the sign of the assumption of changed identity and therefore changed political role and affiliations by a group.

The Mulid *of Salama*

After the greetings):

We have decided with the aid of God the Most High to celebrate as is our custom every year, the birth of our excellent father our Imam (here meaning spiritual guide) Sidi Salama ar-Radi (may God be pleased with him) on the 23rd, 24th, and 25th of the month of Ragab of the year 1385 (Islamic dating) which is the 16th, 17th, and 18th November 1965. A celebration whose lofty execution will be as fitting as faithfulness demands and succession sanctions. I trust that we shall all perform this holy duty in the best possible manner. May God bring success for us and for you in raising the condition of the *tariqa*.

My beloved: By the grace of the Most High the brothers will hold a great procession made up from every area immediately after the afternoon prayer on Thursday 25th Ragab, the 18th November 1965, at exactly 3.30 p.m. from the mosque of Sultan Abu'l 'Ila in Bulaq to the house of the *Mashaikha* (central office) where the reception will be held; an occasion which I hope will be better in appearance, larger in terms of numbers present, and greater in endeavour than in the previous years.

My beloved: It is incumbent on all to whom our invitation has come, and who owe us obedience that they prepare to be present bringing with them the greatest number of their brothers with their banners and should join in the celebration with this splendid procession and blessed (*karim*) *mulid*. And we hope that we will all carry out what is necessary and (show) the zeal and response and mutual cooperation your love demands. For we have decided on the increase of the outward signs (*mazahir*) of the *mulid* this year over the previous year and it pleases us to see the clear and brilliant effect of this in the increase of the number of tents of the *mulid* and their splendour.

(complimentary ending)
Ibrahim Salama ar-Radi

20th Gamadi Ath-thani 1385
15th October 1965

(Text A)

This call from Sheikh Ibrahim to the heads of the *zawiyas* initiates the final month's intensive planning of the *mulid* for his father. For reasons which will become obvious, a great deal of

organization and effort is involved in the project. From mid June
the Sheikh's confidential secretary and the secretary of the Order,
who are in charge of the general administration, are busy with
questions of cost, the lay-out of the different tents, the decorations
of the large area in Bulaq (one of the poorer suburbs of Cairo where
Salama was born and where his mosque and shrine are situated)
where the festival is held, and the summons of the various local
groups to a maximum co-operative effort. In recent years the *mulid*
has grown steadily and its arrangement becomes increasingly
complex. This growth reflects credit on the *tariqa*, but it must be
maintained by ever greater efforts for the sake, quite explicitly,
of prestige and propaganda. The officials are highly sensitive to the
necessity to display an impeccable front[1] to all outside the Order
who will judge it on the general appearance of the occasion. No
pains must be spared to ensure that the setting is impressive and
immune to criticism from whatever quarter. The validity of the
'image', to use a much-hackneyed term, is at stake. Hence the
following:

(To the heads of *zawiyas*)

As a supplement to our previous special communication on the *mulid*
of our Imam Sidi Salama ar-Radi (may God be pleased with him), which
will be held on 16th, 17th, and 18 November, 1965, it will honour both
ourselves and you that the celebration this year should be more excellent
than in the previous years by virtue of an increase in the tents both in
number and splendour. This necessitates of us a double effort and co-
operation so that its fame may spread, its power grow, and its standing
be raised.

And I hope that you will all work and double your endeavour so that
the procession this year will be worthy of you and of this great occasion;
*and that its impression will be one of gravity, order, excellence of attire and
obedience* (underlining in the text) for the glory of its dignity and the
greatness of its standing.

It is therefore incumbent on every one of us to be present in the great
procession, for this is the greatest means to bring to the general notice
the authority of the *tariqa*.

And we warn any one who takes it lightly [despises it] *or fails to appear,
or presumes to make excuses, or stands alone in making a celebration in his
home area far from the official mulid in Cairo* that in this is a clear departure from the highest principles of the *tariqa*; such a departure merits the

---

[1] I use both 'front' and 'setting' in the sense of Erving Goffman, *The Presentation of Self in Everyday Life*, New York: Doubleday, 1959, pp. 22–30.

anger of the members and we take refuge in God from that (happening). [Emphasis in the text.]

General Observations

1. The tents will be ready and lit up on the evenings of the 16th, 17th, and 18th November 1965. For this we hope you will enliven the nights with the presence of all your brothers.
2. I impress on the great and the lesser of you the necessity of sharing in the procession to preserve the appearance of the *tariqa*.
3. That all should know that there is absolutely no place for women in the tents, to preserve the holiness and dignity of the *mulid*.[1]
4. It is hoped that this will be carried out in every respect. May God give ourselves and you success for what He wishes and what pleases Him.

November 1st, 1965

Ibrahim Salama ar-Radi
(Text B)

This almost peremptory missive shows more clearly than any elaboration of field data the importance attached to all aspects of the festival. The stern warnings of paragraph four are an example of the Sheikh as leader to whom unquestioning loyalty and obedience are due. The sanction of punitive action by him is invoked to deter anyone from failing in his duty as a member of the brotherhood.

Some three months before this, the *khulafa'* will have been reminded of the *mulid* and asked whether they wish to have a tent there. In the early years after Salama's death the Order set up only one large pavilion for all the brothers. Later the idea was conceived of encouraging the *zawiyas*, either individually or in groups, to raise the money for their own tents. By 1964 there were sixty-two such; in 1965 there were seventy-one, and the secretary expected that there would be around one hundred in 1966. As he put it: 'The brothers are still not satisfied, they want more and bigger tents.' The *khulafa'* reply giving details of how much they wish to spend and a space is reserved for them by the organizers. The work which the *zawiyas* do not contract privately by themselves is then given out to the best electricians and the firms who erect the marquees on the big public occasions when the President speaks. The central office is prepared to lend the local groups money, but

---

[1] Women are allowed in a special set-off section of the tent. They prepare the refreshments, tea and coffee, etc.

failure to repay it within a fairly generous period means that they will not be allowed to have a tent the following year.

The Sheikh's secretary informed me that out of the eighty or so tents set up he had been in charge of the arrangements for fifty-two. He estimated that the total cost would be around £E3,000, approximately £2,400 Sterling. This gives an average of £E58 for each, with of course wide variation around this figure. There must be added to this the expenses on those of the *zawiya* in transport to the *mulid*, provisions for the stay in Cairo, drinks (cold drinks, coffee, and tea), fruit, and various sweets for the guests, the hiring of some form of entertainment (of which more below), and other miscellaneous items. The real cost therefore of a tent may well come to over £E200 in many cases. One particularly fine example was put up by a number of local centres together; the lighting and furnishing were extremely impressive and it was certainly the largest at the *mulid*. Here the tent and contents alone came to £E300, a fact that was the subject of considerable pride. So we might guess at an overall total including all these items of anything between £E8,000 and £E12,000 (£6,000 to £9,000 roughly), a staggering figure in a country where the average per capita income was only U.S. $125.[1]

The money comes from various sources: the bulk of it is collected and set aside over the year by those groups who wish to participate in this fashion. There is no fixed sum expected from the member; he contributes what he likes and what he can, there being theoretically no difference between the man who gives five piastres and the man who gives five pounds. The credit redounds on all. This ideal picture is not, however, absolutely accurate; it is rather another reflection of that constant insistence on equality in the Order which conceals the differentiation in fact existing.

The organization of a tent is no easy matter, for there are certain functional demands to be met. Apart from all the prior arrangements, in the *mulid* proper there will be guests to be greeted, to be shown to their chairs, to be provided with refreshments and cigarettes, to be conversed with, and all this with a constant stream of people coming and going to and from the tent. Some visitors are more important than others and must be recognized and shown due respect. Perhaps the chief consideration is that people must be

---

[1] Hansen, B., and Marzouk, G. A., *Development and Economic Policy in the U.A.R.* (Egypt), Amsterdam: North Holland Publishing Co., 1965, p. 1.

actually attracted to seek the hospitality thus provided by the particular group of members. The greater the number of visitors and general activity, the greater the reputation and the greater the prestige which redounds on the *zawiya* and on the individuals who have by their contributions paid for everything. And as stated above, all (or most) pay, but some pay more than others. It is these latter who become the *munazzimin*. It is they who, to put it crudely, have the largest stake in the success of the tent, and it is they who are in charge of attempting to ensure that all is in order. The fact that the functional demands are met by this group bestows on them additional prestige over and above the ordinary, whatever may be said of absolute equality. They will naturally tend to come from the better-off section of the membership, to be of the besuited *effendi* rather than the peasant or low-grade worker in the *gallabia*. Despite the protestations of brotherhood, the fact that such brother-hood is susceptible of degrees which in part reflect the standards and status consciousness of the world as much as distinctions within the Order itself is continually demonstrated. Assertions (which are common) that wealth and occupation are of no account whatever do not, then, completely correspond to the realities of the situa-tion. At the same time it is perhaps almost unnecessary to remark that this conscious model of equality plays its part in action; that it guarantees certain forms within which the hierarchization is contained and which must be observed by those in fact wielding authority in the tent. They must appear merely as organizers, no more, though their position has the same ambiguity which we have already noted characterizes that of the *nuqaba'*.

The *mulid* in effect lasts almost a week, though most of the activity takes place during the first three days and the *laila kabira* (main night). It begins with a small procession through Bulaq to the mosque of Salama. This is made up entirely of members from the Cairo *zawiyas*, the brothers from other districts not yet having arrived, and in 1965 was attended by approximately 450. They walk slowly, led by the deputy of the Order and behind the great banner of the *tariqa*, singing some of the hymns written by the Saint. At this time the tents are not set up and only the two small lanes leading to the mosque door and the *Mashaikha* respectively are brightly lit with strings of bulbs. The *hadrah* that followed, in the packed mosque and before the tomb of Salama, was a highly charged occasion. The call for *madad* ('assistance', see Chapter VI,

The *Dhikr*) was repeated at length by the chief *munshid*, and at each plea to Salama cries and shouts of praise burst from the brothers with staccato intensity. This observer's gaze was constantly drawn to the shrine itself, screened in gleaming brass and bearing texts of the Quran around its upper borders. The sense of the Saint's presence, the feeling of immediacy and power, was extraordinarily concentrated, generated by the passionate invocations that filled the mosque with overwhelming rhythmical patterns of sound as the *dhikr* came to its separate climaxes.

Control over the violence of the participants' expressive behaviour was markedly less than for the normal weekly *hadrahs*; officials made virtually no attempt to restrain the extreme enthusiasm that seemed at times to threaten to decline into mass hysteria. Sheikh Ibrahim himself did not on this occasion lead the ritual; that function was performed by his deputy. Attention was thus absolutely on the Saint. Many of the *nuqaba'* did not even participate at all in the *dhikr*, but remained in the *Mashaikha*, talking about the affairs of the Order, the *mulid*, and drinking tea. There was something of the feeling that this was an occasion for relaxing the normal controls and allowing the ordinary mass of members an unrestricted outlet for their devotion to Salama.

Finally, after the reading of a section of the Quran, sweets were handed round to all the members. Such a distribution is a *nafha*, a gift that brings with it *baraka* to those who give and to those who receive. This is a marked feature of the *mulid*, and usually takes the form either of sweets, as in this instance, or of meat sandwiches. It may be labouring the point to present this as ritual commensality of the Order but it is at least true to say that partaking of the *nafha* in this setting is a collective acquisition of grace by the members.

Two days later (Monday, 15th November) there was another procession, again of members of the Order from about sixty of the 120 *zawiyas* in Cairo. By this time preparations were more advanced. At both ends of the quite narrow main street of the area ornamental arches had been erected bearing the name of the *tariqa* in flashing neon coloured lights with lines of ordinary bulbs fixed up everywhere across the street. Above each arch was the word 'Allah' in white lights with a portrait of President Nasser below. Flags of the United Arab Republic (as it then was) were also very much in evidence, as they are at all *mulids*. Members of the Brotherhood spend many hours of their free time (and free labour), often taking days off their annual holidays, in supervising and arranging the tents, the decorations, electricity, and so forth, and in generally ensuring that all contingencies have been taken care of. The Sheikh stays in the central office during the evening giving his instructions for the organization of the festival and occasionally inspecting the work in progress. Those officials in charge were often still seeing to details at two and three in the morning.

By the next day, the first of the *mulid* proper, brothers from outside Cairo had started to arrive and take their share in the last-minute preparations. On 17 November (the Wednesday) what was in fact the 'core' of the *mulid* began when the mass of the brothers came to their tents and the celebrations began in full. All the tents, which occupied every spare space in the area, blazed with light; the various organizers were busy serving tea and coffee, asking in the guests and ushering them to their seats, attending to the wants of the members and doing their best to see that the reputation of the tent excelled that of others. Most had sought to provide some entertainment, usually in the form of singers and small groups of musicians who would perform for hours into the early morning. A great deal, but by no means all, of what was sung was specifically religious in content. Only one tent departed from the traditional by hiring a TV set, and this concession to modernity gained little popularity.

The general atmosphere of these last two nights was one of great enthusiasm, fervour, and good humour. Solemnity had little part either in behaviour or conversation. Though the *raison d'être* of the whole gathering was the honouring of the Saint, like all Egyptian *mulids* there was what would normally be described in common Western terms as a strong 'secular' element. This would, however, be misleading. Whereas it might apply to the Tanta festival where the fairground has become both geographically and metaphorically detached from the celebration to a large degree, in the *mulid* of the *Hamidiya Shadhiliya* the whole framework and social significance of the occasion under which all other elements are subsumed is religious. The universal mood of the *mulid* was well expressed by one member, gesturing with satisfaction towards the chaotic bustle of his tent, as *farah* (joyfulness). There is always a great deal of talking, exchanging of greetings, and of fairly broad joking, even on religious matters. Groups will sometimes hold a *dhikr* for the tent and invite others to join in. Again, and quite as commonly, a reader of the Quran may recite part of the Revelation to large groups of the members. There were not, however, any of the booths and sideshows characteristic of the Tanta and other *mulids* (diversions which once moved the Reverend Swan to censorious castigation as 'recreation of a grossly sensual order'.)[1] There is only the *farah*. Even during the singing of the religious songs many in the audience are flicking their fingers and swaying rhythmically in a way typical of Egyptians when listening to ordinary popular Arabic music. The response is exactly the same, and though when extemporizing the singers will usually end with the name of Salama, it is their skill with word play that delights the hearers. Indeed, a good performer is often the way to the success of a tent, since he guarantees a large number of visitors from other *zawiyas*. If a group can hire a well-known artist, so much the better. As the newcomers hand him up a small sum of money he will greet them by name or area and sing a verse for them.

On the final day the main procession takes place. Reference to the Texts A and B will show the considerable importance attached to this occasion as an opportunity for propaganda by the Sheikh and the central office. Great efforts are made to impress on the brothers the need for exemplary personal appearance on all public festivals, and indeed it would be true to say that the *Hamidiya Shadhiliya* outdoes all the other Orders in its attention to this aspect of their activities. The members first line up by *zawiya* in ranks of three singing hymns of the Brotherhood. When Sheikh Ibrahim arrives they face inwards to form two lines between which, escorted by officials of the *tariqa*, he slowly walks. The wild excitement, the pandemonium of shouting 'Ya Sidi Ibrahim', 'Ya Sidi Salama! Madad! Madad!', the press of people trying desperately to touch him to acquire *baraka*, and the shrilling cry of the women, create a scene of extraordinary mass fervour and intensity. Men who have no connection whatever with the Order join in the demonstration, pushing forward to touch the son of the *wali* whose tomb is in the midst of their neighbourhood. When he has finally reached the *Mashaikha* the brothers again form into ranks of three and walk through the crowded *mulid* area to the mosque and their brilliantly

[1] Swan, G., 'The Tanta Mulid', *The Muslim World*, 1914, pp. 45–51.

lit tents, singing hymns at the top of their voices and calling on the names of Ibrahim and Salama.[1]

The other main feature of the evening is the reception given by the Sheikh for invited notables at the *Mashaikha*. It is attended by the Head of the Sufi Orders in Egypt, the *Sheikh al Masha'ikh*, various high government officials, sympathetic Azhari Sheikhs, and the most distinguished members of the Order. An encomium of Salama is delivered in classical Arabic by a guest speaker, and the occasion is notable for its endless flow of lofty complimentary Arabic interchange at an elevated level of elaborate formal courtesy.

Following this exclusive reception, committees of three, made up of *nuqaba'*, go round the various tents to greet the heads of the *zawiyas* in the name of the Sheikh. He himself does not visit any of them at any time, which reflects the practical problems occasioned by the vast crowds, and the inevitable chaos were he to attempt to go the rounds, rather than any deliberate maintenance of distance. The officials use the opportunity to make a spot check on any previously unnoticed absentees. Should a *khalifa* have failed to attend, then written inquiries are made as to the reason for this disobedience of the Sheikh's commands. If the reply is unsatisfactory then Ibrahim may order a small group of senior members to go to the particular individual to make what amounts to a general investigation into this dereliction. Lack of an acceptable explanation then leads to removal from his position or, the ultimate sanction, actual expulsion should he refuse their decision.

This tour of greeting and inspection over, the celebrations continue into the next morning. During the rest of that day the members and their families pack up their goods and start the journey back, heartened by their visit to the Saint and Founder which '. . . has qualified once more the terrors and ardours of living and has reminded them that he is there, still indefatigably on the job'.[2] The *mulid* is finished for another year.

The Mulid *and the* Tariqa

It is quite obvious that the *mulid* plays a major part in a multiplicity of ways in the maintenance of the Brotherhood. One

---

[1] I would estimate the length of the procession at around a mile. It took over forty-five minutes to pass.
[2] Durrell, L., op. cit., p. 32.

immediately notices the organizational benefits in the carefully encouraged elements of competitiveness which surround the tents. Each endeavours to outshine its rivals, to attract more guests, to provide in its generous arrangement of comfort, refreshment, and entertainment not only for its own members but also for the hoped-for flock of visitors. These latter are often anxiously asked by the more impetuous for their opinion of the tent—how does it compare with its neighbours, and so forth. For all share in the success or failure of the effort, though some of the larger contributors may feel a particular personal involvement. The whole project demands of the local *khalifa* and his followers an intense co-operative spirit and a good deal of economic sacrifice and work. Not only does this increase the solidarity of the *zawiya*, but the fact of making this sacrifice in itself both reflects and enhances the importance of the chief collective celebration of the *Hamidiya Shadhiliya*. Factory workers take the days off from their annual allowance and are prepared, if necessary, not even to spend the whole time at the festival but to return after a day so that another brother may be released from work. Commitment to the *tariqa* as a whole is strengthened as each succeeding year the pressures to provide yet more magnificent a demonstration of the corporate spirit of the Order are built up by the demands of the members themselves as much as by the central office. Each year the brothers want more tents, as the secretary almost resignedly remarked. This growth has reached the point where serious consideration was given to moving the entire *mulid* to the square before Abdin Palace where the most important government public functions are held.

Members attach the greatest possible significance to attending the festival, unless some critical circumstance makes it out of the question. It assumes in their lives a place equal to that of the great feast at the end of Ramadan; only in the *mulid* the immediate and basic framework of co-operative endeavour and celebration is wider than the kin group and embraces all the brothers of the various *zawiyas*. This is not to say that the family has a minor part. Wives and children come to the tents and participate in their different degrees in the activities. The women fill their traditional role of cook and take care of the smallest children. The others join with their fathers and brothers in the excitement of the occasion and share in the *dhikr*, while all the time exposed to the pervading influence of the Saint, which is everywhere in his physical presence in the shrine, in the endless talk about him, in ritual, and in the great procession.

Friends also attend, even though they may not be actually in the Order. Because of the impression that the festival then makes on them new members may be gained through this channel. Furthermore, the *mulid* is a matrix of wider social relations, for sometimes, as one informant explained, strangers come and see the tent for the area from which they or their immediate forbears emigrated to Cairo. Recognized by their appearance, they are effusively invited in, and offered refreshments and cigarettes before the brothers of the village. The singer welcomes them publicly and they are drawn into the hospitality and warmth of the group. Again, brothers from an area outside the capital may stay with friends and relatives in the city and the latter will assist the tent with provisions, whether or not they are under any obligation to another *zawiya* or are in fact members at all. They will make a *ziyara* (semi-formal visit) to the tent of their fellow villagers. Links of reciprocal assistance and hospitality are thus set up, and are sustained out of the *mulid*.

We should not forget that the whole occasion is in a sense directed as much to the wider public as it is to those who already belong to the Brotherhood. This is quite explicit in Text B. My attention was always drawn by brothers to the propaganda element in the display of the tents, and the procession. One object is to gain new members as well as to renew and fortify the devotion of the committed. The *mulid* is advertised in one of the major popular Egyptian newspapers beneath a photograph of Salama, in the hope that as many people as possible will be attracted to it. Those who come must at least carry away with them a high regard for the *nizam* (organization) of the Order and the festival. The fitting and due tribute and commemoration of the Saint must also acquire and enhance the general prestige and reputation of his followers in the eyes of outsiders, especially of potentially critical outsiders. The emphasis on appearance at all levels, is in part to anticipate and spike the guns of opponents of the Sufi Orders; to show that the *Hamidiya Shadhiliya* is not, as the other *turuq* are claimed to be, liable to charges of offering little more than a traditional festival less and less linked with true religion, and pandering to the highly suspect 'old ways'.

The *mulid* further serves as a useful guide to the central office of the degree of effort and devotion of the different *zawiyas*. The procedure in the case of failure to fulfil the expected duties has been touched on. Officials of the Order have the chance to make a personal estimation of the *khalifa* and his members, which could otherwise be obtained only with considerable difficulty. The response to the Sheikh's call is a valuable index of the condition of the local centre, and should any potentially disruptive situation be developing the organization can stifle it more or less at birth. Internal control is thus greatly facilitated, and a regular accounting of trends can be taken.

Finally, and most important, the *mulid* is a crucial factor in the preservation of that feeling of a personal connection between founder and member that is so vital to the Order and its continued expansion. I would suggest, indeed, that it is a functional requirement in this type of organization where the need to preserve the power of the original charismatic impulse is so crucial. The question of the routinization of authority will be dealt with fully elsewhere. We shall merely point here to the critical nature of the transition from the founding charismatic figure to his successor and the inevitable increase in the number and proportion of the members who had never known the Saint. These latter now comprise the majority of the organization and the confidential secretary himself indicated to me the function of the *mulid* in linking these, let us call them second generation brothers, to Salama.[1] It is at the festival that they may establish and recharge a personal devotion at the shrine of the man who is one of that select company of *walis* who, as the preacher at one of the *hadrahs* tells them, 'are living on the Earth until the Last Day' (*'ayshin fi'l 'ard hatta yom al akhir*). Further, they make the pilgrimage collectively, with those formally joined to them in obedience, loyalty, and love to the founder. The entire *mulid* is saturated by his presence. Tents have photographs and portraits of him prominently displayed, and these photos are inexpensively sold to the brothers, so that virtually everyone is as familiar with Salama's face as if he were still alive. He is the main topic of conversation, and from the lips of those who actually knew him they hear of his miracles and his teachings. The Saint is, as it were, diffused into the world of men.

[1] Informants are often not nearly as ignorant as they are made out to be of the sociological realities of their situation! Despite a distressing lack of knowledge of Durkheim and Weber they show themselves very aware of the functions and problems of ritual and organization; sometimes, one suspects, more than the fieldworker gives them credit for.

This occasion is also their opportunity to see their sheikh, the son of the *wali*, from whom they will be physically separated for the rest of the year. True he remains a distant figure, walking slowly with eyes cast down and hand raised to breast in quiet acknowledgement of the brothers' cries of enthusiasm; but he is there, inheritor of his father's cloak and first successor as leader of his *tariqa*. This ritual distance, in dramatic contrast to the high level of socializing and face-to-face contact with other members of the group, serves to intensify the symbolic aspect of his role, upon which the devotion of the members is focused. The whole Order is physically gathered round both founder and leader. It lives together, collectively as it were, for the period of the festival. Brothers meet not only in the ritual context of the *hadrah* as they ordinarily do, but in a wide network of social relations with their confrères. For two days they make visits, eat and talk, perform the prayers, and participate in the *dhikr* together. The Order thus becomes for its members a visible, functioning, corporate entity within which their own *zawiya* takes its place as part of an ever widening organizational system.

III

THE STRUCTURE OF THE SUFI ORDERS

ANY discussion of the internal distribution of authority in a *tariqa* must begin with the basic question of typology. It seems to me heuristically valuable to distinguish at the outset between organization and association as the poles of a continuum. For our limited present purposes we shall regard an organization as possessing a high degree of internal stratification on the basis of differential expertise and/or efficiency. There is greater structural recognition of functional inequality, and a set of over-all, formally articulated controls with an established system of sanctions enforced through a hierarchy of authority statuses. These statuses and their concomitant roles are well defined, as are the values, aims, and functions of the organization, and the means which are adopted towards the fulfilment of these aims. Holders of positions will usually be full-time and salaried professionals, and emphasis is placed on the integrated and directed functioning of the organization as a whole.

It will be at once appreciated that association is differentiated from the above chiefly by degrees of stress. It tends to looseness of structure with a minimal development of a status hierarchy. The voluntary, often egalitarian, nature of the individual commitment is characteristic, together with a less developed division of function and of authority. Officials are appointed for reasons of administrative convenience and are often unpaid and part-time. The pattern of values and norms is more diffuse, as, relatively speaking, are the specific aims of the association. We also find a less elaborate and defined system of sanctions.

The Orders can thus be viewed as lying on this continuum between association and organization, and embodying elements of both. In the majority of cases they are closer to the former type, while the *Hamidiya Shadhiliya* is the best example of a *tariqa* nearer to the latter. It is important to note that they are not necessarily static, but move along the continuum to one type rather than the other. Furthermore, it is obvious that no examination of formal structure in itself will reveal the significant distinguishing features by which a given group may be classified as more of the nature of one than the other. The important factor is the situational weighting of the different elements, the administrative system of sanctions, and the circumstances under which the sanctions are invoked.

Two further points should be borne in mind. In terms of Weber's classic discussion of the nature of corporate groups all the Brotherhoods may be described as 'voluntary associations' (*Verein*), that is, corporate groups 'originating in a voluntary agreement and in which the established order claims authority over the members only by virtue of a personal act of adherence'.[1] Secondly it must be remembered that *none* of the groups claim 'a monopoly of the legitimate use of hierocratic coercion',[2] since all regard themselves as part of the wider framework of Islam derived from Revelation and the *Sunna*.

Structure

The key link is theoretically that of Head of the Order and *murid*; but in practical terms, and of great importance for the analysis of these groups, this link passes through an intermediary, the *khalifa* (head of the local *zawiya*). Direct face-to-face contact with the Sheikh is therefore in most cases of very rare occurrence. All authority, and the allocation of authority positions, lies within the purview of the Sheikh, and the subordinates derive their statuses from him.

There are no significant doctrinal distinctions to be drawn between one Order and another. Not to be a member is not thought to make one any less of a Muslim, nor to cut one off from the possibilities of Paradise. Moreover, it is not in any way 'better', or preferred, from the theological point of view, to belong to the *Rifa'iya*, say, rather than the *Shadhiliya*, and would not be regarded as such by either. There is no sectarian exclusiveness in this regard. Indeed, multiple membership is widespread, though I would speculate that at least in the past in each village and town the local heads of the Orders were members of influential families and kin groupings and the loyalty of the brothers (*muridin*) in given circumstances would actually depend on a complex set of factors operating in terms of the wider network of relations.

[1] Weber, Max, *The Theory of Social and Economic Organisation*, edited with an introduction by Talcott Parsons, New York: Free Press of Glencoe, 1964, p. 151.　　　　[2] Ibid., p. 154.

No doubt the Sheikhs had prestige deriving from their office and their capacity to invoke supernatural sanctions, but equally they may often have been in a situation where they had to compete for loyalty over a particular constituency with other Sheikhs making their own conflicting demands and invoking the same sanctions. Taha Husayn's autobiography indicates that in his province there was a fairly clear division of territory between two rivals, and that when one made a foray into the domain of the other, endless dispute followed, particularly since the visit was usually made with a maximum degree of ostentation and a large retinue.[1] The Egyptian anthropologist, Hamid Ammar, gives details of an election in his village in which a prestige contest developed, involving the grandson of the leader of the Sufi Order there.[2] Certainly becoming the sheikh or local *khalifa* of an Order might be a very powerful card in your hand, both for your local set of relations and because as part of the 'traditional leadership' you might be sought out by the national political organizations of the inter-war period.[3] There is also evidence that in the nineteenth century close connections existed between the *turuq* and the trade guilds, though the precise nature of that connection remains tantalizingly obscure.[4]

Consistent with the fact that a man may belong to several groups at once, and indeed occupy a different office in each, is the diffuseness of the control exercised by the Orders. Most groups do not lay claim to the individual's loyalty over any but the most limited range of behaviour directly affecting the well-being of the particular *tariqa*. The quality and extent of the hold over the members is therefore often weak and limited. However, the degree and kind of mobilization is variable, as is the scope of the adherence required. Berque's evidence suggests that in village politics a primacy which might not otherwise be demanded would be given to loyalty to one Order and the family associated with it.

[1] Taha Husayn, *Al Ayyam*, vol. i, pp. 88–96, for a scathing literary picture.

[2] Ammar, Hamid, *Growing up in an Egyptian Village*, London: Routledge and Kegan Paul, 1954, p. 47.

[3] Berque shows that the head of the *Khalwatiya* Order of Sirs al Layyan was at one time deeply involved in the politics of the Wafd party; Berque, op. cit., p. 66.

[4] André Raymond in his paper 'Quartiers et mouvements populaires au Caire au xviiième siècle' provides interesting details of the rise of the *Bayumiya* among the butchers of the *Husayniya* quarter of Cairo, in Holt, *Political and Social Change*, pp. 104–16. See also Baer, G., *Egyptian Guilds in Modern Times*, Jerusalem: The Israeli Oriental Society, 1964, for a discussion of the relations of guilds and Brotherhoods.

This is not to imply that multiple membership is necessarily a source of organizational weakness. From Evans-Pritchard's account of the *Sanusi* of Cyrenaica (who also had lodges in Egypt) we know that it did not preclude the sway of that *tariqa* in a wide area of tribal political affairs, though otherwise belonging to another group such as the *Madaniya* was quite permissible. And in Egypt in the past this diffuseness meant extreme flexibility and adaptability, cutting quite across lines of stratification and social ties. It is in the modern period that it has proved a handicap.

The mode of entry is voluntary and not in theory a matter of descent, though in certain areas families were traditionally associated with one Order, and children would almost automatically follow their parents' affiliation. Hamid Ammar, on the other hand, shows that in Silwa brothers were not allowed to belong to the same *tariqa*, and he connects this with the socially recognized pressure of sibling rivalry and the maintenance of distance as respect from younger to older.[1] Apart from such factors there is no bar to entry and no test which the aspirant must pass in order to gain membership. He is subject to no examination and is not required to show forth in his life some special qualities fitting him for entry into the group. He swears obedience to the Sheikh, as he may well have done to others in a similar ceremony, and he is a *murid*. What qualitative attachment he cares to make to the Order is largely his affair, for there will often be little if any formal pressure on him to participate in any of their rituals or occasions, save perhaps at the *mulid* of the Saint.

The following basic classification of the *turuq* in Egypt then suggests itself:[2] they are sodality or brotherhood associations of a non-exclusive stamp placing primary emphasis on fellowship as the dominant value. The face-to-face relations of the group, and of individuals in their roles as members, are chiefly within the ritual context, and membership is founded on the devotion of the individual follower to the Sheikh. The latter claims descent by grace (and sometimes blood) from the Saint who established the Order. Their constellation of values in relation to Islamic belief is not markedly different from that of non-members. Their particular social ethic

[1] Ammar, H., op. cit., p. 244.

[2] Though our categories and field of inquiry are different, my general approach to the classification of the *turuq* has been influenced by that adopted by Bryan Wilson in his article 'An analysis of sect development', *American Sociological Review*, vol. 24, Feb. 1959, pp. 3–15.

is minimal; they do not exhort to action in the world, but rather to a devaluation of it and a stress on ecstatic mystical practices theoretically as a step on the way to betterment of the inner self and the establishment and reinforcement of the link between the lover (the *murid*) and the loved (Allah). In terms of the fundamental changes in contemporary Egyptian society they are identified more and more with an introverted, apathetic, retreatist response to the world.

Their organization is characterized by a hierarchical series of ascending ranks, ultimately ending in the Sheikh as the repository of spiritual grace and authority. The Orders do not demand any totalitarian hold over the lives of the members, claiming obedience only in matters strictly concerned with the internal affairs of the *tariqa*. In the past it appears that exceptions to this, determined in nature by their interlocking with the social structure have existed in particular spheres, usually the political. This no longer holds true.

Finally we note that the group with which we are particularly concerned, the *Hamidiya Shadhiliya*, departs from this pattern in one absolutely crucial respect: it is an *organization* in which *exclusive* demands are made on the member in so far as he is not permitted to belong to one of the other Orders. If he does, and then wishes to join the *Hamidiya Shadhiliya*, he is refused and not permitted to take the oath to the Sheikh.[1] Concomitant differences we shall come to throughout our discussion of this *tariqa*, but it is this exclusiveness which is of primary significance.

As is true of any established group, formally an Order internally constitutes a balanced and articulated system of interlocking expectations. The extent to which these operate obviously depends on the scope of the interaction of the members, the settings of the interaction, and the degree of the group's demands of the *muridin* in the fulfilment of their membership. The limited nature of the required participation in most cases has been remarked. Given this limitation the role of member becomes merely one of the individual actor's many roles and is performed within a confined field of action. But the *Hamidiya Shadhiliya*, on the other hand, is distinct in the emphasis it places on the 'total' nature of the commitment to the Order. From being relatively restricted in extent and significance for the actor in his whole system of social identities, that of *murid* here involves important questions of primacy.

[1] See Laws 312–14, and 319 especially, in Appendix.

In a group such as the *Hamidiya Shahdiliya* then the social identity is regarded by the group as being the actor's *dominant* identity and role in the total social system in which he is located.[1] His patterns of behaviour even outside the group setting are expected to conform to certain normative standards laid down by that group. And where conflict or discrepancy arise, he is required to resolve it by acting in accordance with the identity role of member and the norms of the institution. Failure to do so renders him liable to sanctions imposed by the group. Though insulation of his activities from observability by fellow members operates to ameliorate the possibilities of conflict inherent in this situation, he is in theory never regarded as being outside the absolute system.[2] This is as true for a card-carrying member of a totalitarian political party as it is for the sectarian. In both these latter cases it is also true that the identity is especially associated with a group that has its genesis in conflict and is therefore likely to involve its members in some form of opposition to those outside the group. These are therefore only the most extreme examples, for clearly the degree of inherent conflict with 'others' in norms and values varies in these dominant identities. But it always exists, and unless the group withdraws physically from the world, or enters into some revolution against the others in an attempt to convert, conquer, or annihilate them, some mechanisms must operate to minimize tensions.

The more the group accepts (tacitly or otherwise) the standards and authority of the world in certain spheres of action, the less the possibility of conflict. This is in fact precisely what often occurs: namely that 'we' accommodate ourselves to the society in which by force of circumstances 'we' move in those areas where tension may chiefly inhere or arise. This accommodation may take place over time at an almost imperceptible pace, or may, at the other extreme, be compelled, if the group is to be allowed to survive by the society. This withdrawal or limitation of presumptive claims over areas of behaviour and action is an important consideration in the study of

[1] It thus overrides Aidan Southall's major type categories of role which he gives as: (*a*) Kinship and Ethnic; (*b*) Economic; (*c*) Political; (*d*) Ritual and Religious; (*e*) Recreational. See Southall, A., 'An operational theory of role', *Human Relations*, vol. 12, no. 1, Feb. 1959, pp. 17–34.

[2] The concept of insulation from observability is drawn from Merton, R. K., 'The Role-Set: Problems in Sociological Theory', *British Journal of Sociology*, vol. 8, June 1957, no. 2, pp. 106–20.

the adaptation of religious groups to their wider social environment. Thus the founder of the *Hamidiya Shadhiliya* was most specific about the duties of members to perform their occupational roles to the best of their capacities and on no account to neglect work in the world as incongruent with their identity as *muridin*. It is stressed that being a *murid*, like being an ascetic, is an internal state of the actor even more than his external actions. In that situation the dominant role plays only a small part, and the more generalized standard of ethical behaviour (which in any case in diffuse terms of honesty and so forth will coincide with the norms of the Order) is paramount.

On the other hand, the group may attempt to insulate its members as far as possible from the world and this attempt will vary in degree directly with the inherent conflict with Others which is thought to exist. Spatial separation may be sought in the founding of a community where social and physical space are in the relation of referent to symbol.[1] Less extremely, a high degree of participation by members in a continual round of group activities may be demanded as a necessary condition of membership. I would suggest then that in our example of the *Hamidiya Shadhiliya* we find two primary mechanisms for the reduction of conflict which might otherwise prove disruptive: first, the tacit or explicit acknowledgement of separate spheres of influence which is considered justified and tolerable as not affecting the vital, spiritual nature of the individual's commitment; and, second, the maximization of involvement of the member, mainly in ritual occasions.

Such an accommodation is assisted by the fact that an individual's identity as a *murid* has become increasingly a matter of private subjective identification and commitment, as the relevance of Sufi attachments to wider social situations at whatever level has decreased. This process of restricting the boundaries of religious identity to the private sphere has often been discussed for advanced industrial society, but it is present to a degree in Egypt also. Since the Orders are not sectarian in nature, but rather fall within the accepted religious tradition of Islam, the range of significant encounters and relations for which the membership of one of the

---

[1] This was the case in the Orders of North Africa where the full initiates lived in a *ribat* or *zawiya*, separated off from the 'lay' and non-members. See Rinn, L., *Marabouts et Khouan*, Alger, 1884; Depont, O., and Coppolani, X., *Les Confréries religieuses musulmanes*, Alger, 1897.

actors in an Order is in any sense defining is limited. This tendency to 'private' identification is increased by the hostile or indifferent climate in part created by attacks on the *turuq* by the *'ulema'* or in the information media. Since popular Sufism no longer forms an element in the taken-for-granted everyday world of most Egyptians, affiliation is unlikely to be incorporated into an actor's interrelations with others unless he has good reason to suppose them sympathetic. He runs the risk, as the unfortunate *Ahmadiya* discovered in Tanta, of being 'hooted off the stage'.

The Sheikh

Saif speaks of the Sheikh in a series of evocative images: He is the calm light in the veiling darkness, the shade of the verdant tree in the desert, and whosoever entrusts himself to him is safe from the danger of his sins. He is, in an often repeated metaphor, the doctor who cures the *murid* of the sickness of vices and passions, and cleanses the heart, making that which is excellent and good loved. He who has no Sheikh is like someone who goes to a man who is not a physician for a cure (pp. 25–7). Before one listens to the prattle of those '. . . materialists who have appeared in our times and summon to the way of earthly existence . . .' one should go to the *maglis* of one of the Sheikhs and see the light after the darkness. This done, the world is nothing to the Paradise one will enjoy. For one will be in the hands of him who watches over the principles of the Holy Law, guardian of the Truth, one who acts on the Quran in the clearest way and establishes the *tariqa* (p. 26). All Muslims should be taught by him and be cleansed of the love of the world (*hubb ad-Dunya*) (p. 25). To whoever joins him in the way of reaching God (*wusul ila Allah*), he is a spiritual father completely possessing the *murid* who will do nothing save by his opinion or guidance in all affairs and will only leave him to obtain his daily bread (p. 156). *Tasawwuf* began as the curing of hearts and the Sheikh is the doctor of souls and of hearts. Whoever joins him and then deserts him should be rejected as one who has no understanding and merely treats life as a game (pp. 26–7).

The people need him, for he links the worshipper with Allah. The mosque will not be full with folk at prayer or the murmurs of prayer save when the Sheikh is the motivator of it. The Sheikhs work like soldiers pursuing criminals, but instead of punishing them they bring them before God (p. 164). They work not in the mosques, but in the city streets and the villages, gathering the deviators and bringing them to obedience and straightness. For *rak'a* (ritual prostrations of the prayers) is only a kneeling, which does not divert the thief from evil, and he will perform the mere motions easily. But bowing down with the Sheikh is a chain not to be broken, since it is then between him and Allah, and a man will fall into trouble if he breaks it.

The nation also needs him, for when a group is made straight, then they do what their homeland and the government want (this very modern and perhaps slightly forced sentiment is an indication of the political and social climate at the time, 1956, when Saif was writing). They need the power of his spirit over deviating intelligences and hearts (p. 166). The people, he says, feel that the Sheikhs of the *turuq* are inspired men to whose eyes the mysteries of the hidden are unveiled, because they see with the light of God and know what thoughts and confusion are in men's hearts. Nothing can be concealed from them (p. 167). They will not let anything bad pass from their *muridin* (p. 169), and in trouble or enmity they are an ever-present help (p. 179). They rid the world of evil and are respected by all, even thieves (p. 180).

But to attain so exalted a position needs the highest spiritual qualifications and conditions:

(i) He must be godly and fear Allah (p. 157).

(ii) He must possess the moral character to unite and make one homogeneous group of all those various groups of different morals and characters and beliefs.

(iii) He must have both *'ilm* and *ma'rifa* (knowledge and gnosis). His knowledge must be that tasted by the soul and absorbed by the hearts, such as men long for and not the ordinary knowledge of books (p. 158). He must have understanding of the Truth and of the *Shari'a* (Holy Law). For the link of the Sheikh to the *murid* is one of souls; he knows all that is in the student's heart, he is the wakeful night guard, the capable watchman, the honest door-keeper of hearts.

(iv) He should have the personality of teacher and educator (p. 161).

(v) He must have his own way in education, both by example and by admonition.

(vi) He must demonstrate asceticism in the vanities of the world (p. 162). Rich and poor are alike to him. He buys the *murid* and disposes with him as the master does the slave (p. 163: a word having a dual meaning, *'abd*, as slave/worshipper).

The above makes clear the view of a senior member of the *Hamidiya Shadhiliya* but it also accurately reflects the feelings, not only of the *muridin* of that Order, but of the followers of the other *turuq*. The imagery employed indicates the terms in which the brothers think of their Sheikhs, or of what their Sheikhs should be. As we shall see, the 'ideal' elements in the portrait need to be borne in mind in our examination of the social identity 'Sheikh of an Order', and the various statuses which go to make it up.

It must first be said that, *a fortiori*, the position of Sheikh is what I have called a *dominant* role, as specialist roles so often are in 'universal' religions. So that even outside the particular framework of the group in which he acts and of which he is the head, his primary social identity is that of Sheikh, whatever the kinship and political or other relations in which he may also participate. At the same time it is of course true that there is a basic distinction to be drawn between his rights and duties in the we-group and those which obtain in his interaction with 'Others', though the degree of difference will vary greatly according to the part which religion plays in the social setting at large. For his followers, from one point of view, he is never outside his sphere of competence, which extends over the entire spiritual foundation of life. However, he cannot hold the same expectations of behaviour from the non-member as from the member, even while he may well receive considerable deference and respect at a more diffuse level. The less the general value placed upon the identity by the various classes of society, the less respect will be granted. It will depend in addition on other variables such as the range of his charismatic reputation, the social prominence of the Order concerned, its level of activity, and structural significance.

Within an Order he is the supreme authority and the one from whom the *khulafa'* (a word I use here to describe all the officials of an Order) derive their positions. When a man takes the oath (*'ahd*), it is really with the Sheikh, though most will make it through the medium of the local deputy. In his hands ultimately lies the invocation of the formal sanctions for behaviour, usually after consultation with senior members before any major decision, for example of expulsion, is taken. He has an absolute right to obedience from the *muridin* as the following two laws of the *Hamidiya Shadhiliya* indicate: (they would also apply to the other Orders)

44. The student must not argue with the Sheikh nor ask from him any proof for what he orders or makes him do, for the Sheikhs are the trustees of God.

45. Whoever opposes his Sheikh has broken the *'ahd* and is cut off from the Sheikh even though he sticks close to the Sheikh; and the door of *madad* (assistance) is closed to him.

The two most significant terms used of the identity are 'teacher' and 'doctor'; they constitute the warp and the woof out of which the role is woven. Both, it will be noted, are authority roles and both imply asymmetric relations with the 'student/patient'. The teacher transmits knowledge down to the students, directs them, and inculcates the principles of ethics into them. If they fail, he punishes them. The doctor instructs his patient in the course which will most benefit his condition. Not to follow his prescription means continued sickness. The one is the means of learning and piety, the other of health and well-being. Finally the teacher leads his pupil to become *mu'addab* (possessed of pious civility, proper manners, and courtesy), the religiously sanctioned value which Ammar has categorized as primary in the Egyptian village, where the pious son (*ibn salih*) is one possessed of *adab*.[1] Transposed into the Sufi key, the goal of both is in essence the same, the moral and spiritual health of the student/patient.

Consideration of the functions of teacher and doctor brings us to the question of the allocation of the role of Sheikh within an Order. There is a certain tendency to transmission through the specific family, as at a local level the position of *khalifa* apparently often was.[2] Thus the *Bekriya* (whose head was traditionally *Sheikh al Masha'ikh*, chief of the Sufi Orders in Egypt and until this century a figure of some political significance), and the *Rifa'iya* (whose present Sheikh is held to be a lineal descendant from a cousin of the founder Ahmed ar-Rifa'i, d. 1175) are both led by men who trace their ancestry by blood to the original founder (*silsilat ad-damm*).[3] In many cases, however, there is no such

---

[1] Ammar, op. cit., pp. 126–7. I discuss the nature of *adab* more fully in the next chapter.

[2] Berque, op. cit., p. 61, says that the Sheikhs of the *turuq* in the village mostly belonged to families known for having given the community a Saint.

[3] The *Demerdashiya* formerly came into this category as a 'family Order'. The last Sheikh to be of the family fled Egypt in 1952 at the outbreak of the revolution and the post is now filled by election from the twelve *nuqaba'*.

ascriptive principle of succession. Where this is true, allocation may be made by the informally conducted choice of senior men of the *Sigada*, or according to the wishes of the previous incumbent, where he expressed any preference, or to the individual who has, by his reputation for personal holiness or his long experience in a senior position in the Order, become the generally favoured successor. The selection must then be ratified by the supreme Sufi Council. Once the question has been resolved, the new Sheikh takes his place as another link in the chain of grace (*silsilat al-baraka*) which connects him with one of the four great Saints from whom all the Egyptian Orders are ultimately derived—Shadhili, Rifaʻi, Bedawi, and Jilani.

Thus Sheikh Ibrahim of the *Hamidiya Shadhiliya* follows his father in a *silsila* of *baraka*, but members insist that descent is *not* the principle on which he was selected. We may suggest that, given a candidate at all suitable within the Saint's proximate kin group, there will be a tendency, at least in the first generation, to appoint a relative, if only because it is felt that he participates more immediately in the *baraka* of his predecessor. Here the example of Ibrahim is an interesting one, since the degree of his own 'power' is problematic for the members, many of them believing that he performs *karamat* and yet others confessing uncertainty on the question. This ambiguity is a function of the fact that being his father's son he is at one remove, none the less, from the source of *baraka*. Moreover, he succeeded to Salama's position when he was too young to exercise full authority, and the succession itself was a matter of serious dispute (see below). We might expect this ambiguity to disappear in the next generation when the notion of individual *karamat* may well not be present, though the miracles of the Saint and his son will probably continue to multiply.

The somewhat transitional nature of his position is further clarified by a consideration of it in terms of social space and presentation. Our evidence seems to support the proposition that a decline in mystical or political power, or in prestige, in a person, or within a group or community may be compensated for by greater distance, often expressed in the language of ritual, being associated with the particular social identity or institution. An increase in social space can regenerate and sustain the feelings of awe and reverence which may otherwise by some process of change be diminished. It is here, as Goffman observes, that structure and dramaturgy most clearly intersect.[1]

Salama, the original manifestor of supernatural miraculous capacities, was always available to the *muridin*. Though all treated him in terms of high respect, I was told that he was accessible to everyone whether privately or on more public occasions. At the end of the *hadrah* he would stand in the centre of the brothers and make the *musafaha* (mutual hand kiss) with any who wished. In so doing the *baraka*, acquired by physical contact with the Saint, was open to each individual member. Ibrahim on the other hand *never* makes the *musafaha* save under the most exceptional circumstances. Thus on one of the visits to Tanta he was persuaded by the mass pleadings of the very large gathering of the brothers, *but against the advice of his Sigada officials*, to permit them to pass by him one by one and kiss his hand. At the *hadrahs* in Cairo he leaves the ranks of the participants first, while they are still seated on the floor. Wrapped in his father's robe, the symbol of authority, he walks out through the gap in the outer line made for him by the *nuqaba'*, eyes modestly cast down, one hand raised to his breast in humble acknowledgement of the cries that echo round: 'Ya Sidi Salama, Ya Sidi Ibrahim, Madad! Madad!', and the gestures of deference (both hands raised, palms down, to the forehead), while the brothers sitting in the centre brush the carpet where he has trodden with their hands and 'wash' their faces and bodies with *baraka*. Not only does he not make the hand kiss, *but no one is even allowed to approach him as he leaves in order to touch him*.

It is a common occurrence for half a dozen or more of the *muridin* to rush towards him as he goes out of the door of the mosque in order to make some request or to obtain *baraka* by contact with their Sheikh. They are always stopped, and indeed upbraided if persistent, by a group of *nuqaba'* who are ready for such demonstrations of enthusiasm and devotion. On one occasion a *murid* was severely reprimanded for throwing himself at the Sheikh's feet and attempting to kiss the hem of his robe as he left. Ibrahim made no acknowledgement of him. On another occasion in Tanta he explicitly refused to make the hand kiss with any of a group of brothers with whom he had been holding a *maglis*, save the son of the house-owner. The boy, about fourteen years old, was

---

[1] Goffman, E., *The Presentation of Self in Everyday Life*, New York: Doubleday, 1959, p. 241.

covered with an overwhelmed and delighted embarrassment at this singular and rare honour; flushing scarlet and visibly trembling, he repeatedly kissed the Sheikh's hand.[1]

There are, as we remarked above, two major elements here. The first is that of social space in its relation to Ibrahim's structural position, and the contrast with his father. In order to maintain the awe and reverence accorded automatically to Salama, he has to reinforce the diminished degree of *baraka* he possesses in his own right by an increase in institutional space between himself and his *muridin*. The accessibility of the Saint is followed by the distance of his immediate successor. The son participates in the founder's charisma, but the degree to which he does so is an area of ambiguity. By withholding himself from the *murid* the *baraka* becomes more sought after because more difficult to obtain: scarcity brings value. Each week the brothers try to reach him and each week not he, but his officials, keep them away. Any discontent or blame for the separation thus devolves on them, while Ibrahim remains above reproach and the mystery is preserved. On the rare occasions when he may be approached, the blessing and grace is all the more cherished. We saw above how carefully he selects both the time graciously to allow the contact with his devoted followers (publicly against official advice be it noted, and on the deeply emotional occasion of a major celebration), and the recipient(s). Loyalty is thus concentrated and focused on him as the living dramatic symbol and embodiment of the Order and the Way.

The second element, that of performance on ritual occasions in general, reveals another dimension to his behaviour. This is governed by the twofold fact that he is presenting this role at once to an internal audience of the brothers and to an external one of 'Others'. To the former he must maintain the proper humility befitting one who is described as *khadim al-fuqara'* (servant of those in need of God), the deputy (*khalifa*) of a Saint. He comports himself with a grave, modest dignity. Only the raising of his hand in brief but measured acknowledgement shows his awareness of the brothers' cries and gestures of respect and greeting. He looks neither to right nor left as he walks quietly out, his face serious and eyes lowered.

But at the same time he participates in the *collective* performance

---

[1] On the particular attention which the Sheikh gives to the children of the members see below, Chapter V.

directed to the 'Others', who either observe these public occasions directly or hear of them indirectly. He and the *muridin* are collaborators in a presentation in which both must play complementary parts if it is to retain its integrity in the eyes of outsiders. The aim of the group here basically consists in: (*a*) avoidance of any grounds for criticism, particularly by secular or religious authority; and (*b*) in so carrying out the ritual that those who might be regarded as potential recruits to the Order will become interested in or attracted to it. A threat to this double aim lies in the possibility of what I shall call 'over-acting'; that is when the actions of one or more members of the group fulfils, and then goes on to exceed, the requirements of the performance. Thus it is proper for the brothers to show their reverence and respect, and for Ibrahim to give due demonstration of his acceptance of this. But when a brother rushes forward and throws himself at the latter's feet, then the integrity of the presentation is threatened by 'over-playing'. The actor goes beyond the limits in his manner of expressing his legitimate respect in showing what by others may well be regarded as an un-Islamic degree of personal devotion to his leader. The latter is a humble servant of God, and such behaviour infringes on him as such before non-members and the rest of the group. Were he to permit this adulation not only would his performance seem at fault to those in the group, but the collective performance would be open to criticism. Hence the importance of the group of *naqibs* who specifically control manifestations of enthusiasm. In restricting the individual they protect the group as a whole.

The Sheikh's behaviour varies considerably according to the nature of his audience and his relation to them. It was often mentioned to me how Ibrahim lived a fully 'modern' life, in a well-appointed house: that he wears a suit (a necessary sartorial mark of 'modernity', or aspirations to it, in Egypt) for all save ritual occasions. It was repeatedly stressed that he is in no way 'old-fashioned', a charge often levelled at the Sheikhs of the *turuq* by critics, and one carrying dubious political connotations and associations with what is termed feudalism. To a certain extent, therefore, in his life style he adopts the signs of a separation from the traditional, which in so many respects is now held to be blameworthy and reactionary.

On specifically religious occasions, such as the reception given for the *mulid* of Salama, he wears the long *qaftan* and the *'imma* ('turban'—more particularly the head-dress worn by religious specialists). With visiting dignitaries[1] he exchanges effusive formal greetings; but to others who are members of the Order he merely extends his hand to be kissed, paying little attention to those of no seniority or worldly standing and ordering the brothers present (usually officials of the *Sigada*) to various tasks throughout. Nor does this evoke any resentment. His hospitality to the distinguished guests is a matter of pride and his behaviour only that appropriate to their status in the wider society of which the *tariqa* is but one element. The ordinary member, tied to his Sheikh by special comprehensive links of obedience and submission, has entirely other expectations of the Sheikh's manner toward him. And if certain of the brothers are treated with greater courtesy (as some of the 'middle-class' members certainly are), their greater learning and education is justification enough if justification were needed.

I have described the relations between the Sheikh and the *Murid* in the Orders as 'asymmetric', meaning that the rights of the former and corresponding duties of the latter are predominantly stressed. There are, however, countervailing elements. The teacher must teach and the doctor cure; he who is both must possess the necessary skill and understanding to play the combined role to the satisfaction of the 'student/patient'. Where the Order is anything more than an amorphous ritual association, therefore, the Sheikh has certain defined obligations to his followers.

These obligations will obviously be less difficult to fulfil in proportion to the lack of education and sophistication of the *muridin*. On the other hand, the more an Order seeks to attract a wide spectrum of members, the more testing this aspect of the role becomes and the more symmetrical in terms of mutual expectations. The *Hamidiya Shadhiliya* recognize three levels at which the Sheikh must be able to instruct the brothers: the mass must be taught the laws of religion and the *Shari'a* (Holy Law) and the duties of Islam. Those at the middle stage receive a deeper explanation or interpretation of the canonical schools of law, of *tafsir* (Quranic exegesis) and of *hadith*. Finally, learned men of religion and those who have reached profounder understanding are taught

---

[1] In 1965 the Head of the Sufi Orders in Egypt, several representatives of Ministries, including one deputy minister, a number of *'ulema'*, high-ranking police and army representatives, and a high official of the railways board, one or two professors of Cairo University, and others.

of the purification of the heart, the disciplining of the soul (*nafs*), and the control of the passions. We shall see that the incapacity to perform these functions leads to withdrawal or failure to secure support, particularly by the upper educated levels. It was in part precisely the inability of the Sheikhs to provide such guidance that kept growing sections of the population from the Orders. Increasingly, the leadership must be of such an intellectual standard as to attract members from the ever larger numbers who now have secondary or even university training. There are some indications that such leadership is unlikely to arise out of the *turuq* as an organic growth, but will only come through the formation of new groups specifically addressed to Sufism in its most developed forms.

The Sheikh must, finally, pursue a life style that does not conflict with what is conceived of as proper for one in his position. This in turn is linked with the exemplary nature of his role. Whatever the material circumstances of his existence and whatever trappings of modernism he may adopt, he must continually demonstrate the inner humility and personal asceticism that are generally inseparable from the social identity of Sheikh. Given the dominance of the role, this will be expected of him not only by the *muridin* but also by the 'Others'.

The Sigada

The central office (*beit as-Sigada*) of an Order usually consists of a *wakil* (deputy), who acts for the Sheikh when he is absent and who takes precedence over all others, and a group of assisting officials (the *naqibs* of the *Sigada*). These latter are under the direct supervision of the Sheikh and immediately responsible to him. They are recruited from the most senior and experienced members of the Order who have shown their abilities as heads of *zawiyas*. Their role in the *Hamidiya Shadhiliya* is a particularly active one since they are largely in charge of the general administration and running of the Order and have considerable authority in the solving of disputes and in reporting on the condition of the *tariqa* in the different areas. They are as near as any of the Orders comes to an unpaid managerial class. And management is now a very detailed and increasingly complex task. As the group moves nearer and nearer to the organizational pole in order to survive in an industrializing and modernizing society, there is a tendency to growing

centralization and active control over each unit in the total structure. This involves an attention to at any rate the more elementary
bureaucratic procedures:

83. The *Sigada* must have the following books:
One register of all outgoing material
One register of all ingoing material
One register of the *Khulafa'* and the *khulafa'* of the *khulafa'* and the
na'ibs and the *nuqaba'* of the *Sigada* and the *naqib* of the *nuqaba'* and the
wakil
One register of cases (i.e. matters of dispute) and the decision taken.
84. These books must be stamped with the stamp of the *Sheikh as-
Sigada*.

New local centres have to be set up, old ones inspected and where
necessary assisted, official religious occasions (such as the visits to
different *mulids* and the Sheikh's various journeys) publicized and
arranged. Communications play a key part in the process, and the
volume of correspondence increases rapidly in the effort to expand
and consolidate the activities of the Order.

The central body furthermore insulates the Sheikh against the
pressures of direct access by the ordinary members. Though all
power is derived from him and most decisions require his explicit
approval and may be overridden by him, the main burden falls on
them. They thus lighten the weight of administration and, by
selectively safeguarding his distance from the brothers, ensure the
continued strength of his personal *baraka*. In this way they also
form a valuable buffer for any complaints of mismanagement,
injustice, or impropriety, since he is seen to be above such matters
and any fault is laid at the door of the *nuqaba'*. Ibrahim can thus
give his own judgement 'from on high' on any case that may arise.
The charismatic figure appears aloof from the mundane questions
of administration, though an ever-available source of final appeal.

The officials in the tariqa

Every status position is granted only by the Sheikh and no other.
In all the *turuq* he alone is responsible for role allocation within
the Order. In the *Hamidiya Shadhiliya*, however, there is a
further qualification. It is now made quite explicit in the Laws that
none of the offices in the organizational hierarchy, whether within

the *Sigada* or outside it, is to be distributed on the principle of descent.

300. The position of *wakil as-Sigada* (deputy of the Sheikh) is *not* inherited save when the *Sheikh as-Sigada* so recommends [my emphasis].

301. The position of *naqib* of the *nuqaba'* of the *Sigada* and its *nuqaba'* and the *na'ibs* of the *beits* and of the *marakaz* and the *muhafazat* and the *khulafa'* of the *khulafa'* is *not* inherited [my emphasis].

This represents a radical new departure. For in the first edition of the *Qanun*, Salama had laid down that: (*a*) the position of *wakil* of the *Sigada* was to be inherited by the sons of the *Sheikh as-Sigada* by seniority of age; and (*b*) the function of the *nuqaba'* of the Central Office would also go by descent where possible. This was also true of the *na'ibs* of the *beits*[1] other than the *beit as-Sigada* and their *nuqaba'*. All other offices below this level were *not* inherited (see Appendix, The Laws).[2] It appears that the founder initially wished the élite he so painstakingly recruited in the early years to remain a tightly knit group bound by ties of kinship as well as loyalty to the Order. The expansion of the group made it impossible, and the stress on efficiency and spiritual advancement hardly accords with the allocation of office by descent. It has therefore been changed in the new edition (the principle had certainly not operated very extensively for some time in practice). Office has been taken out of the matrix of kinship altogether. The organization as a separate functioning entity is clearly marked off from the traditional loci of authority. Purely local ties are thus diminished in importance and the separate unity and identity of the whole group are stressed. The loyalty of the member is due to an individual strictly in so far as he holds from the Sheikh, and by no claim of kinship, an office in the *tariqa*; and it entails no further structural implications. Status is awarded on the level of achievement and removed from that of ascription. In this way the association which Berque noted of the other Orders with specific elements in the social system of the villages is avoided.

From this other implications emerge. As the group moves towards the organizational pole, and a stress on hierarchy and organization, there is a growing and stricter emphasis on proper

---

[1] A *beit* is a collection of *zawiyas* which are for general administrative purposes placed under one official, the *na'ib*.

[2] *Qanun*, Old Edition, Laws 300 and 315.

role performance which is correspondingly more clearly defined. Position no longer depends on kinship and the location of particular units in the given social system. Rather it is founded more and more on objective, articulated criteria of what constitutes right behaviour and what fits a man for such and such a status. In other terms, one might speak of 'efficiency' of the actor as *murid, khalifa, na'ib,* and so forth becoming a key consideration. Judgement will be made and the individual allocated to certain positions on the basis of the requirements explicitly laid down by the Order where the question of office arises. Rights and duties, which were vague in the extreme in so far as there were *particular* standards expected from members of an Order, tend to be more clearly set out.

But at the same time we must draw attention to the ambivalence which surrounds the very notion of hierarchy in a group devoted to brotherhood and fellowship. It is emphasized on the one hand that the world's standards are not those of the Order, for the former deals in the *zahir* (apparent) while the *tariqa* is concerned only with the *batin* (inward reality); that under the Sheikh all are equal, for all are *muridin* following his Way; that distinctions of wealth and secular status cease absolutely to have any validity within the brotherhood. On the other hand, however, it is recognized that spiritually, to use Orwell's notorious phrase, some are more equal than others. The idea of stages of understanding and illumination is as old as Sufism itself and drawn from the accepted doctrines of Islamic mysticism. None the less there is a certain tension between it and the basic principle of egalitarian association and brotherly co-operation common to nearly all the Orders. The *Hamidiya Shadhiliya* feel it necessary to present the apparatus of organization as primarily a response to administrative demands:

48. Since the Sheikh has work which requires someone to help him, necessity has compelled that every man have a function which he must perform . . .

Nothing of 'since men are not spiritually equal' here, nor could there be in a group that seeks to attract large numbers of adherents from the ordinary mass of the people with an ethic of brotherhood and mutual assistance. The notion of hierarchy continues to be effectively subsumed beneath this rubric of functional requirement. In contrast, the *Demerdashiya Khalwatiya*, which was traditionally an élitist group to which many of the leading *'ulema'* belonged, stress the spiritual stages as of primary importance.[1] This aspect is ritually presented in the *hadrah* of that Order in which the *nuqaba'*, ranged in seniority before the Sheikh play a particular and exemplary role separated from the common members.

Whatever the stress, certain criteria are employed in the allocation of these roles and must be in some way integrated into the value system of the Order. Manifestly, where position was not exclusively tied to descent, the *khalifa* should be able to fulfil his duties of administration and instruction and these will require a minimal level of learning and experience in the *tariqa*. Without going any further we can see at once how quickly in traditional Egypt a congruence might be established between the status system of the world and that of the Order. For literacy itself tended to be the property of a limited class, so that the higher levels of any given group were likely to coincide with those of superior standing in society at large. This congruence persists in a more limited way even in contemporary Egypt, allowing for the great diminution in the extent and social range of membership of the *turuq*. Of the twelve *nuqaba'* of the *Demerdashiya*, for example, there are two senior sheikhs of the Azhar, two prosperous jewellers, one engineer, one senior official in the Inland Revenue department of the Government, one described as a house-owner of considerable private means, two well-to-do merchants, one carpet merchant owning his own premises and a member of many years standing, one employee in a department of the Civil Service, and the last a worker (the precise nature of whose occupation was not forthcoming. This man was also head of the *nuqaba'* of the *Rifa'iya* Order, ranking third after the Sheikh and his deputy).

The status of senior officials at least will only be open therefore to those of some relatively developed degree of education or exceptional piety and commitment to the Order and all its activities. As indicated above, in the *Hamidiya Shadhiliya* the general requirements are explicit:

50. It is necessary for the *khalifa* not to make the office inoperative; he must have students so that the *tariqa* will spread and the people will benefit from it.

---

[1] The *Khalwatiya* appear to have been traditionally an élitist preserve. See Heyworth-Dunne, J., *Introduction to the History of Education in Modern Egypt*, p. 9. Also Gibb, H. A. R., and Bowen, H., *Islamic Society and the West*, London: O.U.P., 1957, vol. i, Pt. II, pp. 197–9.

51. He must know a large section of the Holy Quran and how to make the ritual ablutions and the ablutions with sand; how to wash and pray and the regulations for fasting. He must have a sound belief in *tawhid* as has been mentioned in our book *Murshid al Murid*.

52. When he has students he must hold a *hadrah* or *hadrahs* for the remembrance of God in a *zawiya* or house.

53. He must discuss religion with his students and what will be of benefit in their way to God; he must teach them good behaviour in the *tariqa* so that their souls will be refined and their hearts purified.

54. He must read the books of the Sufis and the explanation of the aphorisms of Sidi Ahmed ibn 'Ata' Allah and the *Ihya'* [i.e. the *Ihya' 'Ulum ad-Din* by al Ghazzali: see footnote translation of law 54, Appendix], and the books which we have put in the *tariqa* and what is like that.

The *khalifa* may be selected directly by the *Sheikh as-Sigada* (see Law 49) or may be brought forward to the latter's attention by one of the other officials because of his devotion and efforts for the Order:

326. Every student or *naqib*, or *naqib* of the *nuqaba'* may ask permission of his Sheikh (here meaning his local *khalifa*) to hold a *hadrah* in which he gathers those who love the *tariqa*. And he unites their hearts. If his Sheikh finds him suitable he gives him the permission; and if the Sheikh orders some of the brothers of that student to attend the *hadrah* with him to help him in learning from what occurs in that *hadrah* then this is good. If the Sheikh finds him suitable to be a *khalifa* he may bring him forward to the *Sigada* to make him a *khalifa*.

This Order lays great emphasis upon the fitness of their *khulafa'* for office. In his book *The Guidance of the Murid* (*Murshid al Murid*), Sheikh Ibrahim prescribes a test of the candidate so that the *Hamidiya Shadhiliya* can become through him a 'centre of illumination' and a place to which the mass can turn for religious opinions.[1] He must know the duties of the position and be capable of correcting, warning, and instructing the brothers by kindness and charity.[2]

As one of the *khalifas* put it to me, his duties have two aspects, the worldly (*dunyawi*) and the other-worldly. He must at once both help and assist the *muridin*, visiting them, taking a personal interest in their problems, and he must also try to guide them on the Way of

---

[1] *Murshid al Murid*, p. 3.   [2] Ibid., p. 4.

the Saint as their religious teacher. In this, my informant said, his position was different from that of the *'ulema'*: their knowledge is of *fiqh* (Islamic jurisprudence) only, and they have no spiritual connection with other Muslims (a common charge by members of the Orders against the guardians of the orthodox tradition); whereas the *khalifa* must continually encourage new members, ask about the brothers and any difficulties they may be having, and at the same time beware of becoming proud or conceited. In short, he has to demonstrate his profound concern with every aspect of the well-being of the *muridin*, and remain humble in his responsibility.

Running parallel to the question of fitness is the individual's efforts on behalf of the Order, chiefly in the field of recruitment. This is one means by which a *murid* becomes a *khalifa*, a *khalifa* of the *khulafa'*, and finally the *na'ib* of a *beit*. There is a constant stress in the *Hamidiya Shadhiliya* on the growth of the *tariqa* and the officials play the key part in this process. They must show ability for recruiting as well as leading those who join. At each stage they have this dual responsibility. And each level supervises those below it and is supervised by, and passes information about its activities to, that above in a highly centralized network of positions ultimately leading to the Central Office. This hierarchy stretches from the *nuqaba'* who assist each *khalifa* (see Appendix, The Laws) through the officials of the administrative areas and the *na'ibs* of the *beits* to the Sheikh himself, the source of absolute authority.

The Muridin

We have noted in our discussion of the roles of the Sheikh and the officials some of the duties of the brothers, and what being a brother is held to imply. The *murid* is the student to be guided, the sick man to be healed by his Sheikh. In theory, he has absolute obligations of obedience in any and every area of his life over which the *Murshid* (guide) chooses to exercise (usually through the *khalifa*) his authority; in practice, the comprehensiveness is limited by non-observability of behaviour, and by the tacit withdrawal or non-assertion of the claim to authority (influenced by situational factors) over a wide range of action.

In explaining the obligations of brother to brother Sheikh Ibrahim of the *Hamidiya Shadhiliya* distinguishes five major points:

(i) That a *murid* must not sin, or commit wrong, or gossip against his brother.

(ii) That he should help him if he is in material difficulty or financial trouble.

(iii) That he should always seek to put the good before him by example and by encouragement.

(iv) That he should take by the hand one who is in straitened circumstances (whether morally or materially), and should lead him away from what is disapproved of (*makruh*—reprehensible).[1]

(v) That the *murid* should not utter one evil word about his brother, but should guide him to the proper goal if he errs.[2]

He must make his brother guard against his faults until both together succeed in moving with one united purpose. For brotherhood is encouraging each other to actions which show forth that quality called in Arabic *birr*.[3] In secular use Gibb points out that this extremely comprehensive term '. . . indicates the paternal and filial relation, with its attitudes of affection, obedience, and loyalty.[4] Sura 2, verse 177,[5] of the Quran makes clear its specifically religious sense:

It is not righteousness (*birr*) that ye turn your faces in prayer towards the east and the west, but righteousness is of him who believeth in God and the last day, and the angels and the scriptures, and the prophets; who giveth money for God's sake unto his kindred, and unto orphans, and the needy, and the stranger [*ibn as-sabil*—the traveller, M. G.], and those who ask, and for redemption of captives; who is constant at prayer and giveth alms; and of those who perform their covenant, when they have covenanted, and who behave themselves patiently in adversity, and hardships, and in time of violence: these are they that are true, and these are they who fear God.[6]

Birr is '. . . the crown of true belief, when the believer at last realises and responds to the ever-presence of God in all his thoughts

---

[1] One of the five divisions by which all actions are classified under Islamic canon law. They are: *wagab*—obligatory; *mandub*—recommended; *mubah*—indifferent; *makruh*—reprehensible; *haram*—forbidden. See article, 'Shari'a', *Shorter Encyclopedia of Islam*, pp. 524–9.

[2] *Murshid al Murid*, p. 72.

[3] *Murshid*, p. 9.

[4] Gibb, H. A. R., 'The Structure of Religious Thought in Islam', in *Studies in the Civilisation of Islam*, London: Routledge and Kegan Paul, 1962, p. 191.

[5] Gibb cites it as v. 172. My numbering is taken from the Cairo edition.

[6] Sale, George, *The Koran*, London: Warne, n.d., pp. 24–5.

and conduct'.[1] It is important to bear the Quranic context in mind, since it is this which makes it so evocative a word to the pious Muslim. For whether he is literate or not, the Quran is in his memory, chanted in the *hadrahs*, quoted extensively in conversation, its sacred verses in ornate calligraphy on the walls of his home, bringing *baraka*, and recited over the radio and the television; the Quranic context is immediately familiar to him. The word is therefore rich in emotive power and association drawn from its setting in the Divine Revelation, and evokes a whole system of beliefs and values of cardinal significance in his being as a Muslim.

The *murid* is expected to show a constant willingness to co-operate with and help his fellows; to visit them if they are sick; to contribute to any funds which may be collected for the benefit of a member in want, providing always of course that he is financially able to do so; to treat the brother's needs as his own; and to assist and take part in their corporate rituals and activities (again we note that the particular demands, whether ethical or concerned with the degree and scope of participation, which an Order may make of its members in their interaction with one another as members, varies greatly from one group to another). He must seek that ultimate end of brotherhood which is knowledge of the way of connecting the good of one individual to another for their mutual help in what is good in this world and the next (*Murshid al Murid*, p. 9). In everything he should manifest in his outward devotion to the *tariqa* the quality of that inward condition which is so much the concern of Sufism at all levels of its elaboration and development.

Conclusion

We have attempted in this chapter to set up a simple model—of association and organization as poles on a continuum—and to use this model in an analytical description of certain formal aspects of the Orders. In general the *turuq* are characterized as being closer to the first pole. Though their structures are all superficially similar, a hierarchy of officials theoretically based on spiritual understanding and the local *zawiyas* under *khalifas* dependent on the Head Sheikh for their authority, we saw that this structure is in reality extremely tenuous. Taken as functioning entities, most

---

[1] Gibb, op. cit., p. 192.

of the Orders are highly amorphous.[1] The *zawiyas* usually operate as self-regulating units and the complex of rights and duties around the various social identities is very imprecisely defined. To all intents and purposes, as mediator of the link between the Sheikh and the *murid*, the *khalifa* has in fact complete local autonomy. And in so far as it appears that such positions were connected with the social structure through kinship and inheritance, the *tariqa* reflected aspects of that structure rather than having an 'independent' existence.

Furthermore, plural membership was, and still is, very common. The commitment demanded of the brothers is highly attenuated, though we remarked on the possible significance membership might have in the political sphere (with particular reference to the *Sanusiya*).[2] To talk in terms of mobilization of members *qua* members, and to think of the Orders as 'organizations' at all, would be extremely misleading, not least because they are ultimately based on charismatic inspiration and authority. And, as Weber pointed out, a group subject to, and founded on, this principle tends to be opposed by its very nature to that rational and bureaucratic authority characteristic of organizations.[3]

Nevertheless, one group, the *Hamidiya Shadhiliya*, has attempted to strike a balance between association and organization, to make the Order an integrated, cohesive, and functioning whole— more, that is, than merely a series of loosely related separate parts. Two key steps were taken here: kinship ceased to be the principle on which office was allocated, and the Order insisted on exclusiveness of membership, with a corresponding stress on the *dominance* (as I have used the term) of the role of *murid* of the *Hamidiya Shadhiliya*. However, the greater the stress on hierarchy and office on an achieved basis, the more crucial the position of *khalifa* becomes, and the more likely to be the focus of tension and conflict (as we shall see later). The same is true, *a fortiori*, of the position of *Sheikh as-Sigada*, and especially at the critical period immediately following the death of the founder. The case of the *Tijaniya* may

[1] Brunel, *Essai sur la confrérie des 'Aissaouia au Maroc*, Paris: Paul Geuthner, 1926, refers to the 'absolute lack of cohesion' of the Orders.

[2] See also Lewis, I. M., op. cit., for an interesting discussion of the political importance of the Orders in Somaliland. For a comparative survey see the same author's introduction to Lewis, I. M. (ed.), *Islam in Tropical Africa*, London: O.U.P., 1966.

[3] Weber, M., *The Theory of Social and Economic Organisation*, p. 358.

be cited as an example. In this North African Order bearing a sectarian and exclusive stamp, even though the Saint himself (Ahmad al Tijani) appointed a successor, the Order split into dissident movements on his death as the chiefs of two major *zawiyas* pursued their rival claims to leadership.[1] Lings mentions the considerable hostility of other *khalifas* when the Sheikh al 'Alawi broke away from the Order he then belonged to and founded his own.[2]

In the *Hamidiya Shadhiliya* also the succession to Salama provoked a crisis. When the Saint died, his son Ibrahim was only a boy of thirteen. Though Salama is said to have preferred him (and I was told by one informant that he had actually seen a letter to that effect), some of the brothers wavered. The old Sheikh's death had left a tremendous sense of loss, and many were worried that Ibrahim was too young and inexperienced. The *wakil* of the *tariqa* then declared that he (the *wakil*) would assume the vacant position, persuading some of the brothers to take the oath to him. With the help of a committee of the loyal *muridin* who went to the Sufi Council and secured its approval Ibrahim was made the Sheikh. He then took over the sole control at the age of nineteen. The split within the group was not healed, however, until four years ago (1962), when the one-time *wakil* was allowed to rejoin the Order (without any rank whatever).[3] The possibilities are thus always present at these vital times of succession to leadership, whether in the 'association' or 'organization' type of *tariqa*.

Nevertheless the *Hamidiya Shadhiliya* have realized what most of the Egyptian Orders are only now beginning to see, the importance of some degree of centralized control, or obedience to the bureaucratic imperative, for survival. Salama ar-Radi had this insight into the nature of the changes occurring in Egypt over fifty years ago and the *tariqa* is profiting from his understanding. In the following chapter we shall see the further implications of the framework he laid down for the control and maintenance processes in the Order.

---

[1] Abun-Nasr, Jamil, *The Tijaniyya*, London: O.U.P., 1965, p. 53.

[2] Lings, Martin, *A Muslim Saint of the Twentieth Century*, pp. 82 and 87.

[3] It was extremely difficult to obtain information on this crisis of succession. Quite naturally, members were not keen to discuss a serious conflict, even though it is now resolved. I was told that only 'a few' of the brothers had followed the *wakil*, but I was unable to obtain precise figures.

IV

SYSTEM AND SANCTION

IT is a truism that all organizations and associations have to face tensions and conflicts that arise from the circumstances of their origin and from their constellation of values. Traditionally the Orders did not act as unified, society-wide groupings with centralized control from the capital. They were important precisely because of their localization of authority, the multiplex roles of their leadership, and their incorporation into the social and normative universe of the people. They were part of the cultural and social universe which it was not necessary to *teach* because it was *lived in*; they belonged to the axiomatic world in which men grew up. Sanctions, means of recruitment, and the maintenance of certain particular symbols and values only became problems when this organic nexus of Orders and society was broken. Since they are no longer part of the 'nature of things' and cannot assume that individuals share a common collective outlook, a group such as the *Hamidiya Shadhiliya* has to set out specifically to inculcate certain concepts, motivations, and loyalties in its members; to persuade them to *be*, as well as belong to, the *Hamidiya Shadhiliya*.

The evolution of what are considered appropriate means of control is, of course, intimately linked with the ultimate purposes of the group and will vary considerably. We must also remember that a group may find that organizational requirements in themselves cause it to act in ways which directly or indirectly lead to a result contrary to its original purposes. Here processes of internal regulation play an obvious and important role, for they create problems as well as solve them. Dislocation may occur precisely because of an excessive fidelity to the system of rules; to take a well-known example, rules in an administrative department which are designed to achieve maximum efficiency in performance can lead, by what Merton has termed 'bureaucratic ritualism', to a diminution of organizational effectiveness.

For the purposes of analysis it is convenient to describe the means of regulation in the *Hamidiya Shadhiliya* under two headings.

The first is overt formal control, the prescribed rules and principles which govern the group, and which direct members'
action, and the system of sanctions which can be invoked to
guarantee those rules. The second concerns concealed informal
controls, which operate often in ways of which the members are
unaware. Each type of control has in turn two aspects. Since the
group is not a sealed unit, it must of necessity be in some relation
to the wider society and we find therefore that the means of control
are as often directed to the maintenance or establishment of a
desired pattern of relations with the 'others' as to internal regulation. In the nature of the case this involves a whole number of
sets of 'others' more or less constituted as organizations, groups,
or classes—government agencies, religious specialists, the bourgeoisie, industrial workers, peasants, etc.—and the aims and
expectations of the group may well be different for each different
set. The first three above in our particular example of the Orders
constitute actual or potential opposition or threat. The government
and the *'ulema'* possess in their varying degrees power and
authority over the *turuq* whose relation with them is thus extremely
delicate. No opportunity must be given to either to find the
brotherhoods wanting in their religious or social functions. The
lower urban classes, the workers, and the fellaheen, on the other
hand, are the primary sources of recruitment, a target of propaganda, and the mainstay of the membership. The efforts of the
Order and the presentation of itself must be directed to them in
a very different way. The more active an Order is and the more it
seeks to gather recruits, the more complex the problems of control
will be with reference to the many divisions of the external society.

The specific difficulties inherent in any organization founded
round the link of the individual member to the charismatic religious
leader have been well-nigh exhaustively discussed. The central
paradox which confronts the Orders, particularly an actively
recruiting *tariqa* such as the *Hamidiya Shadhiliya*, is easily grasped:
quantitative and by implication geographical expansion of the
group is an explicit goal, but achievement of this goal makes it ever
more difficult to preserve this key structural link between Sheikh
and *Murid* and the primary emphasis on the total system of relations.
Either the organization evolves ways of balancing the tension
between expansion and group solidarity based on a constant and
intimate set of personal relations, or it must change or modify some

of its aims and structure while seeking to keep intact its values. Some accommodation there must be, the ways in which this accommodation is made vary greatly.

Formal Controls

The setting forth of the *Qanun*, the Laws of the *Hamidiya Shadhiliya*, is the major element in the control system of the Order. Though other groups have had a 'rule', in the sense of a general series of religious prescripts,[1] none have the written elaboration of a detailed hierarchical bureaucratic network for the functioning of the group and the precise delineation of the role of each office.[2] The founder provided a text to which recourse might be had for guidance and to which formal appeal through the interpretation of the Head of the Order could be made. The effect was to 'fix' the formal structure of the *tariqa* almost at its inception far more clearly and unambiguously than is normally the case.

Certain stipulations and requirements made in the Laws deserve special attention. The most striking is the rule (316) that: 'No one who has joined us may join a *tariqa* other than ours.' As we have noted before, the *Hamidiya Shadhiliya*, in contrast to all the other Egyptian Orders, demands an exclusive commitment on the part of its members. Taking the oath to Sidi Salama bars one from affiliation with any other Sheikh. The group is thus clearly set off from its peers and its boundaries unequivocally drawn. Further, it will not accept individuals from those *turuq* into the *Hamidiya Shadhiliya*, and makes provision for dissociating from itself anyone who already belongs to an Order before coming to it (319). Members may not share in *hadrahs*, processions, or any of the official religious occasions with what are in effect regarded as their competitors, and are prohibited from taking guidance from them (312–13). Such basic definition and establishment of identity is essential, as Salama clearly understood, to any group seeking to retain autonomous existence over a long period of time with a carefully worked out set of aims and purposes. If the pervasive influence over the member's life which Salama conceived of as a characteristic

---

[1] See Bannerth, E., 'La Khalwatiya en Égypte', *MIDEO*, 8, pp. 1–74.

[2] One might speculate perhaps as to the influence on Salama of the bureaucratic organization in which he worked for so long. He was one of the first generation of Egyptians to have personal experience of Western bureaucratic organizations.

of the movement was to be realized, a first requirement was a complete absence of any ambiguity as to the boundaries of the group.

Viewed in this context the full significance of the commitment contained in the covenant with the Sheikh (made either directly with him or through the *khalifa*) becomes clear:

The Covenant

[*al-'Ahd*: see also the full translation of the laws for complete text]

Law 328. The instruction of the Order amongst us is that the student places his hand in the hand of the Sheikh then the Sheikh administers the covenant to him: that he takes the Sheikh as a Sheikh for him before Allah the Most High on the way of Sidi Abu'l Hassan al-Shadhili and Sidi Salama ar-Radi, may Allah be pleased with them, and on the *Tariqa Hamidiya Shadhiliya*. And the Sheikh says: O God, verily I have received him as a brother before God the Most High—then the Sheikh says 'There is no God but Allah' three times and the student says this after the Sheikh once in a loud voice; then the Sheikh reads the verse of the taking of the allegiance which is: 'Verily those who take the allegiance to you take it to Allah'—to the end of the verse. Then he (the Sheikh) instructs him in the *wird* which is asking God's forgiveness, and the Prayer for the Prophet (May God bless and preserve him) and the *Shahada*. All of this one hundred times and he seals it with 'There is no God but Allah and Muhammad is the Prophet of Allah. May God bless him and his family and his Companions and preserve them' said once according to what is recorded in the section of the *wird*. And the Sheikh orders him to do what he thinks suitable for him of the *awrad* [daily offices] of the *Shadhiliya* and their *ahzab* ['sections', i.e., of prayers]: And he says: 'Have you accepted me as a Sheikh and Spiritual Guide before Allah the Most High?' Then the student replies: 'I have accepted.' And the Sheikh says: 'Have you accepted what I have laid down for you?' Then the student says: 'I have accepted.' Then the Sheikh says: 'And we have accepted.' Then the Sheikh and the student recite the *Fatiha* on that; then they repeat 'There is no God but Allah and Muhammad is the Prophet of Allah' once. Then the Sheikh prays for the student and those present and then they (the Sheikh and the student) make the formal hand kiss.

This ended the ceremony of covenant-taking in the first edition of the Laws which was in force until February 1965 when the second revised edition was issued (the question of these changes is also dealt with in the Appendix with the full translation of the *Qanun*). There is, however, an extremely important addition in the revised version which amounts almost to a creed. I give the translation in full as it follows rule 328 above:

The form of instruction

[*not* in the first edition]

I ask pardon of Allah the Most Great—than whom there is no other God, the Living, the All Sustaining, and I turn in repentance to Him. I have turned in repentance to Allah and returned to Allah—and I regret what I have done—and I have determined that I will not return to sin ever again—and I say with my tongue—believing in my heart I witness that there is no God but Allah and Muhammad is the Prophet of Allah.

I have faith in Allah and His angels and His Books and His Prophets and the Last Day. And in destiny with its goodness and its evil according to the way of the people of the Sunna and the consensus[1]—according to the purpose of Allah and of His Prophet.

O Allah: Verily I bear witness to You and Your angels and the bearers of Your Throne and Your Prophets and Your Messengers and the sufficiency of Your Creation and You are the Best of witnesses—that I have taken and agreed and accepted this my brother as a brother before Allah and as a guide to Him on the path and way of my lord 'Ali ibn 'Abdullah Abu'l Hassan al-Shadhili—and my lord (Sidi) Salama ibn Hassan al-Radi, may God be pleased with them.

And verily I have covenanted with Allah and I pledge myself to Allah and I trust myself to Allah and take Him as a witness to me that I have taken on myself total obedience to this Sheikh and I shall not oppose him with my heart or my limbs or my tongue and I have made this a solemn pledge to Allah on me and a legal, true, honest, determined, whole, absolute covenant, both outwardly and inwardly, while I live and on the intention of this my Sheikh; and I stand for it in this world and the next. And I am responsible for it before Allah. And if I oppose my Sheikh or deny him or stand against him or change or exchange then I will be a traitor and faithless and an oath-breaker of the covenants of Allah and His promises and I take refuge with Allah from that. And we hope to remain faithful to what we have sworn—and what we have pledged to Allah; Allah is the Trustee of what we say.

Then the Sheikh says in a lowered voice but so that he may be heard:

O Allah: Verily I have subjugated myself to Allah and accepted this my

---

[1] *ijma'*. One of the four *usul* (roots or principles) of Islam. The others are Quran, Sunna, and *Qiyas* (analogy). See *Shorter Encyclopedia of Islam* article on *idjma'*, p. 157.

brother and taken him as a brother in God and accepted whoever has received this our instruction who has come to us whether he be related with us or not. And he has become a member as have all of us in the way of the *Shadhiliya*, and we have become of their children and entered into their circle and their protection—O Allah: Turn us not away from Your Presence—and do not cut us off. Praise be to Allah for that.

Know, O my brothers, that the Prophet, may God bless and preserve him, taught the Imam 'Ali the *Dhikr* (remembrance) and it has come to us by the blessed chain[1] from Allah (may He be exalted)—to His approaching angels—to the Lord of the totality of men (the Prophet Muhammad), may God bless him, and his family and his companions all together and the Followers—and whoever follows the Followers—and who followed them in excellence to the day of Religion; then it came to our Sheikhs until it reached us, then it came to you—say with me 'there is no God save Allah' three times, the chain of the instruction comes to you.

The Most High said: 'Fulfil the covenant of God when you have sworn and do not break the oath after its confirmation; and you have taken God on yourselves as a surety.' Allah the Most Great has spoken truly. And the Most High said: 'Verily those who take a covenant with you only take an oath with Allah; the hand of Allah is above their hands. And whoever breaks (it) only breaks (it) on himself. And whoever fulfils what he has covenanted with Allah for, then He shall give him great reward.' Allah the Most Great has spoken truly.

(The Sheikh then says alone in a lowered voice but so that he may be heard):

Praise be to Allah and blessing and peace on the Prophet of Allah and on his family and his Companions and who follows his guidance—I entrust you and myself with belief in Allah the Most Great and obedience to Him—and I warn you and myself against disobedience to Him and opposing Him. And know that you have made a covenant with Allah and His Prophet and a true legal covenant with your Sheikh (according to Islamic Law). And you have made it a pledge on yourselves not to be broken ever after that. Its fulfilment is incumbent on you for what you have covenanted and what you have vowed to Allah the Most High; you will have success and prosper and Allah will be pleased with you. And know that this is a covenant of God and His promise—this is a trust of Allah on your necks—Allah will ask you of it when you stand before Him. He glorifies Allah who glorifies the way of Allah; and he pours scorn on Allah who pours scorn on it.

---

[1] The reference is to the chain of blessing connecting Sheikh Salama to 'Ali, the Prophet's son-in-law, fourth (and last) of the orthodox Caliphs.

The contrast of this with the simplicity of the first version is striking. We notice the stress on repentance for sins past and the idea of starting, with membership in the *Hamidiya Shadhiliya*, a new and sinless future. The oath thus more clearly marks off the postulant's past, his life outside the pale of the Order, from that which is to come in his newly entered-on brotherhood and obedience. After this separation the *'ahd* builds up to an extraordinarily weighty and solemn undertaking of the most abject obedience to the Sheikh sworn under the sanction of the wrath of God against one who is '. . . a traitor and faithless and an oathbreaker of the covenants of Allah and His promises . . .'. No compact could be more comprehensive in its demands. It is also a completely asymmetric agreement with no guarantee for the student other than the Quranic assurance of great reward; the Sheikh makes no reciprocal undertaking.

This spelling out of the nature of the link which the *murid* now makes with the Sheikh, the extreme tone of the language, and the invocation of the Divinity as trustee of the promise, may be seen as part of the attempt to assert the primacy of the Sheikh and his relation with his students at a time when the growth of the Order means that he is more and more physically separated from large numbers of members. The all-embracing character of the authority to which the individual subjects himself is quite explicit; once in the organization under such terms before God, one is absolutely committed to Sidi Salama the founder and to his son. And it is this latter who has thought it necessary to introduce this addition to the *Qanun*. As we noted in the previous chapter, the death of the charismatic leader leaves his successor more dependent on formal, ritual promises of a loyalty that the Saint, by virtue of his sanctity, could rely on obtaining from those who followed him.

It will be recognized, however, that the covenant is backed by a sanction, God's displeasure, that is distant and diffuse as well as being in another sense the strongest. It is further the most extreme and covers the ultimate case of reneging on the promise; the organization requires means to ensure the cohesion and discipline of members in the less demanding circumstances of everyday administration and maintenance. For the whole point is that every effort should be made to ensure that no one comes to the state where the ultimate needs to be invoked. This involves constant supervision, so that the central authority should be informed of the affairs of every local centre and of the actions of the deputies, in order to anticipate and deal with any possible conflicts or backsliding before they become serious and thus a threat on whatever scale to the functioning of the group. To this end reports and supervision by officials (see Laws 67 and 71) have always been made. Again, however, there are significant additions to the old *Qanun* which we may relate to the growth of the Order, its wider geographical distribution, and perhaps to the attention of a Government wary of the possibilities of illegal opposition under the cover of the most active Sufi Brotherhood in Egypt. The following regulations are *only* in the new edition of the Laws:

73. The *khulafa'* and the *khulafa'* of the *khulafa'* and the *na'ibs* at their different levels must send detailed reports to the *beit as-Sigada* on their activities and the activities of the brothers of their circles at least once every three months.

74. The *khulafa'* and the *khulafa'* of the *khulafa'* and the *na'ibs* at their different levels must fill in the following form and send it to the *beit as-Sigada* and inform (it) about every change which is in train for the future; and the secretary of the *Sigada* is responsible for receiving these forms and he must write it down in the register set aside for that:

[the form]
Complimentary greetings:

It is our desire to secure the advancement of the *tariq* and to discover the condition of our brethren. We hope that you will fill in the items written in the attached form in order to facilitate the visit of a committee of the brothers of Cairo acting on our behalf to communicate with you and co-operate with you in whatever you want them to discuss with you which will contribute to the advancement of the *tariq*. This information must return to us within ten days in detail from its date (sending date) because of its extreme importance. Greetings.

The Servant of the *Fuqara'*
Ibrahim Salama ar-Radi

The *Hamidiya Shadhiliya Tariqa*

Report of the brothers of the *tariq* in the district   *markaz* governorate   to the central office of the *Sigada* of the *Hamidiya Shadhiliya* in Cairo presented by:

1. Name and address and nearest telephone to the responsible *khalifa*.
2. Names of the *khulafa'* in the district.
3. Nights of the weekly *hadrahs* and the time of their beginning and the places where they are held.

4. Nights of the meetings of the brothers and their times and places.

5. The visiting of the brothers to the neighbouring districts.

6. Was any disagreement or disharmony found between the brothers or the brothers of the district or the brothers of another district and what is it?

7. Number of the brothers in the district   the average number of people who gather in the *hadrah* and the meeting separately.

8. The way of reaching the area (the communications from Cairo).

9. The way of reaching the place of the meeting of the brothers or to the *khalifa* of the district.

10. Do the brothers have a special *zawiya* or mosque?

11. Important general notes on the advancement of the *tariq* in the area.

> Signature of the presenter of the report
>
> Signature of two
> of the brothers

Even more relevant to the question of control of members' actions and central direction and supervision is the following, which is *not* in either edition of the Laws, but was drawn up in 1966. This second form is confidential between the Sheikh, the officials of the *Sigada,* and those making the report (I would be personally inclined to see it as a response to the trial of the Muslim Brotherhood which took place in 1966 and possibly to direct Government instruction). I was informed that the Sheikh had set up committees to go round the different *zawiyas* in Cairo (of which there are now some 175) and the provinces, each committee composed of two people selected from the officials and senior trusted members of the Order. The visit is made on the night of the *hadrah.*

The Form:

1. The organisation (*nizam*—order) of the *hadrah.*

2. The number of those in the *hadrah.*

3. The manners (*adab*) of those in the *hadrah.*

4. The attention paid to the general *hadrahs* by the *zawiya.*

5. The instructions (*mudhakirat*) of the head of the *zawiya* to the beloved.

6. Were 'the cries of truth' read in the *hadrahs*?[1]

---

[1] Literal translation of *saihat al haqq*; this was explained as being a reference to the general conduct of the leader, the propriety of his conduct, remarks to the brethren, manner, etc.

7. The performance (*tashkil*) of the hymns.[1]
8. The effort put into the great *mulid* and the general occasions.
9. The effort of the head (of the *zawiya*) for the beloved.
10. The length of time in which the head has performed his duties.
11. Any proposals of the *zawiya* for the welfare of the Order.
12. The opening of new *zawiyas* in the neighbouring districts.
13. The instruction of the beloved in the manners (*adab*) of the Order.
14. Notes of the committee of the *zawiya* and its proposals.
15. Was there any quarrel between the beloved of the *zawiya*?
16. Signatures of the members of the committee of the *zawiya*.

Observations:

(i) The members of the committee of the *zawiya* may neither begin the *hadrah* nor give them (the brothers) the hand kiss.

(ii) Meetings are held for the decision of the central office to direct the *zawiyas* as they need to be directed.

It could justifiably be said that the main office of the *Hamidiya Shadhiliya* has gone to the bureaucratic limit in its attempt to maintain central direction of all the branches of the group, with its precondition of close supervision and detailed knowledge of the particular workings of each *zawiya*. I have indicated that in doing so it may have been motivated as much by external pressures, arising from political circumstances in the wider society as a whole, as by purely functional demands for broader control over the local groups. The immediate effect is to increase the organizational predominance of the *beit as-Sigada* in a very direct way at the expense of the *zawiyas*; to reinforce the centripetal aspects of the Order and to bring the Sheikh's authority closer in a practical sense to every member, and especially to the *khalifas*.

A further important effect of this centralizing tendency with the network of subordinate investigating committees reporting back (others are sent out on tours of inspection when the Sheikh feels it necessary) is to emphasize the role of the central office as a major control agency rather than as the fount of religious excellence and exemplary spiritual guidance that is its own sanction for devotion. It should be stressed that Sheikh Ibrahim preserves his aura of sanctity; it is even, as previously suggested, enhanced by 'distancing', the concentration of power, and the strengthening of the administrative and therefore the spiritual link with the entire

---

[1] i.e. all the hymns were sung in *absolutely perfect detail*, for no mistakes are allowed.

membership. To attempt a projection into the future, however, one might speculate that his successor, lacking the intimate personal connection with the founding Saint, and probably also the reputation for the capacity to perform *karamat*, will more and more rely on the highly institutionalized channels for asserting his authority; and further, that the essence of that authority will have undergone a significant *de facto* change in character which can be very crudely expressed as shading off from the charismatic pole to the legal and the bureaucratic.

At the same time as provision is made for supervision of the *khalifa*, care is taken to set out clearly the boundaries of his and all the status positions in the hierarchy of the *tariqa*. This is of great significance for the integration of the role set of the organization and the reduction of conflict that might otherwise arise through a lack of definition of the spheres of authority, rights, and duties. Such definition is of two kinds: Vertically, as between roles in a subordinate/superordinate relation—from *murid* to *khalifa*, *khalifa* to *khalifa* of the *khulafa'*, and so on up to the *Sigada* and to the Sheikh himself, who possesses total authority and is its only source; and horizontally, between actors occupying the same status within the Order and each of whom yet has his own sphere of competence and particular function which fall outside the legitimate realm of any other. The risk of strain is always present in either case and is indeed inherent in any role set, but clear demarcation of boundaries reduces the possibility of its occurring. Broadly speaking, the officials and the brothers know precisely their formal structural relation to equals, superiors, and subordinates in the Order, and potential areas of tension are anticipated in the *Qanun*. Four of the Laws have an immediate relevance here and are useful illustrations of this point:

305. It is not permissible for a *khalifa* or higher than he to receive in the *hadrah* which he holds in any town, even if he is a follower of the *beit as-Sigada*, a student who has taken the *tariqa* from a *khalifa* or higher than that in our Way *except with the permission of the khalifa from whom the student (originally) took the tariqa*; if necessity compels the matter may be brought up before the *Sheikh as-Sigada*.

(my italics; this is an example of the way in which the link to the particular *khalifa* from whom the student took the covenant on first entering the Order is emphasized. It is not an attachment that can be trespassed on or diminished in any way by divided loyalties that may arise.)

318. Everyone who has taken the *tariqa* from the Sheiks of our Way and then from us [i.e., Sheikh Ibrahim] is our student and not the student of the person from whom he first took the *tariqa*. [Of immediate relevance to the above; the only authority which can intervene over a *khalifa* is that of the paramount link of Sheikh to *murid*.]

308. It is not permissible for a *khalifa* or higher than he to give the *tariqa* to anyone who has taken it from the Sheikh of the Order or from a (different) *khalifa* or higher than him in our Way. [A complement to the preceding two regulations.]

(Reference has already been made to these two regulations which establish the supremacy of the oath taken to the Head of the Order over all others.)

311. It is not permissible for a *khalifa* or higher than he to issue an order to one of his rank; nor may he issue an order to anyone lower than he in rank unless that person is his follower; and he may not under any circumstances stop [i.e., expel or keep from his duties] a *khalifa*.

Since the role system is to be a perfect mechanism with expectations, rights, and duties constituting a harmonious set, the minimization of ambiguity in these laws covering areas of possible conflict plays a major part in control. But in an imperfect world norms are violated, infractions occur, conflicts arise. Since the *Hamidiya Shadhiliya* demands a complete involvement from its members and expects to exercise its authority over so many aspects of their lives (at least in theory, whatever modifications may in practice tacitly be made) the field for dispute, and for failure perfectly to fulfil all obligations, is greatly widened. Such contingencies are anticipated in the elaborate machinery for conciliation, settlement, and, where necessary, the prescription of some form of penalty contained in the *Qanun*.

Dispute and Judgement

Disputes or arguments between members are very often settled by fairly informal means; either by efforts by individual friends of the protagonists, or by the *khalifa* personally taking an interest in the issue. He may even, if he judges it necessary, send a few of the brothers of the *zawiya* privately to those involved and they then report back to him for his decision on the question. His verdict is more than likely to be accepted, sanctioned as it is by the authority vested in him by the Sheikh. Indeed such decisions are generally regarded as being binding on both parties.

More serious cases occur, however, for which such procedures are inadequate (though we must emphasize again the fact that, according to informants, the vast majority of disputes are in fact sufficiently minor to be covered by these personal means through friends or, failing that, by the ruling of the *khalifa*). In these circumstances, somewhat more elaborate procedures may be followed though the *Sigada* can always send the deputy of the Order (or a delegation) to end a dispute if the Sheikh sees fit. If this is not thought suitable, then the matter has to be taken to one of a series of 'courts' set up for this purpose. Reference to the Laws 268–99 will give the reader the full details of the composition of these courts, the nature of their powers, and the distribution of the latter.[1] Here I want only to draw attention to the main points of these particular regulations.

We note first that the authority of the Sheikh is put over all and that:

274. (With regard to) every judgement which issues from one of these *maglis*, even if from that of the *beit as-Sigada*, the Sheikh may carry it out or not or order it to be renewed. And he may elect other than those who discussed the question in the first place.

When the Sheikh has agreed in writing, then the judgement may be carried out. These 'courts' are not resorted to save where all else has failed and their verdict must, as a final check, be ratified by the highest authority. Thus even though a *khalifa* may expel his own student (298), such an expulsion would in fact require the Sheikh's approval. The registering of the case has to have his seal on it. He represents the ultimate source of appeal by any member against any decision:

284. All the judgements which are over a *murid* or *khalifa* or higher than he may be appealed against to the *Sigada* for it to examine.

This would extend particularly to the execution of the most severe ruling that can be made, the expulsion of a brother from the

---

[1] I was unable either to attend or to obtain records of such a 'court'. I was informed that they are rarely resorted to, and I did not meet a member who claimed to have participated in one.

tariqa. The official attitude to this critical situation emerges clearly in the following two regulations:

286. As for the greater matters such as going out from the *tariq* and not paying attention to it or displaying disobedience or harming some of the brothers or doing something to their detriment or committing any of the great sins,[1] advice must be given on this from the beginning: if one comes forward and demonstrates his repentance and then returns again [to the Way, M. G.], he may be received in again with his punishment such as being kept away [literally 'stopped'] for some days or months or other than that—if he does not come forward and continues in his error he may be expelled for ever and it is necessary in what is particularly concerned with the expulsion of the *khulafa'* that the matter be set forth in the *Sigada*.

296. If there occurs the expulsion of a *khalifa* or higher than he by order of the *Sigada* then he may not be received in a *hadrah* or a procession or in the assembly of our *tariq*; it is not permissible to walk with him in a procession or a *hadrah*; if he has students and they leave him at that time then they are followers of the *Sigada* and it orders them with what it sees fit; if they follow him at the time of his expulsion *then the judgement of expulsion is applicable to them too*; if among them there are *khulafa'* or higher the *Sigada* decides what it sees fit for those *khulafa'* or any higher. [My emphasis.]

No member of the *Sigada* may be barred save by express ruling from the Sheikh himself (299).

The second general point to remark about these regulations is that a member is only subject to judgement by his superiors and *not* by his peers. What is more, the lowest of the courts begins well up in the hierarchy at the level of *na'ib* of the *mudiriya*.[2] Neither the *khalifa* nor the *khalifa* of the *khulafa'* can hold such a *maglis* (271). However, when the *maglis* is held all the members have an equal voice, though they differ in rank (273). In this way any problem is dealt with by some of the most senior and experienced members of the Order in a group where each man's opinion ideally carries the same weight.

---

[1] The orthodox differ as to the exact number and nature of the 'great sins'. Some give as many as seventeen. Hughes quotes a tradition of the Prophet which lists the following: *shirk*—the associating of anything with God, magic, killing without reason, usury, the unjust appropriation of the property of orphans, fleeing from the infidel in battle, taking an innocent woman in adultery. See Hughes, article 'Sin', *Dictionary of Islam*, London: W. H. Allen & Co., 1935.

[2] Administrative division of a governorate.

I was informed that should a member actually commit an offence against the criminal code of the State, this action would not come before these courts of the Order, always assuming that it became known. Officially, as the Sheikh put it, *al hukm min sha'n al wali*—legal judgement is the concern of the ruler.[1] If an individual secretly confesses to such a crime to his *khalifa* or to the Sheikh, he is urged to make private restitution and some form of spiritual penance. It is not felt that he should be handed over to the secular legal agencies—his detection and punishment are their business.

The Minor Punishments (Munasefat)

The courts dealt with above represent very much the last resort in the internal control of the *tariqa*. The vast majority of the infractions are of what one might at first consider a minor character. This covers matters such as the failure to recite the daily *wird* (office) of the Order, making a mistake in the singing of the hymns, failing to behave in the way required of members on a public religious occasion, and so forth. Individuals either come forward at a meeting of the *zawiya* before their brothers to say that they have done or neglected to do such and such a thing, or their lapse is noted by others. In either case, the rules governing the *munasefat* (215–21) are of great importance, for these small details are crucial in the process of internalizing the standards and values which the Order demands. Failure to say the *wird* once in a morning, an action which begins the day with a religious duty imposed by the *tariqa*, must be *felt* by the member to merit penance of whatever degree (to the public nature of the admission of fault and imposition of the *munasfa* we return below). He may be told to recite the *wird* ten times, or to look after the shoes during the *hadrah* for a month, or to make a visit to the tomb of a local saint. But he must *feel in need* of this 'correction and benefit' (Law 216) for the betterment and purification of his internal state and moral character, and accept without question its legitimacy. With this aim in mind his brothers must judge him as they would wish to be judged (Law 217), making allowance for his age, seniority, and other circumstances. What is prescribed is laid down by them all in a communal

---

[1] This reflects very much the classic attitude of the '*ulema*' to the agencies of political authority.

decision in a spirit, not of censure, but of charitable concern for the brother's spiritual well-being. This is rather the consensus of equals than discipline handed down by a superior, and it is thus more closely in accord with the basic values of the group.

Informal controls

Confession

Consideration of the *munasefat* leads us to those controls which I have termed informal: that is, mechanisms (or simply patterns of action in the loosest sense) whose manifest purpose or effect is not the regulation of the functioning of the Order, but which are nevertheless important in that respect. As previously suggested, such controls are equally significant for the maintenance of the integrity of the group as are the formal means, and may indeed have crucial implications for its proper functioning. In this regard the most striking institution of the Brotherhoods is that of confession (*'itiraf*).

It has for long been asserted that the confessional mechanism was not present in Islam, but it may well be the fact that it has existed for a considerable period of time. It lies beyond both the scope of this book and of my competence to discuss when and how it may have originated and spread; nor unfortunately do I have the comparative data for all the Orders in contemporary Egypt. One can only advance this as a topic for further inquiry and confine discussion here to the *'itiraf* as it now exists among the *Hamidiya Shadhiliya*.[1]

The difficulty about using the word 'confession' at all as a translation of *'itiraf* is, of course, its immediate Christian (more particularly Roman Catholic) association for the western reader. An essential point of distinction is that there is no forgiveness given or absolution promised by the Sheikh, nor is it within his power to do so. This is linked with the notion of the Absolute Transcendence of the Omnipotent God, and with the nature of Islam, as a religion in which the relation of works to faith is not so crucial and intimate as it is in, for example, Catholic doctrine. Certainly the sense of sin, of the fall from grace, of spiritual guilt and the whole theodicy of suffering are virtually absent from Islam by comparison with

---

[1] My only source of comparative data is the *Fasiya Shadhiliya* where the *'itiraf* is of the same nature and subject to the same interpretation.

most of the Christian Churches. None the less, in an Order directed to the moral condition of its members in a comprehensive way, the questions of 'sins' (*dhunub*), of lapses from the moral norms, is one of great importance. They offend not only against one's spiritual condition and status as a Muslim, but more particularistically against one's membership in the *tariqa*; they violate what Sidi Salama has taught and the Laws which he and his son have laid down for their followers who are bound to them by an oath of the most solemn nature. The Sheikh is their leader, teacher, spiritual guide in every matter, and successor to the Founder of the Way; his deputies act for him in the local *zawiyas* with his authority. He knows all and should be informed of all, for everything in the members' life is his concern.

Whatever the offence may be, therefore, from the failure to recite the *wird* to a major moral deliction, members are encouraged to admit to it. Unless it is of the highest magnitude (adultery for example) it is preferred that they declare their fault before one of the meetings of the brothers and to the Sheikh, rather than only privately to the latter, though the member is free to follow his own choice in this matter. For *tasawwuf* (Sufism) is not passive, but rather a courageous facing of facts.[1] One is seeking an outer and then an inner humility and it is better to confess and repent in front of the brothers than secretly as an individual to beg God's mercy. Since the Sheikh is closer to God, his prayer for forgiveness is more likely to be effective. Moreover, once having admitted his fault to the Sheikh the *murid* feels confirmed again in the Way and ashamed to return to his failing.[2]

It should be emphasized that the *'itiraf* is not regarded as either an absolute duty for the member, or as an absolute requisite for proper fulfilment of one's spiritual obligations. It is nevertheless very much encouraged in the brothers by the hierarchy as being an instrument for their inner improvement and sanctioned by Sidi Salama. One could argue as a layman that confession probably acts for the individual as a kind of catharsis or psychological release mechanism. Its significance for us more particularly resides in its place in the moral universe of the Order. The disjunction between act and intention, the outward form and the inner truth, is always crucial to a religious and ritual group that constitutes itself on the

---

[1] Saif an-Nasr, op. cit., p. 69.
[2] The interpretation is that of the Sheikh's private secretary.

ground of shared identity under an ultimate authority. Men must be what they seem. For the *Hamidiya Shadhiliya* is defined not only by the rules for and acts of its members but by the creation of a shared moral vision and belief, a collective conscience, and a collective consciousness. The *Hamidiya Shadhiliya* must produce and constantly renew and rehearse their consociation and common apprehension of the world. Brothers entering the Order must be instructed not just in a pattern of activity but more profoundly in patterns of motivation and consciousness such that, among other matters, they feel the *necessity* for *'itiraf*. Since in their daily lives, in a society in which there is increasing social differentiation, most of the members move among non-members in a complex urban environment, the Order seeks constantly to reinforce the inner commitment of the brothers. *'Itiraf* draws them into a common set of relevances and criteria of significance.

It is not simply that one lays before one's Sheikh the great or lesser failings, but one admits them humbly before one's brothers. They also participate and 'brotherhood' acquires a deeper meaning in this intimate awareness of personal shortcomings revealed before a gathering of the members. In this reduction of inter-personal space to a minimum, a sense of closeness, of a shared knowledge of the individual's life and character which lies at the very root of the whole notion of brotherhood, is thus produced. The confession strengthens the vertical link of *murid* to Sheikh and the horizontal tie of brother to brother.

The profound involvement in the Order of the *murid* and correspondingly the influence over him of the group are in this way increased. We might add, moreover, that the *'itiraf* serves to impede any break which a member who has participated in it might contemplate. This would probably be particularly the case in the smaller communities where the individual is most likely to come into fairly constant contact with his fellows in the normal course of the daily routine. It has already been pointed out that in the group there is a continuous stress on regular communal ritual and the legitimate benevolent interest of the *tariqa* in every aspect of the followers' lives. The confession gives this control an extra dimension as well as providing an institutionalized channel for the expression of feelings or the admission of sins of commission which might otherwise prove disruptive and impair the quality of the individual's devotion to the Order.

Adab

Even the most casual observer is struck by the high level of courtesy both in verbal address and respect behaviour with which inter-personal relations within the Order are conducted. Egyptian Arabic abounds in pious complimentary phrases, and their use is by no means confined to members of the *turuq*. The brothers do, however, employ these phrases almost as a continuous and necessary formal part of their conversation, together with liberal quotations from the Quran and from *Hadith*. Modes of address tend to be of great civility, the most common terms being *Hadritak* or *Siyatak* (there is no satisfactory English translation: both words, and particularly the second, indicate deference and respect). Since most compliments have a 'symmetrical' proper response, interchanges often assume to the rude Westerner a mandarin air of a courtly, balanced exchanging of phrases[1]—*Allah yahfazak* (May God protect you), *Allah yakhallik* (May God preserve you), *Allah yakrimak* (May God be generous to you), and *Allah yebarak fik* (May God bless you). Pauses in discussion are interspersed with a murmured *Allah, Allah, Allah*, or *Madad ya Sidi Salama, ya mawlana* (Assistance O Sidi Salama, O our Lord, or *La hawl wa la quwa illa billah*. (There is no power and no strength but in God. When members wish to decline an invitation of some kind or to insist on some point in argument they will swear on the founder's life—*Wahyat Sidi Salama* (By the life of Sidi Salama)—and address their importunate would-be host or interlocutor as *Sidi* (literally, 'My lord').

There are variations. Senior members might well permit themselves joking liberties in the way in which they speak and behave to the junior, younger men, which would never be returned in kind but always replied to in deferential responses. Whereas younger *muridin* would at least go through a great performance of respect behaviour, illustrated, say, in refusing a cigarette offered by a member of an older generation; or they would offer the senior one without themselves smoking. This conforms to a common 'traditional' norm that a son does not smoke before his father, his father's friends, or indeed those of his father's generation. Junior members may ultimately allow themselves to be compelled, after

[1] The son of one of the older members once remarked to me that he and his friends referred to these exchanges irreverently as 'ping-pong'. He was neither a member of the Order nor his father's delight, it should be added.

the most elaborate invocations of Salama's name, to take the cigarette but only if it appears to the company that they do so under
duress, to please their persistent senior by accepting his generosity,
and following his indication that formal norms may be somewhat
modified in the particular situation or relationship between them.
Otherwise this expression of the respect relation between genera-
tions in Egyptian society is reflected in the Orders.

This display of *adab* between members of the Sufi Orders has,
as Lings points out, '... almost a methodic aspect as a means of purification'.[1] Two of the *Qanun* of the *Hamidiya Shadhiliya* make clear
the general type of behaviour required:

19. It is necessary that a man be merciful to his brother and therefore
he should not argue with him nor quarrel with him, nor insult him, nor
slander him behind his back, nor envy him, nor say he is a liar, nor
harm him; and (he should) be kind to him and humble with him; and
soft in speech and (should) advise him with friendliness without humiliating him so that he may be a help to him against his *nafs* and his
devil [*shaitan*] and not help them against him.[2]

214. If one of the brothers makes a mistake in his opinions (observations) [*mudhakra*], or his ignorance appears in it, the brothers must not
reject his opinion or embarrass him but rather they must receive it well
and teach him with kindness and civility [*bilin wa bilutf*].

In the studies, we are told, one may not call a brother a liar even
indirectly; one must avoid conceited language, use gentleness and
civility, put up with any breach of courtesy and any impoliteness, and
only allude to the fault or sin of another indirectly. Further, one
should not insult or talk about someone who is not present (204–7).
Failure to observe these prescriptions would, of course, be met by
invocation of the sanction of the *munasefat*.

Two important elements should be noted. First, that in general
the closer the personal relation between individuals, whether in
terms of kinship or positive affective content, the less was the regard
paid to the convention of formalized mutual respect behaviour we
have shown *adab* to mean in this context. The reverse also holds
true: That in the case of 'affective neutrality', where the individuals
are perhaps strangers or slight acquaintances, or entertain negative
feelings of hostility and antagonism, the prescribed rules were the

[1] Lings, op. cit., p. 71, footnote 3.
[2] *Nafs* in Ghazzali's sense as 'flesh', or 'lower nature', which must be
disciplined.

more closely adhered to. And second, the conventions of behaviour were more marked in situations where the interactions of the members occurred specifically in terms of their respective status in the structure of the Order; where, in other words, the formal rights and duties of the roles involved were being invoked. In each rank the actor is laterally the equal and brother of all others, since they occupy the same structural position within the *tariqa*. But he is not equal to those in the rank above from whom he must under certain circumstances take direction. In addition to this, however, there is the underlying theme of a general equality to which we have previously alluded. In this perspective the ranks are mere functional conveniences for the assistance of the Sheikh under whom *all* are in fact *muridin*. Officials are not expected, or indeed encouraged or allowed, to assume an impersonal orientation of contacts either with one another or with those 'lower' in the hierarchy. Where this ambivalence in the nature of the distribution of authority and the question of organizational status exists, the institution of *adab* acts as it were as a buffer between role performances and mutual expectations which might otherwise in the particular circumstances come into tension and conflict.

Then it is, of course, also true that while the equality of brotherhood is the ideal of the *tariqa*, social discrepancies in the world's terms exist in addition to internal differentiation. Men are of varying levels of education from the University graduate to the illiterate; they are stratified occupationally so that the unskilled worker or peasant may come into contact within the specific context of the Order or outside it, with one whose 'brother' he is but who works as a senior bank clerk or as a civil servant. Even in a culture where the distinction between the office and the man remains a clear one and respect is accorded rather by reference to the latter than the former, this can still pose further problems of possible conflicting role expectations which formal civility will at least effectively cloak. *Adab* gives men a common mode of address and manner through which to conduct their interaction with their brothers.

Finally, there is the simple proposition that in any group in which membership involves constant participation in a network of face-to-face relations, often at an intimate level, personal tensions will arise. Brothers or not, temperaments may clash and the ideal be publicly and awkwardly infringed. *Adab* provides a channel for individuals who feel in this way to address each other with little risk of such a difficulty. As it is a means of 'distancing' the interchange on the neutral level of elaborate courtesy it helps to preserve the norms of the brotherhood.

Ziyara

Some of the other means by which the organization, values, and commitment of the membership are maintained have been touched on already elsewhere. We have seen the importance of the *mulid* of Salama in gathering together large numbers of the brothers in a festival devoted to the founding Saint, and we related this functionally to two problems: (*a*) that posed by the increasingly large proportion (now the vast majority) of members who never knew Salama, and (*b*) the geographical dispersion of the group that is the necessary correlate of its success in expansion and recruitment. Both these problems are of key significance for the *tariqa*, and their resolution is attempted in various formal and informal ways. The Saint is now firmly enshrined, not only literally in the place of pilgrimage that his mosque and tomb have become, but in his writings, the biography of Saif an-Nasr, in the oral transmission of tales of his *karamat*, his character and his spiritual excellence, and in the person of his son the Sheikh.

The second question of geographical distribution and the preservation of the sense of total group unity extending over the various local centres in a network of *personal* relations of the brothers is a more intractable one. Adaptive measures may well change in the future; it is even conceivable, for example, that there will be less attention paid to proselytization if the central authority comes to feel that the organizational integrity is being imperilled by too widespread a growth in numbers and locations. Alternatively, and much more probably, it may be considered that a greater degree of organizational looseness is not an excessive price to pay for an increase in the membership and that central control and the *mulid* can effectively perform the same tasks that the present emphasis on face-to-face contact fulfils. The latter may therefore diminish with the development of the *tariqa* more and more into a formal bureaucratic organization. Means change, and with them subtle shifts in the character of the Order occur which bring with them their own problems of maintenance and control. As remarked before, we appear to be witnessing the transition stage after which the *Hamidiya Shadhiliya* will become more 'fixed' in its structure and modes of regulation.

At the moment, however, there is still predominant the *gemeinschaft* notion of the individual face-to-face relations of all the brothers to each other as the active ideal. The chief instrument of this is, of course, the *mulid*. But there is a further important principle which is laid down in the Laws and which was particularly close to Salama's heart:

13. One of the principles of our *tariq* is friendly relations, *mutual visiting*, and love. [Emphasis supplied.]

We may distinguish four closely linked kinds of *ziyara* (visiting) here. It refers in the first place simply to the giving and receiving of personal invitations by members. And when, to give a more particular instance, one of the brothers is ill it would be regarded as improper if the *khalifa* himself and a few friends neglected to pay a visit and inquire after his health. We may include here, too, those occasions when a member presses all his brothers in a particular *zawiya* to accept his hospitality after a *hadrah* in the evening. His guests will be served coffee and tea and spend an hour or two reciting the Quran or listening to hymns of the Order sung by various members, or telling stories of the life of Sidi Salama.

Secondly, there are those visits of the brothers of one *zawiya* to another, usually on a reciprocal basis. These are of particular significance where the host *zawiya* is newly established and receiving its 'senior' neighbour branches. In these instances it is part of the policy of the central office to make sure that new groups are involved in a series of such occasions to help to put them on a firm basis. The visitors will share in the ritual of the *hadrah* with their hosts, and will attend a fairly informal gathering afterwards at the house of one of the brothers. The visit will then be reciprocated and a network of relations thus initiated which will be regularly renewed, sometimes over quite wide areas. At a *hadrah* of the reconstituted *zawiya* in Alexandria, which I attended, a group of the brothers from Damanhur (fifty kilometres away) were present as well as some who had travelled in from a village in the Delta just outside the town. These trips are extremely pleasant for the members and eagerly looked forward to and arranged. As a minor point they also furnish a personal experience of the increase and success of the *Hamidiya Shadhiliya*.

Mention above of the policy of the central office in this matter leads to the third type which may be termed 'the *ziyara* for administrative purposes', since the social aspect is subordinated to the more strictly organizational. Here we are referring to those trips undertaken by formally or informally constituted committees from the *Beit as-Sigada* or lesser positions in the hierarchy (see Laws 67 and 71). Officials who go round to make the elaborate reports sent back to the central office do so under the guise of visiting the brothers. If there is a new *zawiya*, then it is common for a representative of the *Sigada* to attend a *hadrah* as a 'guest', when his primary purpose is in fact to inform the Sheikh of the general condition of the group. This was particularly true of Alexandria where, as we shall see below, the administration had cause for special concern and took special pains to supervise the early months of the new local centre. The *khalifa* thus has the direct opportunity to make any representations first hand that he may wish to the representative of the *Sigada*, as indeed have the members themselves to whom is demonstrated the concern that the Sheikh feels for the well-being of their group.

Finally there are those visits which the Sheikh himself undertakes and which involve large numbers of members, sometimes as many as 1,500 to 2,000, from many local groups. At present these are usually made to Tanta, which serves as a useful gathering place both because of its central location in the western delta and because of the celebrated shrine of Ahmad al Bedawi in its large central mosque. On such occasions two or three bus-loads of the brothers from various *zawiyas* in the capital make the journey and perform the *dhikr* with their fellow members after the Friday noon prayer. *Muridin* come into town from the villages around to share in the opportunity thus presented to see the Sheikh of the Order himself with whom they will otherwise have little direct contact. He leaves the mosque immediately after the completion of the *hadrah*, in spite of the tremendous efforts made by many to touch his garments or to speak to him, and goes to the main Tanta *zawiya* to hold a *maglis* attended only by the senior members. After this he and the Cairo group drive to one of the villages nearby to visit the brothers there before returning late at night.

A visit like this may take place four or five times a year, though the administration hope to make it once a month, and in different key areas all over the country, so that the Sheikh may personally be seen by as many of the members as possible. This would in effect be a return to the journeys which Salama made, especially after his retirement, round the centres of the then still young *tariqa*. Expansion has meant that Ibrahim is little known to some sections of the brotherhood, and the officials of the *Beit as-Sigada*, regarding some tangible indication of that vital link between follower and supreme leader as being of continued necessity and relevance, are attempting to ensure that some contact will be made through the visits and the great *mulid*. Though structural and spiritual distance must continue to be stressed, the whole character of the Order would be changed were the personal connection which lies at its heart allowed to disappear or fade into a vague amorphous connection with an unseen figure known only to the hierarchs of the *Beit as-Sigada*.

In this way the *Hamidiya Shadhiliya* attempts to ensure a constant round of personal and collective interaction, in spite of the difficulties that expansion creates for relating the parts to the whole in a face-to-face network. Within the local *zawiya* members are expected to attend *hadrahs* and meetings very regularly, to participate in any further activities of the group, in the great *mulid*, in any other celebrations of Saint's Days which have the approval of the *Sigada* (which encourages this sort of devotion to the company of *walis*), and in the visiting of brothers to brothers and *zawiyas* to *zawiyas*. The members are encouraged to a full involvement in the *tariqa*, with all that this entails in terms of obligations to the Order as a whole.

Given this high level of participation demanded, and the pressure for the individual to place his life within the orbit of the brotherhood as far as possible, the primary indirect sanctions are at once apparent. Absence from the rituals is immediately noticed by others and questioned; if a man fails to attend a *dhikr* for some reason, perhaps little comment will be made, but should he miss a series of such occasions speculation and gossip will be rife, and he will very probably be visited by friends or a delegation from the *khalifa*. It is hoped that any back-sliding will be sufficiently felt to be such by the individual that he will wish to confess the matter to a gathering of his fellows in the intimate atmosphere of brotherhood and group solidarity. His personal, financial, and domestic problems may well be known to the Sheikh, or the *khalifa*, whose guidance he will have sought, and the greater the depth of this commitment the greater obviously are the sanctions against any form of deviation.

But the high incidence of personal contacts in this continual series of group occasions also serves to reduce in another way the possibility of any conflict, tension, or personal dereliction arising. Members have the chance to discuss and to 'talk out' virtually all matters relating to the Order whether directly or indirectly. Such conversations among the brothers deal with any and every topic. Advice, criticism, explanation, and opinion flow freely in the coffee shops after the *hadrahs* or in the meetings. Members swiftly come to know the feelings of others on particular issues of concern to them, and matters which might otherwise well give rise to dispute, were there less personal communication, are fully ventilated. Complaints or grievances can be produced in the relaxed surroundings of a coffee shop which, failing such a forum, might have to be far more formally and perhaps acrimoniously raised in an official meeting specifically summoned to consider the question. The whole affair could then become a matter of official decision, the overt assertion of authority, and the calling into play of the various mechanisms, touched on above, whereby judgements are awarded and enforced. As it is, a kind of membership democracy operates in this very informal way without the explicit channels of conciliation and judgement being employed by the hierarchy. It appears reasonable to suggest that a large number of disputes which would threaten the unity of the *tariqa* were they to become 'official' and cast within the rigid framework of complaint, claim, and counterclaim are thus anticipated or neutralized almost before they can take on a definite shape and structure. Furthermore, group visits not only extend the process of discussion on internal and external affairs through a number of local centres, but they are the basis for comparison of the *zawiya* with its neighbours and the same element of competition present in the *mulid* of Salama operates, to the strengthening of the Order as a whole.

The External Orientation of Control

At the beginning of this chapter we drew attention to the fact that both formal and informal controls have an external aspect. That is to say that they are directed, or have reference to, the 'significant others' as much as to the members of the organization. It was indicated also that the 'others' fall into various groups or classes and that the aims of the Order with regard to these might be significantly different.

A four-fold division of these 'others' would follow the lines of: (a) the agencies of the Government concerned with internal affairs, security, and information; (b) the 'ulema', (c) workers, fellaheen, the popular masses, and the lower-middle economic and occupational strata; and (d) the 'middle classes' on a fairly neutral ground in between. Groups (a) and (b) may be said to represent a threat to the Orders in direct terms—the *turuq* could be repressed, or their activities severely curtailed—and in less direct terms through discredit heaped upon them by the 'ulema' as being contrary to orthodox religious practice. The third level is the most fertile field for recruitment without which the *turuq* would necessarily wither (as indeed most of them have). Those of the last section are perhaps of least immediate concern, and therefore must only not be stirred into actively antagonistic attitudes, which might arouse sympathetic reactions in higher authority, or percolate down to those levels from which new members are needed and sought.

It is reasonable to suggest that these general conditions were true, *mutantis mutandis*, before and at the time of the founding of the *Hamidiya Shadhiliya*. It is also reasonable to infer from internal evidence in the *Qanun* and from what senior members have said of the Saint that he was as acutely aware of the problems he would face in this field as he was in so many others. Certain of the Laws make this quite explicit:

22. It is necessary for the brother to adorn himself with humility and dignity and avoid too much laughter and joking so that hearts should incline to him and thus people come near to the *tariq* or at least the *tariq* will be respected by them.

21. It is necessary for each one who is attached to the *tariq* to be faithful to his religion; and not to speak of what he does not know; nor to pass on any distorted *hadith*; nor (do) anything like that. Rather he must be certain of what he says lest he fall into what is forbidden and be held ignorant by the people.

These are quite obviously directed in part to the 'ulema', on whose opposition to the Orders we have remarked. But, as with all the rules mentioned here, they have many purposes—internal discipline, the avoidance of criticism on the grounds of un-Islamic practice (from whatever quarter it might come), inculcation of the proper norms of behaviour and correct belief, and as an indirect 'exemplary' means of recruitment.

The insistence on orthodoxy of belief and practice is a constant theme of the *Qanun* and Salama returns to it again and again. Sometimes he deals with practices which have altogether died out or are prohibited by the Government. Law 41, for example, forbids the eating of glass, cactus, etc., and cutting with the sword (self-inflicted wounds, at one time a common feature of Sufi celebrations).[1] Men must not behave like women or vice versa (Law 30); they may not mix with the 'possessed' (*magazib*);[2] they must not shout out *hadith* in public places. He further forbade the use of musical instruments in the *dhikr*, a practice still found in some of the Orders (Law 37).

There are more insidious dangers to be guarded against, however. Excesses in spiritual practices, which were sometimes put to dubious use by those of insufficient capacity to bear them, must be eliminated, not only because they are bad in themselves, but because they justify damaging criticism by non-members of whatever level. Ascetic practices are therefore not only dangerous to the general, but also to the *tariqa* in so far as their abuse may be brought to the attention of unfriendly 'others'. Salama's concern is spelt out in some detail:

36. Every *khalifa* or higher than he who teaches his students names which are not Arabic, or makes them enter the *khalwa*,[3] or orders them to pray unlawful *awrad*,[4] or orders them to make a *dhikr* with 10,000 names in every day and night; or orders them to devotions which stop the eating of all things which were alive; or to make a fast for many months; or to use the *djinn* or anything like that; he is responsible for what he does and the consequence is on him, for the *tariqa* is free from that.[5]

---

[1] See Hughes, op. cit., article '*Zikr*' for an account of self-wounding in the rituals of the *Rifa'iya*.

[2] Those thought to be in some special relation to the Divine, or to have great power, usually on the basis of being harmless lunatics '. . . vulgarly regarded by them (the Egyptians) as a being whose mind is in heaven, while his grosser part mingles among ordinary mortals'. Lane, E., *Manners and Customs of the Modern Egyptians*, Everyman Library, 1st edn., London: J. M. Dent, 1908, p. 234.

[3] Cell or place of seclusion.

[4] See *Qanun*, Section vi of the full trans., for note on this.

[5] We remember Salama's own early excessive reliance on such practices.

249. [After stressing that seclusion is of the heart not bodily action, an internal state is not a physical removal] . . . Every Sheikh who orders his student to enter seclusion must beware of its dangers, for in entering it there is a danger of which most of the people of the Way are unaware. For much fasting and hunger and much sleeplessness and *dhikr* will lead to dullness of the brain and will create mental illness or disturbance in the mind. Or he [the student] will come by chance upon a *shaitan* in his seclusion who will harm him so that he will speak that which has no meaning. Or the devil will set forth something to him and some of the people will think that he has become a Saint of God. Or light may by chance come upon him, or he will see an angel or a *wali* and he will not be able to hear what he sees and he will go out of his mind. . . . Then he who has no capacity for this should be deterred by fear of God from going ahead with that or ordering anyone to do it . . .

These two laws together involve a comprehensive interdiction of practices which have always been associated with popular Sufism both in fact and by reputation. The whole syndrome of ecstatic/ascetic behaviour, often becoming extreme in its nature, brought the Orders into increasing discredit in Egypt in the nineteenth century, and particularly in the last decades. Salama's mission seems to have been in this regard very much a reforming one, purging Sufism of the dross of these abuses of techniques of the mystical way and extreme practices which are of value only when properly employed by the initiated. In internal terms they are at least a peril, at worst a perversion; externally they present to a world growingly hostile or apathetic, an image of unorthodoxy, backwardness, and superstitious practices to increasing numbers either repulsive or irrelevant. The *Hamidiya Shadhiliya* was to be free of all grounds for criticism, or for 'guilt by association' links with the practices of other Orders.

The Processions

Given these circumstances, the most favourable 'front' must be presented by the Order and the most favourable setting assured. We shall note the strict regulation of the *hadrahs*, those formal religious occasions when the group is most strikingly on show before outsiders. There are other major occasions, the processions, when the same requirements are necessary.

256. Walking in the procession must be perfect, with dignity and

complete order. It must be free from what dishonours the *tariqa* and its members.

As an added detail there is the following regulation which has some bearing on the element of 'propaganda' to which members constantly drew my attention in the chief religious occasions:

266. Everyone affiliated to the *tariq*, whether young or old, must wear on his chest a green band whose breadth is 15 centimetres with only the words 'The *Tariqa* of the *Hamidiya Shadhiliya*' written on it.

These rules have their effect. The public appearance of the *Hamidiya Shadhiliya* is in great contrast to that of the other *turuq* in dress and organization. They walk in ranks of three with hands linked in each rank and each man wears his best clothes and the band of the Order. Hymns of Sidi Salama are sung as they move slowly through the city under the watchful eye of the officials who keep the group under close control. It is difficult to fault the performance at any point and the members are proud of the impression which the *mawkib* (procession) makes on outsiders, both in negating criticism and in the awakening of interest. The bystander cannot but appreciate how different they are from the other groups in order and appearance, one of the main objects of the exercise. To achieve this purpose every brother must play his part in the presentation and co-operate to the full with the rest of the group; failure of one compromises the whole before an audience which will be quick to see any lapse in the performance and to suspect the 'front' or collective representation of the actors as in some way or degree not genuine. The dramatic distinction between this and other groups has to be absolutely maintained for the positive and negative reasons of showing what the *Hamidiya Shadhiliya* are, and from what they are to be distinguished.

But important though the religious occasions are for the Order in terms of its corporate presentation to the 'others', they do not constitute the only times at which the group and the individual members must strive to ensure the integrity of their performance. In this respect all the Laws dealing with personal behaviour are relevant (e.g. Laws 22 and 21 cited above) for this external, other-directed reason. For in a sense, wherever the individual is before non-members aware of his affiliation, the quality of his performance is critical. Certain regulations which are set down to govern apparently quite minor aspects of the member's life are not only a means to the widest possible control of the Order over the brother, but also a guarantee of his presentation to the outsiders, even on the most informal occasions and outside the immediate framework of the *tariqa.*

154. The brothers must wear clean clothes even if they are cheap or torn. And they must be well behaved in eating and behave with restraint though not avoiding eating. They should eat politely without being greedy. For whoever is most polite and his clothes clean though they are torn, will precede the other who may have the better dress or be rich.

161. It is necessary for anyone who is eating that he should not blow his nose at the time of eating, nor cough, nor laugh loudly, nor sniff, nor belch, except after turning away from the food. He must break the bread into small pieces and chew it for a long time and not despise the food.

162. The brothers should not lick their fingers while eating, nor pick their teeth.

163. It is better that they speak of the right-doers (*as-Salihin*) and those like them while eating.

This goes beyond a simple set of regulations on table manners. It is an attempt to inculcate into those whose circumstances in life have not been such as to impress a great degree of refinement in behaviour a certain common denominator of appearance and civility (as with the *adab,* also very important in this respect) which they can achieve whatever their financial, occupational, or educational position may be. It is not expected that the brother can dress well, the means of the vast majority do not permit it, but he can dress cleanly whether or not his clothes are torn or of poor quality. He must play his role.

The Crisis in the Alexandria Zawiya

Having given an outline of the means of control which operate formally and informally in the *Hamidiya Shadhiliya,* I shall now turn to an example of a major breakdown in the Order and one whose remedy occupied a great deal of the attention of the Sheikh and the *Sigada.* We have seen what controls and sanctions act on the individual member; an examination of the difficulties in the main *zawiya* in Alexandria will show how the organization responded to critical circumstances involving an entire group. The data are in many ways unsatisfactory for our purposes since they are scanty in the extreme. Members are no more enthusiastic about discussing embarrassing crises in their *tariqa* than one might expect, and details were difficult to obtain. Quite naturally in an Order as dynamic as the *Hamidiya Shadhiliya* and as tightly regulated, inquisitive questions on a delicate subject are liable to be brushed aside and the conversation turned to the perfection of the administration and the general success of the *tariqa* under the wise leadership of Sidi Ibrahim. With this caveat in mind the following sketch gives what I believe to be a substantially correct account of the main factors.

A very senior *khalifa* died about ten years ago and his passing left the *tariqa* without one of its most experienced members. He had spent about twenty years in the Alexandria *zawiya* as its head and knew all the brothers there intimately, and (as the informant put it) he could control everyone as he was familiar with the habits of them all. He had built up the centre, one of the first to be founded outside Cairo by Salama, in whose heart it always had a special place. It is said that at one time there were even more members than in the capital, though I have no way of judging the accuracy of that estimate. Suffice it to say that it ranked with the major *zawiyas* of the Order.

A tremendous altercation followed the death of the old *khalifa*. The brothers split into groups, each one supporting their candidate against the others, and, as the situation was getting out of hand, Sheikh Ibrahim ordered one of the senior *muridin* to be the *khalifa* on probation. (It should be remembered that this was around ten years ago when the administration was less centralized and control less rigorous than it is now.) He proved, however, not to have the qualities demanded by the extremely difficult situation. Some of the rival groups were alienated, and apparently he failed to show the firmness and tact required. He also lacked energy (*nashshat*) in the running of the *zawiya*. The predictable result was a decay in the organization of the group around him. Finally about four years ago the *zawiya* was wound up by the *Sigada*.

The Sheikh's secretary explained to me that as a general principle in cases such as this the central office does its best to help the *khalifa* in his task and only in the very last resort do they dismiss him from his post or dissolve the local group. In this case, for whatever reasons, their help was insufficient and dissolution

became inevitable. The Sheikh was furious and decided on a complete restoration of the *zawiya*. For this purpose he travelled to
Alexandria and saw the old members to sound their opinion, but
found them divided as to the course of action to be followed.
Eventually he found a number of the old brothers and some of the
younger men, including the sons of other members there, and
appointed the senior *khalifa* from one of the Delta towns who
changed his job and moved to Alexandria. Members of the central
office spent the best part of a year travelling to and fro, advising,
encouraging, and assisting in recruitment and in the summer of
1965 the *zawiya* was officially re-established.

The procedures followed to strengthen the new centre, and to
build it up, are of considerable interest in the practical application
of means of control and maintenance. It was subject, as mentioned
above, to continued supervision by the most senior members of
the *Sigada*, and with the personal direction of Sheikh Ibrahim.
When not under their scrutiny it was visited by the neighbouring
zawiyas who were instructed to make a point of making a *ziyara*
and setting up the links of reciprocal hospitality already referred
to. At the *mulid* of Sidi Salama in 1966, the members were accorded
special treatment by the Sheikh and a tent was provided for them
near the central office as they were then too few to raise enough
money on their own account. When the Sheikh makes his periodic
visits to Tanta they are all encouraged to go unless there is a good
excuse for not doing so. Meetings after the *hadrahs* have been made
a regular part of their activities.

More particular techniques have been employed to stimulate and
reinforce the member's devotion to, and involvement in, the
zawiya, and his obedience to the *khalifa* and to Sheikh Ibrahim.
The name of the latter as well as of his father was used in the *madad*
(supplication for assistance in the *dhikr*)—a thing unheard of in
Cairo. Great emphasis is laid on the notion of interrelationship
and interdependence between the brothers, and this notion is given
symbolic expression in the ritual setting. At the end of the *hadrah*
every individual kisses the hand of every other person present (the
musafaha—symbol of mutual love and co-operation), and the
khalifa himself walks at the end of the line also greeting each one
in this way. He then invites those who for some reason wish the
brothers collectively to recite the *fatiha* for them or for their friends
or relatives to stand up and make their request. On this occasion a

student asked for their prayers that he might succeed in examinations; another because he was going on a journey, and that he might arrive safely; and a third that God might help him to solve the difficulties besetting him.

The *khalifa* then delivered a short speech of general advice and instruction. He exhorted the brothers to obey all the *Qanun* and to follow the ritual laid down in its ideal form without any failing or imperfection. He asked them to make a point of visiting each other and one man complained that he had been ill and the brothers had not come to see him. The *khalifa* explained that he and some others had in fact gone to his house on learning of his condition, but that he had been out. He went on to advise them to avoid the coffee-shops unless they had good reason for entering them. They might meet strangers there not of the *tariqa* and go to the way of the devil (*shaitan*). One member asked what was wrong in going in for a glass of tea and was told that it was all right provided one wanted to meet someone in particular in the coffee-shop and could not do so at home, if there was some proper purpose. But simply to go in to drink coffee and play backgammon might take one far from the Order. At each point in the discussion the *khalifa* ended his various remarks with *kadhalik ya ahbab?* (is that correct, O beloved, i.e. is there general agreement?). Throughout there was general questioning and a seeking of consensus on the different topics, though his view was always acceded to. He explained that a mutual responsibility united them all; that they were making a society and that they should look after each other and ask one who is not good in behaviour to come back to the proper way of behaviour. They made the ritual together, and if someone did not attend it might be because he was sinning. At the meeting afterwards he presided and gave permission to smoke, remarking 'praise to God' when no one did.

A certain rigorousness and tendency to asceticism in daily practice were noticeable here, thus making the way of life associated with the *tariqa* as distinct as possible; to demonstrate that it made special requirements which set it off from the everyday routine of the world; and that it was a total and clear commitment, entailing a degree of personal sacrifice for the proper fulfilment of membership. The member is joining a collectivity which expects from him certain behaviour, and which offers him in turn certain benefits and advantages. All exist for all and are bound by ties of assistance and obligations of responsibility in the maintenance of the new group. The insistence on the nature of this link and the use of the techniques outlined above are some indication of the need the central office feels to 'impose', as it were, patterns of action externally. That is to say that the norms of brotherhood are perhaps not yet felt to be fully internalized and that constant insistence on what is demanded, constant stress on the obligations of membership, is necessary before one can safely assume an automatic response in accordance with expectations. This is part of the 'socialization process' and it takes this form of an almost exaggerated statement of what being a member means in its widest sense. Like the supervision from outside, the need for it will diminish as it accomplishes its purpose, as the network of face-to-face relations becomes self-reinforcing, and as the feeling of group solidarity increases and the outward form takes on inward content.

Conclusion

I have tried to show what kind of controls the *Hamidiya Shadhiliya* employs and is subject to, and how these are fitted to the purposes, values, and structure of the group. There is, I suggest, a dynamic relation between the two as parts of the total system, a relation whose processes are not fully realized by the participating individuals. Each profoundly influences the other, and the over-all form the Order takes over a given time is a *product* of this relation that may differ markedly from the initial model set up by the founder and his core of disciples. In our particular example the dynamic is peculiarly apparent, since the organization is passing through the transitional stage whose characteristics have been previously indicated.

Controls operate in two ways, formally and informally, and each type refers not only to the internal workings and maintenance of the group, but to the interaction of the group with the external society—that complex of 'others' with whom relations of different kinds must be set up and maintained. It has been shown that the *Hamidiya Shadhiliya* are aware of the crucial nature of this interaction; of the absolute necessity, if the group is to continue to *exist*, let alone expand, of presenting to the different strata of society a total performance that will accomplish its separate purposes and ends in regard to the particular sectors addressed.

Even within the system of control there is a dynamic 'field' between part and part, by which one may act against tendencies set in train by another. The trend to bureaucratization, to the separation of the *Sigada* as almost a 'managing body', of which the Sheikh is Chairman and Chief Administrator of the Departmental Rule Book, is at the moment counterbalanced by the charismatic force of the leader reinforced by personal distance, by the principle of face-to-face relations itself, and by democratic decision-making and (to a degree at any rate) the informal means of resolving conflict.

Given that the Order is committed to centralized administration and the expansion of membership, a major problem was seen to arise out of increasing geographical dispersion with the possible attenuation of links between group and group, and between group and *Sigada*. Connected with this is the question of maintaining the link of the Sheikh and the *murid* and keeping the *khulafa'* as an integral part of the system rather than as independent units. These difficulties occur, moreover, at a time when in the natural course of events the growing majority of the membership never knew the founding Saint.

In the resolution of these important problems there is a factor to which attention has been only indirectly drawn, namely the potential of the media of communication. There are indications that Salama himself was influenced in his organization of the *tariqa* by his experience of departmental work in the Civil Service—the Laws are only the most obvious example here. He was also aware of the possibilities for administration that a postal service, the telephone, and the railway offered. Absolutely new means became available during his life of regulating and supervising, to a degree previously impossible, the activities of the brothers as a whole. There resulted this elaborate network of committees, forms, and reports which has only recently been further expanded to give the Central Office direct connections with virtually every local group. What is more, through that other modern medium of communication, photography, his image is forever before his followers. In pocket-books, on calendars, in portraits with his son, hung in the place of honour in members' reception rooms, his picture gives the *murid* a sense of his presence, and of a personal and immediate contact.

How far these means of control will affect the balance of formal administration and face-to-face relations one can only guess. The latter principle also benefits by the advances in communications and transport, and it continues to be emphasized. In a sense the increased domination of the *Sigada* does bring with it too a contact between the *murid* and Sheikh, however indirect, that is of considerable importance. It contains, in itself, counters to the depersonalizing, bureaucratic, rationalizing tendencies, but they may well ultimately predominate, after the death of the founder's son. That they should do so may be the key in fact to the survival of the Order in the future.

V

SOCIAL ETHIC AND RECRUITMENT

THE tradition of Sufism has flowed through two channels: that associated particularly with the name of al Ghazzali, has allied itself closely with the Sunna and the Law; the other has been devoted to the individual perception of the Truth (*al haqiqat*), often in a strongly ecstatic and emotional mode, set apart entirely, or to a great degree, from the prescriptions of the *Shari'a*. These it has necessarily tended to regard either as of primarily symbolic significance, as an allegory of the human experience in its relation with the Divine, or as an actual barrier to the essential religious existence, and as such to be rejected altogether.[1] The former are the *salikin*, those journeying on the ordered path of God, the latter, the *majdhubin*, 'embarked without restraint on the broad sea of their feeling of God's drawing them and attracting them to himself'.[2]

In either case it might seem profitless to search for any foundation on which a coherent and comprehensive social ethic might be constructed. For it is of the very kernel of Sufism, as of all mysticism, to dwell on the inner experience and illumination, the intuitive vision of the individual seeking the ultimate goal of gnosis or the *unio mystica*. In this the Holy Law itself, the *forum externum*, can be only of limited value as a first step of the way, whose primary aid is meditation and the constant remembrance (*dhikr*) of God. It is the quest of the self that has meaning, and not the striving of a society in history which then becomes largely irrelevant. Its concern is not with the workings of the social process through time, but with the progress of the spirit in realms where time itself is meaningless in the pursuit of a transcendent fulfilment. The events of mundane existence pass without effecting the inner advance through the stages (*maqamat*) on the *tariq* to God. 'He that knoweth God loveth Him, and he that knoweth the world abstaineth from it'[3], a saying that is complemented by a phrase often

---

[1] See article 'Shari'a' in *Shorter Encyclopedia of Islam*, pp. 524–9.

[2] Macdonald, D. B., *The Religious Attitude and Life in Islam*, Beirut: Khayats, 1965, p. 258.

[3] Hassan al Basri, d. 728. Quoted in Lings, op. cit., p. 46.

heard from the *muridin*: 'The closer one is to this world, the farther one is from the next.'

For the core of Sufism is the establishing of the personal link between the lover and the Loved, rather than the distance separating worshipper from the transcendental, omnipotent God; the state of the heart (*qalb*), not the quality of man's actions.[1] And though there is a very real sense in which 'the fully realised mystic is the most practical of men',[2] since the complete Sufi possesses 'on the earthly plane, an integral human perfection, which implies not only a static flawlessness but also, dynamically, a perfect reaction to every circumstance of life',[3] the mundane always remains of essentially secondary significance. Gibb puts the point in the bluntest terms: 'As for ethics, nothing is incumbent upon God; our concepts are quite irrelevant to Him. He rewards and punishes as He wills and cannot be called to account.'[4]

Yet there are certain other factors also which are of special relevance to the study of mass, as distinct from individual, Sufism. The founders and sheikhs of the Orders have always had a keen awareness of the different levels of spiritual capacity and attainment. To the broad majority of their followers, therefore, they have been guides to, and interpreters of, the basic duties of Islam and the *Shari'a*,[5] providing at least a minimal definition of right behaviour. Absorbed in Egypt into the fabric of the daily lives of their communities, and, at another level, to such a degree integrated into the established authority, their *irshad* (guidance), both formal and informal, was no doubt quite as much a reflection of the social and political interests of the different strata as a force for shaping and channelling those interests. Yet this educative function, in all its variations on the central theme of Revelation and Sunna, preserved and constantly reproduced the social meanings of Islam with all the flexibility and accommodation that religious systems must have to survive as living forms.

---

[1] *Qalb* 'approximates to the English "heart" only in that it suggests the inmost, most secret and genuine thoughts, the very basis of man's intellectual nature.' Macdonald, op. cit., p. 221.

[2] Lings. op. cit., p. 107.

[3] Ibid., p. 106.

[4] Gibb, H. A. R., *The Structure of Religious Thought in Islam*, p. 205.

[5] Ling's statement, 'It was a principle of the Alawi Tariqah that the first thing to be done with a novice was to teach him his ordinary religious obligations according to his capacity', op. cit., p. 107, could be applied to any of the Egyptian Orders (the standard of teaching would of course be very variable).

Further, we should not allow understanding of the meaning of submission to the Will of God (the literal meaning of *Islam*) and to His predestination of events to blind us to its potential as a spur to human action. A belief in the predestining hand of God, and the so-called 'fatalistic' attitude, do not *in themselves* involve a passive world acceptance, as Weber so clearly illustrated from the history of European Protestantism. Nor has Islam since its inception been lacking in movements which have sought a dynamic fulfilment of the Divine Purpose with all the fierce energy that such a sense of mission brings. In recent times the *Sanusi* Order of Libya, the *Mahdiya* of the Sudan, the *Wahhabis* of Arabia, and the Muslim Brotherhood in Egypt are only the most immediate examples that have sprung from this source. Each of the founders indeed had his roots in one of the *turuq*, though the latter three in varying degrees transformed their organizational framework, and reconstituted the pattern of demands made of the *muridin*. There is no parallel to the Protestant stress on the performance of the worldly occupation (the *beruf*—'profession' in the sixteenth century sense) as the sign of election; but the *da'wa* (calling) was of what we would term a profoundly political nature in its objectives, remembering that the category 'political' was completely subsumed into the overriding *din* (religion) in each of these movements. Each aimed at the founding or moulding of an Islamic state by a community of the believers. If sanctions for behaviour were supernatural and eschatological, they were none the less sanctions for actions in the *dunya*, not only for the internal and moral condition of the worshipper with eyes only for *al akhira*. Ultimate reference is to the Divine Plan, but as it is revealed for this world in its relation to the next. Far from being irrelevant, History became of crucial significance.

The supra-mundane concerns of *tasawwuf* do not imply therefore that we are dealing with an exclusively other-worldly orientation from which no coherent pattern of social action can flow. Whatever his teaching, the Saint with his followers plays a role in the world, in men's attitudes and valuations of it, and their behaviour in respect of it. If this behaviour has often been of the passive, ecstatic type, and devotion has been to the demonstration of thaumaturgic acts rather than to a set of ethical demands, the latter have not been lacking. The particular colouring popular Sufism has taken on in any given context has been to a great extent a result of the external political, economic, and social circumstances. The relative stress on faith, or on faith complemented necessarily by works, on asceticism as entirely directed to the internal betterment of the *murid's* soul, or bearing a more outward application, is likewise largely a function of the same factors. Some Orders have provided only a means for emotional release in unrestrained *dhikr* circles: others, to an example of which we now turn, have taught certain obligatory standards of actions and patterns of values.

The Hamidiya Shadhiliya

The Sheikh of the Order puts forward the following set of qualities for the guidance of those who are attached to his *tariqa*:

As for the stages through which the *murid* passes, they are: the following of the Sunna; Quran; Islamic Jurisprudence; obedience; adab; (good) behaviour; night vigil; persistence; suspecting [the *nafs* or lower nature, being careful not to allow it to mislead, M. G.]; visiting; self-control; conformity; blessedness; passionate devotion; dignity; dependence (on God); brotherhood; submission; endeavour; truth; dedication; self-effacement; leaving the people of vanity; a friendly disposition; contentment; the taking of sincere advice; excellence of thoughts; the service of the brothers; endurance; blessedness of the heart; the fulfilment (of the duties) of brotherhood; compassion for the creation of God [i.e., all created things]; not assisting the *nafs*; humility; forgiving; patience; purity; beneficence; altruism; magnanimity; the keeping of the '*ahd* [the oath of the Sheikh, see above]; *dhikr* [remembrance of God]; study; thought; examination of the conscience; striving [in the way of God]; the increase of repentance; the abundance of supererogatory good works; contemplation; moderation [or contentment with one's lot]; asceticism; trust in God; gentleness in the heart; fear (of God); control; being wholly absorbed in Allah; the keeping of the divine ordinances; certainty; religious awe; the proper qualities of religion.[1]

In this general statement of what should characterize the *murid* little relation to a programme of action appears, save in so far as it is so internally directed to the soul. Nevertheless external actions are linked with the spiritual well-being of the individual. For he must conform to the demands which the Holy Law makes of him, to the works which God has enjoined upon the Muslim. Study, submission, dependence on God, obedience, contemplation, and

[1] *Murshid al-Murid*, p. 58.

repentance must be accompanied by brotherhood (with all the practical obligations we have seen that to entail), endeavour and dedication, altruism, and a fulfilment of the duties of fellowship after the comprehensive design of the *Hamidiya Shadhiliya*. And these can only be shown forth and have meaning in the context of the individual's behaviour to, and relations with, others. What one *does*, as well as what in the profoundest sense one *is*, is therefore of significance; what is apparent in one's actions is intimately related to the hidden condition of one's essence, a premiss upon which ultimately the practice of the confession is based. So that dependence on God does not mean a resignation of individual responsibility for what one does, nor does it absolve one from carrying out the duties of the *Shari'a* and of the *tariqa*.

The Sheikh also isolates five requirements for those walking in the way: trusting in God in what is secret and what is open or revealed; following the *Sunna* in word and deed; avoiding vain people's company; being content with God in both little and great; and returning to Him in happiness and misfortune.[1] The brother must lose his own volition (*irada*) and in searching for God become one who wishes only for the Beloved.[2] He must be totally directed to God and perpetually lodge Him in his heart, resting always under His command.[3] For the founder of the *tariqa* taught that *tasawwuf* means the purification of the souls by the avoidance of blameworthy characteristics; that its subject is the deeds of hearts in a pure way, and of the inner essence so that they may be cleansed; that its fruit is coming to eternal happiness and spiritual victory in the pleasure of God; its excellence lies in its being the highest of the sciences, since it is connected with deeds leading to God;[4] its link with the other sciences is like that of the fruit to the tree. It is God Himself who is its author, for He has revealed His signs to teach praiseworthy qualities. The *murid* need only follow the Prophet and those devoted to him, the Sufis.[5]

But labour in the world has its place. We have already drawn attention to Salama's insistence on the proper carrying out of the demands on one's occupation. And we stressed the exceptional fact that the Saint himself continued in his work, despite his leadership of the *tariqa* and the burdens which that imposed. His example to his followers is clear: work has positive value as maintaining the

[1] Ibid., p. 56.   [2] Ibid., pp. 27–8.   [3] Saif, op. cit., pp. 181–2.
[4] Ibid., p. 19.   [5] Ibid., p. 20.

reasonable material condition of the believer. This does not at all imply, however, that it is an index, or a means of spiritual achievement, or in any sense a sign of grace or election. The pursuit or gaining of occupational success, in whatever terms this may be measured, is of no intrinsic merit or significance; it is not an outward criterion whereby others may judge the true worth or condition of the *murid*. Though Salama rose to be the head of his department, thus demonstrating his practical capacity in that limited, mundane sphere of his life, it is the quality of his relations with his colleagues, of whatever status, and the fact of his undertaking a task, that is the real lesson to be learnt. This is the key point, and his rise in position is almost entirely marginal (we shall return to the importance of this question of status below). One does what occupation requires, or more accurately, what provides oneself and one's dependants with adequate sustenance. There is to be no turning to God for succour in distress, if it lies within one's own power to alleviate it, nor reliance on Him for help when one possesses the abilities to acquire that little which is necessary. And if the brother is enjoined to be ready to give financial help to his fellow, this is not assistance obtainable as of right, regardless of circumstance.

The *murid* is therefore responsible for his material condition, and has a duty to strive to accomplish the daily task that the maintenance of life demands, for the disciplining of the soul (*nafs*) and the good of his religion (*din*).[1] For if the member is lacking in material wealth, if he is a *faqir* in the literal sense of being poor, he must work with his hands *to preserve his dignity* (the phrase is Sheikh Ibrahim's). And he must give alms with part of what he earns that he may show mercy (*rahma*) to the weak and the needy.[2] He must help them, comfort the oppressed, and take the blind by the hand on the way. In all things he must co-operate, a word which is a *leit-motif* in the doctrines of the Order, with righteousness and due religious reverence and sense of God's might.[3] It is in this that the value of work resides; in its employment as a means to help others and to sustain a style of life that furnishes one with the essentials of existence, no more and no less. For ultimately work is devoted to God and founded on love, and without that devotion and that foundation it has no worth and no meaning. The poor man who grumbles because he has little pay and feels his life

---

[1] *Murshid*, p. 75.   [2] Ibid., p. 70.   [3] Ibid., p. 71.

is useless should not be misled: his sheikh tells him that the world is only for fulfilling one's duties on the way to Paradise, and one should be grateful to God whatever one's poverty.[1]

This world is thus not to be totally ignored or turned from in rejection since it is an integral part of the Divine synthesis. But its true significance resides only in so far as it relates to the next, and it is awareness of this 'reflected' meaning that the *murid* must attain. It is only a preparation for what is to come, and though by no means intrinsically evil or a place of darkness, one must realize that its function is to serve as a prolegomenon to the ultimate reality. As the heart must be freed from vices and passions (*shahawat*), so it must be cleansed of love of the world by the agency of the spiritual physician to whose authority one is unreservedly committed. For *hubb al dunya* (love of the world) distorts the understanding of experience. To take the world of and for itself is meaningless, and action in it on those terms is consequently also meaningless. It is only action which at root is directed to what comes after the *dunya* which is of inherent worth. Mundane achievement *per se* is therefore at best of neutral concern and at worst a spiritual danger in that it clouds the worshipper's understanding and infects his heart. The *murid* is not opposed to the world and its social system; he does not protest against it, but rather moves within it, so qualitatively informing his personal relations with men as to enter into the contentment of God. To its economic and political institutions he is indifferent, since they have no relevance for his (individual) faith. He therefore neither withdraws from, nor interferes with, the social order and social action, but his evaluative analysis of it, and of his own experience, is drawn from spiritual criteria whose nature his Sheikh has put before him.

It follows from this attitude to the world that riches may be a negative element, while poverty is a positive one, since to be judged poor in the world's terms indicates a right view of the essential lack of value that attaches to anything that exceeds necessity. To be a *faqir* means both to be needy in material terms, and to be one of those who recognize their need of God and devote themselves to it. The brothers are thus *fuqara'* (poor) in the interior meaning, whatever their exterior wealth. Nothing prevents the rich man from belonging to this group of the needy, but before the Sheikh he will

[1] Saif, op. cit., p. 175.

sit with the worker (*sic*, Saif, p. 61). And he will learn that the increase of means in this world is a danger to the soul, and of the Saint's dislike for one who did not use his money for the well-being of his brothers. We remember too that it was to the poor and those who he felt were despised by other religious leaders that Salama directed his mission. His grandfather had taught that poverty is health, and endurance in time of need is *jihad* (holy struggle). The transmutation and giving of an internal reference to this concept are of some significance, for in the beginnings of Islam status in the religious community was granted largely on the individual's role in the *jihad*.[1] In the *tariqa* it has become internalized, a function of a very different effort, having no relation to his endeavours in the world, but only to his fortitude in want and distress. The measure of a man in the final analysis is the amount of his faith (*iman*), and in this respect all are needy, and all equally sit in front of the Sheikh covered in his love and filled with the love of God.

Clearly, however, we do not find here a radical transvaluation of poverty whereby it is exalted as a special condition of God's elect, any more than we find a radical rejection of the world. Wealth is lawful, and its possession, though potentially a danger, does not necessarily impinge on the interior quality of the believer's essence. While it is meritorious to give to the poor, there is no Franciscan-like stress on the special grace of their state as contrasted with that of the rich, though certainly the ethic of the *Hamidiya Shadhiliya* contains comfortable words for the humble. Nor have the élites of the Orders performed the dramatic virtuoso spectacle of Cistercian or Benedictine obedience and self-negation in monastic seclusion. In the Christian tradition the world as the place of the flesh, sin, and temptation is a problem to be overcome by its denial through heroic asceticism, or the mediation of the Saviour and the Church, or its mastery by men as instruments of God. Where man is fallen through original sin, Paradise is always uncertain because of the only partly observable operations of divine grace. The constant interrelation of works and faith then becomes central to the attainment of heavenly reward and the avoidance of damnation,

---

[1] We note also that a parallel change has occurred in the meaning of the word '*higra*'. This originally referred to the flight of the Prophet and his Companions from the hostile city of Mecca to Medina and is usually taken as the date for the founding of the Islamic community (A.D. 622). In the Orders, however, it is used of the act of becoming a member of a *tariqa*.

whether through the hierarchy of religious specialists or the severe 'unpriested' communities of Protestant saints.

In Islam, however, salvation is not imperilled by man's inherently sinful nature, and his endless need for penance and the renewal of intention. There is no theodicy in the cognitive sense of the term, for the will of the Transcendent Creator One God which is in essence unknowable determines all things. Suffering, therefore, whether just or unjust, of the individual or of the community, is not a dominant mode of purification or redemption or a path to salvation; it has no positive soteriological meaning crystallized in the symbol of the human-divine crucified Saviour or the persecuted community in exile. Man submits, obeys, and in awe fears God in an attitude of confidence, taking that word in its most fundamental sense. The Covenant once accepted and the declaration of faith made, the tensions of sin, atonement, and redemption lose their significance and the question of unjust suffering does not arise. Though charity and the giving of alms and assistance to the needy are cardinal virtues, whose demonstration gains merit for the donor, as does making the pilgrimage or participating in the *jihad*, the recipient is not a means of transferring mystical powers to the giver nor does he serve as an intermediary with the source of those powers.

Of the apparent aspect of asceticism we have already seen examples in the early career of Salama. He adopted a series of extreme, though characteristically Sufi, practices designed to free him from the sensual self and to discipline his soul. If he never went into actual physical seclusion (*khalwa*), believing that the Sufi remains in the world and faces up to circumstances, he adopted other equally demanding techniques to mortify the body and turn his concentration entirely on God. He renounced sexual practices and devoted himself to a rigorous and continual series of *dhikr*. But he eventually came to see that such practices associated with *zuhd* (asceticism), however useful they may be in the inculcation of self-discipline, do not make up its essence. That lies rather in an internal abjuration of what is vain, and in the purification of the heart (*safa' al qalb*). There is no element here of a dynamic inner-worldly asceticism seeking to achieve mastery over the material. Such an ethic would be considered basically meaningless. The *murid* is clearly directed inwards to his soul and upwards to his God, for therein lies his true path. The brother should therefore observe restraint and moderation in his life, and should follow the ascetic practices recommended to him by his *murshid* and suitable to his particular level of advancement, remembering that these are only praiseworthy means to an end, and do not constitute the end in itself.

There is thus a pattern of key principles central to this Order. They revolve around brotherhood under the authority of the Sheikh and an intense solidarity of communion among members. As Troeltsch saw, the absolute individualism that comes from the religious idea of pure-hearted love of God leads to an equally absolute fellowship among those united in God.[1] Though by definition the mass is excluded from the highest reaches of the mystical path that is accessible only to the spiritual élite, they may yet join together in a corporate body in devotion to the founder, join in a society where the value and normative system derives entirely from God's prescripts and the Sheikh's interpretation of the right existence. This fellowship, the basis of whose interrelations is love and fraternity, seeks as a group to experience an awareness of the personal link that binds lover and Beloved in the *dhikr*. It attempts by the corporate repetition of the names of God, and in the concentrated emotion of the ritual, to escape from the finite world of sense, and to participate, to whatever degree, in the infinite. It looks, in a way that the sober institutions of orthodox Islam cannot accommodate, to attain to a feeling of immediacy in relation to the Divine. What the formal abstract system of the '*ulema*' has failed to provide, the richly personal ethic of the *tariqa* offers in abundance.

The *Hamidiya Shadhiliya* thus constitutes a specific system in terms of belief and ethic. For the actor, his normative reference is directed inward to the brotherhood, and his valuative reference directed to Divine Revelation and the teachings of the Saint. Comparison of status and behaviour are made within the group of brothers rather than to any collectivity of others. For while the latter are equally Muslims, they move within conceptions of an ethical universe that are recognizably different in regard to the weight they give to certain elements; interpreting the world in ways which, valid in themselves, yet do not correspond in their totality to the *murid*'s vision. The question then, 'Whom do you compare yourself

[1] Troeltsch, E., *The social teaching of the Christian churches*, vol. i, London: Allen & Unwin (4th impression), 1956, p. 56.

to ?', can only have one answer from the member, 'to my brothers', and the standards by which he judges both them and himself proceed directly from God through the mediating *wali*.

There is therefore no appeal to, or utilization of, resentment, no radical reinterpretation of the world and man, no outside comparative reference, no set of expectations linked with the amelioration of social inequalities, since these are empty of significance for the *tariqa*. Members live in what they still feel to be a Muslim society whose constituent individuals have the same hope of Paradise; *muridin* of the other Orders, though in some ways they form a group with which the *Hamidiya Shadhiliya* explicitly points an unfavourable contrast and from which it takes care to differentiate its practices, have no lesser claim to God's love, or lesser chance of attaining His contentment. Indeed this is true of all, for as we have seen there are no external ways of measuring a Muslim's worth because the quality of his faith, not his worldly activity, is the only criterion.

Social Implications

Turning from the particular example of the *Hamidiya Shadhiliya* to general considerations, we recognize the essential flexibility and multiplicity of variations to which such a system is inherently open. Intellectualist and non-intellectualist, ecstatic and ascetic, it could and did support egalitarian groups, characterized by intensity of communion, and placing primary stress on ecstatic and uninhibited emotionalism with only secondary importance attached to teachings; while on the other hand it was as well associated with a strong emphasis on hierarchy and order predicated on advance in the spiritual path of the founder, each to his proper place. As part of a universal religion with its own distinctive spectrum of beliefs and complex of symbols, *tasawwuf*, of course, stands to some degree outside its human carriers and representatives at any one moment, limiting the range of correspondence which they might find in it to their human condition, and for the ordering and understanding of their moral and physical universe. Following Weber, it is not at all my contention that 'the specific nature of a religion is a simple "function" of the social situation of the stratum which appears as its characteristic bearer, or that it represents the stratum's material or ideal interest-situation. On the contrary, a more basic misunderstanding of the standpoint of these discussions would hardly be possible'.[1] Both interact in a constant dynamic relationship. But accepting this in-built flexibility, we may still attempt to identify those basic elements and concomitant social implications which might lead to an understanding of the predominance for so long in traditional Egyptian society of Sufism and the Brotherhoods.

In a doctrinal system guaranteed by Revelation and derived from the Divine through the Prophet, the Orders presented a perfect 'closed' model of the grounds of human experience. Immutable, with all the stasis of certainty, it offered an explanation for the universe of a dominantly agrarian or non-progressive Time in which the historical process and linear Time is of but marginal significance. Rather than a concern with possibilities out of which the what-is-to-come might be forged, the Brotherhoods pointed to a withdrawal inward on the constant Way after the example of the Saint and in a religious community rooted in the great conservative impulse of consensus. In such a world the mysterious predestining hand of God became a passive force leading to world-indifference, not the motor for the dynamic fulfilment of the Omnipotent Will.

The *turuq* direct and directed attention away from the external material and the physical condition to the soul and the participation in ascetic and ritual practices which link the individual with that ultimate power which gives his life its meaning. To official dogmatics, in which the gate of individual interpretation had for centuries been closed, they added the capacity at once to release and to absorb the charismatic personality. They offered in communal ritual and collective celebrations those joint experiences which appear to be vital to the maintenance of an organized religion, and provided a set of social networks based on a common Muslim identity. Combined with this was a freedom in modes of expression which made popular Sufism adaptable to every social level. In one whole were incorporated the means of attaining blessing (*baraka*), the hope and promise of the intervention of grace in human affairs in the *karamat* of the Saint, and the psychological liberation catered for by those whom Weber calls the 'plebeian technicians of orgiastics'.[2]

In its identification of status and spiritual understanding of the commonly accepted and 'lived-in' religious system, the Orders

[1] Weber, M., 'The Social Psychology of the World Religions', op. cit., pp. 269–70.   [2] Ibid., p. 269.

supported a minimally differentiated society in which the highest position was that of Sheikh and *'alim*.[1] They both taught and reinforced (as they still do) the primary values of a stable society where occupations are relatively few and non-diversified, and upward mobility, that great solvent of certainty, highly limited; a society where the vast mass of the population, the peasants and unskilled artisans were '. . . ignorant, illiterate, apathetic, and in bad health',[2] sharing an almost total lack of resources to alter a subsistence-level existence and haunted by perennial want.

In the towns there was the close interrelation with the guild organizations, themselves called *tariqas* and led by 'Sheikhs' who headed a series of ranks through which the member might, after initiation, progress.[3] In an Egypt where power was located in a distant and separate, not to say foreign, administration, and authority vested in the traditional leaders and literate guardians of the Book, I have already suggested that there was a 'fit' in status between the Orders and the social system in general. The structure of the society was such as to allow a homogeneity of values. Social identity in the *turuq* was complementary to and supported that in each community; the primary value system of both was coterminous and mutually renewing. In this aspect, world and religion were one. And membership in the Orders was an integral part of Muslim life, the means by which the beliefs of Islam were inculcated in him, the setting for his major collective festivals and his ritual life, a main source of his leisure activity.

Rather than compensation for lack of status and the furnishing of totally other criteria for awarding it, which Pope has suggested is characteristic of sectarian groups,[4] there was justification and legitimation for the world order as it was conceived as a congruence of *din* and *dunya*.

However, if Sufism is a system capable of many different interpretations and yielding a wide range of meanings and referents for social action, it is markedly less amenable to some interpretations than to others. An ethic derived from it ceases to be of much relevance to a society which was submitted consecutively to

---

[1] Lufti as-Said, A., 'The Role of the *'ulema'* in the early nineteenth century', in Holt, *Political and Social Change*, discusses the decline in power and prestige of the *'ulema'* under the impact of Western influence.

[2] Hansen, B., and Marzouk, G. A., op. cit., p. 1.

[3] Baer, *Egyptian Guilds in Modern Times, passim*.

[4] Pope, Liston, *Millhands and Preachers*, New Haven: Yale U.P., 1942.

conquest (by the French in 1798, a date usually for convenience regarded as the beginning of the 'modern' period in Egyptian history); to a regime of a degree of centralization and control unprecedented in the recent past of the people (that of Muhammed Ali who ruled the country from 1805 to 1849); to a considerable and forced increase in foreign influence and penetration ultimately leading to colonial occupation (by the British, an occupation which cannot be said really to have ended until the withdrawal from Suez in 1956); and finally to sweeping changes in the system of land tenure,[1] and the secularization of education and politics.

Nor has it much to say to those who, in a society where the 'political' (which in the present context centres round the ideology of Arab Socialism) and the religious become ever more separate, are firmly committed to the former; nor, *a fortiori*, to a revolutionary army élite, which, having overthrown the old parties and landed power factions, has taken over and refashioned the apparatus of government explicitly to bring about rapid and fundamental changes in the distribution of power and of wealth. How strong could we expect the ethic of the Orders to remain in a society where there have occurred major shifts in the means of production, and high rates of urbanization and industrialization; where a demographic explosion of critical magnitude coincides with a rapid growth in the complexity of bureaucratic administration and of an economic system that is of its nature deeply bound up with factors largely outside local control in the world fiscal and export markets? Popular Sufism is of little relevance in the fluid economic and social situation in which the emerging 'middle class' of civil servants, officers, engineers, doctors, lawyers, academics, journalists, business men, and associated professions finds itself.

I shall return to these topics in some detail later, but even so crude a catalogue indicates the ever widening inapplicability of *tasawwuf* as it developed in Egypt to the new circumstances and new alternatives born of an ever more apparent linear historical process. In this situation, with its confusing multiplication of occupation and status, and the formation of different economic and educational social groups, I suggest that Pope's observation is becoming increasingly true of contemporary Egypt; that in fact

---

[1] This very complex question is fully dealt with in Baer, G., *History of Land Ownership in Modern Egypt, 1800–1950*, London: O.U.P., 1963, and Saab, G., *Land Reform in Egypt (1952–1962)*, London: O.U.P., 1967.

the Orders are in part *now* functioning as sources of religious status for those who lack social status. The overt secularization of so many social and political institutions has left the *turuq* more and more a haven for those who, for whatever reason, either do not seek or have no place in the new order. It is those sections of the population which have only a marginal place or interest in the processes which I have outlined, and which still adhere largely to the traditional world view that the Orders expressed and inculcated, who continue in limited numbers to turn to them.

In the main the bulk of the membership is drawn from those sections of Egyptian society which are not as yet fully committed to, or accommodated by, the new order as it is developing. That is to say, from groups which still strive to adhere to the old homogeneous system of values, to interpret the world on the same stable set of propositions and expectations; those before whom new ranges of alternatives have not yet opened and who are largely unaffected by, or in some way marginal to, the processes of social upheaval; and finally those whose social circumstances have been relatively static in the midst of flux.

Negatively we also find little participation by those whom we have loosely characterized as the 'middle class'. For these latter have emerged in an Egypt where the Orders were no longer the primary social institution, holding to a value system profoundly altered by intellectual trends in the Islamic modernist and nationalist movements,[1] and employing standards and criteria of judgement in part acquired in an alien (European) setting. Moreover, such groups have a positive interest in fundamental changes in their milieu, unlimited by traditionalist restrictions. They occupy those strata most subject to social mobility and the rationalization of means in a framework in which economic values are increasingly significant and individual efficiency, expertise, and achievement constantly stressed.

From the point of view of structure and social interest the 'middle class' exhibits a more complex pattern than do the agricultural and proletarian masses that are still only minimally literate,[2] and live

[1] I refer particularly to the influence of Jamal ad-Din al Afghani (1839–97), and Muhammed ʿAbduh on Islamic and nationalist thought. The best discussion of this whole topic is that of Hourani, A., *Arabic Thought in the Liberal Age*, London: O.U.P., 1962.

[2] Details of literacy rates are in Hansen and Marzouck, op. cit., p. 38.

with no marked increase in either real income or consumption over the same sixty years which have seen the rise of the former.[1] Their religious needs present a correspondingly far more heterogeneous picture than those of the traditional sectors. This is not to say that, as a necessary function of social status or occupational and educational position, they have lost a belief in the tenets of Islam, or that they reject it as an ultimate value system. Rather it is that a new complex of what we might call 'proximate' values and goals have assumed what is now in many areas of their existence a dominant importance. Sufism in its advanced or higher forms may therefore well continue to answer personal psychological and intellectual requirements for the members of this 'class'. But Sufism in its popular institutions, the Orders, is unlikely to gain their adherence or support.

Nor, even assuming the need, are there any alternatives in the traditional system. Islam has no Church, in the limited sense of congregations regularly coming together as a particular group of 'parishioners', and the organs of religious authority, outside the Orders, have been canon lawyers and not priests. They have therefore no traditional or residual attachment to any formally constituted body playing a role even remotely parallel to that played by the denominations and sects in Western Europe and America in the history of the 'middle class'. Their growth has thus taken place almost entirely without association with the framework of religion as manifested in its formal institutions. Not until a radical reinterpretation of action in the world on the basis of Islamic precepts appeared in the Muslim Brotherhood did any religious organization succeed in gaining large numbers of members from their ranks.

Though I did not carry out any random sampling of members in terms of education, occupation, and income, it seems clear from observation that the vast proportion of *muridin* come from the ranks of the fellaheen and the lower grades of workers. These are the ones for whom the *turuq* can remain a major source of emotional gratification, enabling them to come to terms with life. Their lives are carried on in physical and material circumstances such as to warrant the famous description of 'nasty, brutish, and short'. Financially extremely depressed, their diet is inadequate,

[1] O'Brien, op. cit., p. 2. For a discussion and figures of occupational distribution, see Issawi, Charles, *Egypt in Revolution*, London: O.U.P., 1963, pp. 86–90.

and they exist on or below the level of subsistence. Even on the internal relative indices of average income they are in poverty and deprived.[1]

It is difficult to say how far awareness of the changes in Egyptian society has percolated down to them. Most are certainly within reach of the burgeoning media of communication, particularly the radio (very many coffee shops possess one) and the television (often publicly installed by the government). Without full information, however, it is impossible to know to what extent they comprehend the inequality of their low economic and social status, or what comparative reference they make, and how far they contrast the situation and attributes of others with their own. We might safely suggest at any rate that they are the group least directly affected by the processes of change, and with the lowest expectations of upward social mobility. For them in one sense at least, all is still as it was.

Moreover the Orders in general help to keep it so. As far as the economic status of the members is concerned, the *turuq* make no attempt to raise or improve it. Having no interest in the world in that respect, they reinforce the restrictions on consciousness of these strata. No encouragement for effort or material advancement or political change plays any part in their teachings. Indeed they may often be said not to teach at all, but merely to provide opportunities for the kind of emotional expression we discuss in the *dhikr*. They will therefore tend to assist in maintaining the static elements in the situation rather than contributing in any way to change in the material circumstances of members.

In as much as they have any educational or socializing function left (a point to which I shall return) it is not of a kind to equip the *murid* with an understanding of the developments in modern Egypt and their implications for himself; it is not such as to cause him to place any value on economic achievement, or political action, or effort in the world outside the sphere in which he moves. In a very limited sense (given the very tenuous links within most Orders and

[1] Per capita income is given as U.S. $125 in Hansen and Marzouck, op. cit., p. 1; many will of course have an income considerably below this figure. O'Brien comments that there was no real rise in the previous half century; O'Brien, op. cit., p. 31. More recently: 'In 1960 Egypt embarked on a development plan that, helped by devaluation in 1962, all but hit its target—a growth in income of 4% a year', *The Economist*, 1 Apr. 1967, p. 15, though this report gives no actual figures or break-down of the real distribution of income.

the narrow spheres of action in which they function) the Brotherhood may act as an adaptive mechanism assisting him in a situation that is changing for reasons beyond both his control and his comprehension. In addition to the psychological comforts which the ethical system offers to those who remain within it, and the order it preserves in an increasingly confusing external environment, an Order may fulfil more material purposes of mutual help between members over and above what might be expected or required from the kin group, and serve as a secondary matrix of social relations outside ascriptive groupings. But in all things the *tariqa* will bolster the traditional, and in the face of the break up of the old social units and patterns, the increasing reorganization of society on other terms, and its fluidity or even apparent fragmentation, assert a simple but total system from which life continues to take its unchanged and unchanging meaning.

It is true that these are not the only social levels represented in the Orders. Though the *Ahmadiya Idrisiya* of Aswan is almost entirely made up of members from these strata, others such as the *Demerdashiya Khalwatiya* have already been instanced as stressing notions of the spiritual élite and teaching, and we have drawn attention to the social composition of the *nuqaba'* of that *tariqa*. Nevertheless it was also indicated that this élite is of the traditional kind, learned men of religion from al Azhar and representatives of the older trades and professions. It is, furthermore, a very small group. A senior brother of the Order put the number of active members at approximately three hundred. Of the Sufi Orders in general, therefore, only one, the *Hamidiya Shadhiliya*, has succeeded in making any real breakthrough in the social status of the membership it attracts beyond the lower 'class' of peasants and workers.

The Hamidiya Shadhiliya *and its membership*

That this is so is due in major part to the Laws of that *tariqa* and the great attention paid to the internal organization and the proper arrangement of the public occasions. As we have shown, the *Hamidiya Shadhiliya* lays considerable stress on the functioning of the group as a whole, and an intensive round of ritual occasions, visits, and meetings. Their *dhikr* are rigorously controlled so that, while offering gratification to the uneducated and barely literate, it yet is possible for others to feel that the stricter tenets of Islam are being observed, and that emotion is not being indulged in for its own sake. No 'undignified' behaviour is permitted, and the Sheikh emphasizes the character of the *dhikr* as means rather than as an end in itself.

What is more important, the Order has a distinct, corporate, and highly regulated identity. The amorphousness which characterizes the other groups is conspicuously absent. It is quite clear to each member what being a *murid* implies for him, and he is intimately involved in the collective activities of the *tariqa* which takes a comprehensive interest in his spiritual, physical, and material wants. If he is ill, members will come to visit him in anxious solicitude; if he has personal problems in his life, for example in his family situation, his Sheikh and some of the senior brothers are sympathetically ready with practical as well as spiritual advice and assistance.

If he moves from one area to another (an important factor in view of the increasing geographical mobility of growing sections of the population), from his village into one of the towns, then the local *khalifa* will put him in touch with *muridin* in his new environment. If he has no accommodation, they will help him find some; if he is in financial difficulty despite his own efforts, they will give him limited funds; if the education of his children involves material hardship, the *tariqa* will ameliorate the problems. The brothers will take great pains to make the alteration in his job, or the change from the rural to the urban setting, with all its attendant problems and difficulties, as easy as possible. He will be able to rely in any major town in Egypt on entering the same close fellowship that he knew in his home district and his adaptation to fresh circumstance is correspondingly made the easier. The Order may even be responsible for his geographical or occupational shift, since it acts in part as a network to help brothers who so wish to find new employment where it has connections. So that if he comes from a village and leaves the kin group on which he will previously have relied, the *tariqa* will more than assume its functions in the town and act also as an important socializing agent in the process, as a buffer between him and the less ordered and coherent world in which he now finds himself a part. It will be the medium of inculcating in him what is new in the normative standards of the urban setting. He thus belongs to a brotherhood that effectively acts as such over a wide field of action, and quite outside and across ascriptive links, whether of kinship or neighbourhood.

In this brotherhood he is instructed as to his own individual responsibility in his worldly task or occupation; that work diligently carried out on the model of the Saint has its own proper part in the life of the *murid*, and is to be positively valued. Though achievement as such is not a mark of religious advancement, there is a definite encouragement to effort which is in considerable contrast to the other *turuq*. It is thus true that in the *Hamidiya Shadhiliya* with its elaborate hierarchical organization laying great stress on the different levels of understanding and capacities of members for progress on the Way, the *new* status order that has developed is accommodated by that of the *tariqa*.

We here come again upon that familiar duality of equality/inequality inherent in the nature of all Sufi Orders. The ambivalence is particularly present in the case of the 'middle-class' members of the *Hamidiya Shadhiliya*. Though *muridin* of whatever social standing take great pride in the fact that they are all brothers, that each makes the hand-kiss with each, regardless of secular station, and that, for them, the company director is the same as the peasant and the rich man as the poor, the pride is of a slightly different kind at either end of the social scale. The peasant is delighted with the 'levelling down' symbolized in the *musafaha*, though he acknowledges the economic and educational advantages of his brother; the company director is also delighted at the assertion of a common humanity and identity as Muslims, and at his own capacity to stoop, briefly perhaps, to those whose economic and educational inferiority he clearly sees. Both ultimate and proximate values are in this way asserted.

Those members of the 'middle classes' who join the *tariqa* for whatever personal reasons thus enter a group that provides some accommodation for their particular interests. It places a religious value on their work and assures them that they follow the model of the Saint himself in their scrupulous carrying out of their task. It instructs them that asceticism (*zuhd*) is an inward state, the quality of which is not impaired by worldly wealth, so long as they understand its true nature and their hearts are not tied to the *dunya*; and it adds to their secular status a religious one that transcends the former at the same time as it imparts a higher meaning to the totality of their existence. The Order allows them to relate

themselves to the ultimate value system of Islam through a corporate body in which they form the élite of those closest to the
Sheikh. In his *maglis* he directs the discussion of religion and his
teaching to them, while others of lower understanding can only
sit silent.

Though I was unable to acquire any quantitative data of this
group, my observations suggest two main points. The first is that
several of the members in this 'class' have risen in occupation *since*
joining the Order, and that they have initially become *muridin* when
their social position was considerably lower. The private confidential secretary of Sheikh Ibrahim, as an example, entered the *tariqa*
as a young man. His parents, who were peasants in a small village
outside Cairo, both died when he was young and he was brought
up by a poor farmer. He had some friends in his village who
belonged to the *Hamidiya Shadhiliya* and used to talk to him about
Sidi Salama who was still alive. Being, as he put it to me, 'very
religious', he determined to go to Cairo to see this man who worked
karamat. He therefore came to the capital and took the oath from
Salama, whom he attended faithfully until the death of the latter.
He also joined a small commercial company run by the British, and
over a long period of years both gained the close confidence of his
contemporary Ibrahim, and rose in his job to be under-manager.
After the company was taken over by the Government, he became
general manager, his present position. As private secretary to the
Sheikh, he is perhaps the single most important official in the
Order and devoted to its head. As another member put it: 'He
does not go to sleep until the Sheikh tells him to.'

I came into contact with several other cases broadly of this type.
The individual joins the *tariqa* as a young man in a low social
position and rises to one of the occupations we loosely labelled
'middle class', retaining his loyalty to the group. This tends to
support Bryan Wilson's suggestion that in membership in religious
groups there is often what he terms a 'lag' effect; that is, that the
group may have ceased to fulfil the latent functions which motivated entry (Wilson's word is 'conversion' which is not appropriate
in our context) and has come instead to perform overt functions
as a repository of sentiments, ideals, and associations, and as an
integrating factor in life.[1] Providing membership does not actively

---

[1] Wilson, B., *Sects and Society*, Berkeley and Los Angeles: University of
California Press, 1961, p. 321.

clash with the change in the actor's situation, then, but offers some accommodation to his altered circumstance, he may well maintain his attachment to a collectivity he would not perhaps, as one of the 'middle class', enter.

Such an example is likely to be particularly frequent in a society such as that of modern Egypt. The increase in the range of education at all levels and the multiplication of job opportunities all the way up the scale to top management means that the occupational and educational situation is fluid.[1] Individuals may, in a relatively short time, effect major changes in social status, while still retaining loyalty to an institution which embodies those patterns of values in which they were initially trained.

The second point my researches on this aspect of membership suggests is that the *Hamidiya Shadhiliya* also recruits individuals who, though they in one way partake of the new dispensation, yet do so in a more or less marginal sense. They are, as it were, *en passage* in terms of changes in their social position and values. They are thus in an unusually difficult position in which the old certainties are being called into question, but not satisfactorily replaced by new ones. Further, though occupational opportunities have increased, and the number of those formally educated up to university standard has grown enormously, in many cases the main effect of this process is to raise expectations and a vision of alternatives which cannot in the nature of the circumstances be fulfilled. For the aspirants far outnumber the jobs available at the level of expectations which these aspirants now entertain. Coming often from families of low status, they have completed secondary or university education only to find that instead of the avenues to high status being open, they are still firmly blocked. The degree student (especially in Arts subjects) thus finds himself employed as a bank clerk, or a minor executive in a large business company. His hopes have been raised, and their realization checked. In his perhaps shifting and uncertain world, where anomy may threaten and the grounds for existence seem to move beneath his feet, the Order reconstitutes in fraternal certitude and security the norms to govern his behaviour and the values to which he may redirect himself.

The *tariqa* assures him of his worth in ultimate terms, and that the status system of the world is of minimal significance; that in a

[1] O'Brien, op. cit., p. 246.

sense it does not represent 'reality', but is only a potentially dis-
tracting appearance. It tells him of the importance of his greater
understanding (gained through education), but that this importance
is not to be measured by any occupational or material advancement.
It lies rather in its use as a means to progress on the inner spiritual
way to Truth. The sphere in which he had acquired those expectations, which were later frustrated, is thus devalued. He is now led
to perceive it as a set of secondary values that are but marginally
related to the primary religious values taught by the *tariqa*. The
conflict of anomy which threatened is dissolved, since the whole
disjunction between ends and the possibility and means of achiev-
ing them is now seen as basically irrelevant.

Both the above observations induce caution in any discussion of
'middle class' membership in the *Hamidiya Shadhiliya*. For in the
first category we were dealing with individuals who had joined
the group while of one status and then risen to another within the
classification 'middle class'. And in the second we were concerned
with those who were perhaps first generation 'lower middle class',
drawn into patterns of education, occupation, and values not those
of their fathers, and experiencing all the conflicts and problems
inherent in such a situation. In neither instance were these
examples of individuals who were born into this stratum. Without
detailed sociological evidence and quantitative data we should
therefore be careful in discussing this aspect of membership. But
we may at least suggest that the *Hamidiya Shadhiliya* offers an
ethic and corporate activity that is not isolated from cross-class
relations, as the other *turuq* in the main are, and is not tied exclusively to the needs of those lowest placed in the social order.

The Channels of Recruitment

This discussion of the social ethic is of particular importance at
the present time. For in contemporary Egypt the Orders have
actively to *attract* members, rather than relying on their now-lost
position of being the major religious and social institution of
traditional Muslim society. Instead of the automatic membership
of nearly every individual in one or several of the groups, they now
face a situation in which individuals must be persuaded by members
to join. They are no longer the dominant agency of association
beyond strictly ascriptive groupings; they must therefore set out

to provide organizational functions which will be of significance
to members of the transitional society to the point that, as a matter
of conscious choice, they wish to enter the collectivity. I shall try
to show in the final chapter that only the *Hamidiya Shadhiliya* has
comprehended the implications of this and its importance for continued survival. As we have seen in its ethic, which it delineates
with far greater clarity than do the other *turuq*, it offers some
accommodation to the changes in Egyptian society which its fellow
Orders largely do not. Its membership is correspondingly on a
broader social base and includes some representatives of the 'middle
classes', as well as drawing on the mass of the lower-strata peasants
and workers.

But we have yet to answer the question, through what channels
does the *Hamidiya Shadhiliya* recruit its members, and to what
extent do they seek to expand membership? It has been explained
that traditionally the Orders could rely on an assured and continued
process of renewal. Now it is almost impossible for them to do so.
Most have declined markedly in quantitative terms over the past
sixty years, in part because of their passive attitude to the whole
problem of recruitment. In their loose, amorphous associational
character they have failed to comprehend the growing need for a
mission if they are to continue as viable institutions.

Salama on the other hand had a clear conception of active
recruitment and the publishing of his call; he devoted a considerable part of his early career as we have seen to the rigorous selection
and training of the core élite of the *tariqa* who would set up the first
zawiyas in and outside Cairo. Furthermore, he made the whole
principle of recruitment a key function of the officials of the Order.
They were and are constantly encouraged to expand their activities
and the size of their particular local centres. It is indeed one of the
imperatives of their office:

Law 50. It is necessary for the *khalifa* not to make the *khilafa* (i.e. the
position of *khalifa*) inoperative; he must have students so that the *tariq*
will spread and the people have benefit from it.

Advance in the hierarchy is also in part predicated on their success
in this field. To become a *khalifa* of the *khulafa'* the individual
must bring forward others whom the *Sigada* regards as worthy to
be *khalifas*. The *muridin* too are urged to gain members for the
tariqa and the fellowship of Sidi Salama, and pride in their group

makes them very ready to proselytize within their own range of social contacts.

The formal establishment of a new *zawiya* usually takes the following pattern. The members concerned go to a mosque in a town or village at the time when the greatest concentration of people will be present, the Friday noon prayer. They ask the leader of the prayer, the Imam in charge of the administration and upkeep of the building, for permission to speak to the congregation about the Sheikh, the *tariqa*, and the brothers. They then announce that a *dhikr* circle will be held after the prayer and invite all to attend. Brothers from the neighbouring villages and *zawiyas* have been assembled and a group of the hymn singers brought together. They duly perform the ritual with those who stay, and encourage them to take the oath (*'ahd*) to the *tariqa*, making careful note of the names and addresses of those who do so. The first (and temporary) head of the new group, usually a senior and experienced *khalifa* from near by, can then count on every assistance from the central office in his consolidation of the *zawiya*. When this has been accomplished and there are twenty or thirty brothers, they will be asked whom they would like appointed *khalifa*, and providing that the *Sheikh as-Sigada* approves, the person selected then takes over the leadership of the local centre.

A particular area and location may be chosen for any one of several reasons. Members of the Order may move there and wish to set up a *zawiya*; some of the brothers may have kinship, affective, or other links with a village where the *Hamidiya Shadhiliya* is not represented, and suggest it to the main office as fertile ground for the mission of the Order; or a *khalifa* of a neighbouring group might be particularly energetic and zealous in the advancement of the *tariqa* and so make great efforts in his area to found a new centre. Whatever the case, a major effort to attract members is made initially through the prayer in the mosque, so often in Islamic history the setting for the proclamation or founding of religious, social, and political movements.

Many members join the Order through the more informal agency of friends or kin. This is often allied with the principle of *giran* (neighbourliness), which may operate in recruitment, and especially in the urban immigrant situation. Where people who have come from the same area tend to live in the same quarter in their new urban setting, they may be drawn into the *Hamidiya*

Shadhiliya by those of their number who already belong. They attend one of the *hadrahs* as guests, and are thus introduced to the society of the members. Perhaps swayed by the power and control of the ritual, the eager explanation which their hosts give of the activities and benefits of the group, and of the powers of Sidi Salama and Sheikh Ibrahim, they are persuaded to take the *'ahd*. Particular attention is then given to inquiring after them and to making every effort to absorb them into the world of the *tariqa*. For men who feel themselves 'strangers' away from their home environment, the Order then serves, as we have noted, as an important adaptive and integrative mechanism into their changed circumstances.

Yet others come to the *Hamidiya Shadhiliya*, not as the result of an introduction through any personal relations with the brothers, but after witnessing as an outsider one of the 'occasions'—the processions, the *mulid*, or the *dhikr*. The great care taken over performance in its every aspect, and the marked and immediate contrast with the other *turuq* make a strong impression. Moreover, officials are always ready to invite an onlooker to take part in the occasion, and to urge upon him the special character of the organization, the importance of the Laws of the Saint, and the doctrinal propriety of the ritual.

Finally there are two significant internal means of recruiting to, and maintaining, the *tariqa*. The first is the preference which exists for marriage within the limits of the Order, or in other terms a limited 'religious endogamy'. There is no insistence on such a marriage pattern, no prescription in the Laws on the subject which the member is bound to follow. But the brothers are encouraged to seek wives from the families of the *muridin*, rather than from outside the group. And we remember in this connection that Salama's daughters married members of the Order (see above, p. 13), which furnishes a precedent in the life of the supreme authority.

Such a pattern is, of course, by no means uncommon in religious groups. To different degrees institutions as disparate as the sectarian Plymouth Brethren and the Roman Catholic Church both advocate it, and employ varied sanctions against those who infringe what is for them an article of doctrine. This extreme position does not hold true of the *Hamidiya Shadhiliya*. Nor could it. For being an orthodox Sunni *tariqa*, any exclusiveness it claims does not extend to the theological sphere; there is correspondingly no emphasis on the need for the preservation of doctrinal purity and the avoidance of kinship and 'blood' links with outsiders (variously regarded as damned, or spiritually unequal, to the faithful). The contrary is in fact the case, and we have already seen that the non-member is regarded as having no less a claim to be a Muslim than the member.

As an element which reinforces the extension of the influence of the *tariqa* over the most intimate and personal areas of the member's life, and which ideally leads to the establishment of a network of affinal relations between the 'brothers', this form of marriage preference has important implications for the maintenance of the organization which will be at once apparent. All the more so, because of its significance for 'second generation' membership, the other important internal channel of recruitment. It has already been explained that belonging to the *tariqa* is a voluntary act by the would-be initiate, and is not dependent on descent. The agent is not *born* a member of the *Hamidiya Shadhiliya* (as one is in many cases born a member of a particular sect or denomination). There is therefore no assurance of the continuation of the group from within, no structural principle guaranteeing the maintenance of the Order, at least from this source. But the limited preference for 'endogamy' does mean that children will be raised in a primary kin group for whom the *tariqa* is the chief agency through and from which the norms and values by which the individual lives are largely derived; that much of the socialization process will be profoundly influenced by the intense commitment to the *Hamidiya Shadhiliya*, to whose rituals the child will be taken.

The Order thus attempts to ensure a continuity of recruitment through the families of the members, as well as by attracting outsiders. The Sheikh pays great attention to the sons of the brothers (we recall the illuminating instance of this cited on p. 77 above, when he singled the boy out, over his seniors, for the particular honour of kissing his hand): he takes pains to inquire about them to the group. This policy is followed by the *khalifas* in the *zawiyas*, one or two of which in Cairo have started small youth sections for children under the ages of thirteen or fourteen. Everything is done to make the family one of the most significant channels of recruitment.

VI

RITUAL: THE *DHIKR*

THE central ritual of the Sufi Orders is the *dhikr*, or 'remembrance' of God. This is the mystical practice of the repetition of the Names of Allah in order to achieve '. . . knowledge (*ma'rifa*) of God by way of contemplation . . .'[1] So important has it been in the history of Sufism that Lings holds that 'It is the Quranic use of the cognitive term "remembrance" rather than "love" which has, perhaps more than anything else, imposed on Islamic mysticism its special characteristics.'[2] To be of value and achieve its full purpose it requires a *niya*, or intention, and presupposes in theory a general preparation embracing the whole life of the participant. As is so often the case in religious ritual, unworthiness in the participant or some insufficiency of intention negates the purpose for which the rite is performed. In a more limited and immediate way, the recitation of certain litanies and sections of the Quran prescribed by the founder of the Order (the *hizb* or *wird*) fufils the function of preparation for the *dhikr* proper and establishes the appropriate psychological 'frame' for its performances.

The Sufi writers distinguish between the *dhikr al-khafi* or hidden *dhikr*, the repetition being in the mind or muttered in a low voice, and the *dhikr al-jali*, the open recitation in which the worshipper recites aloud. They further differentiate between the *dhikr* of the tongue (*al-lisan*), the heart (*al-qalb*), and the innermost being (*sirr*).[3] Each is a succeeding stage, attainable only by increasing spiritual excellence, on the path that leads by total capture of the thought, heart, and most inward part to separation from the world and complete concentration on the Divine. This process is assisted

---

[1] The Sheikh al Alawi quoted in Lings, op. cit., p. 58. It should be pointed out that Lings was himself a member of that Sheikh's Sufi circle.

[2] Ibid., p. 45.

[3] See Anawarti, G. C., and Gardet, L., *La Mystique musulmane*, Paris: J. Vrin, 1961. Also Gardet, L., 'Dhikr', *Encyclopedia of Islam*, new edn., vol. 2, Leiden: E. J. Brill, 1965, pp. 223–7; and Brown, J. P., *The Dervishes*, London: Trubner & Co., 1868.

by specific techniques of breathing intended to facilitate the
absolute involvement of the worshipper in the *dhikr* by the regulation of his physical nature.[1]

Divine sanction for the practice is drawn from many references
in the Quran concerning the excellence of the remembrance of
God, and from the Traditions of the Prophet, the *Hadith*.[2] Occupying from the beginning of Sufism a key place in the meditations of
the mystics, the *dhikr* was taken up communally with the rise of
the Orders. What originated as an arduous ritual often associated
with total dedication to the mystic life, became a popular means of
arousing collective religious enthusiasm. We therefore distinguish
between the specialist and the folk tradition and practice; the
latter, the *dhikr* of the commonality (*al'awamm*) being our chief
concern. In all its variations, the *dhikr* has continued to be the
most emphasized of the means to spiritual advancement in the
Way.

As a type of religious action the *dhikr* is not of course unique to
Islam. The repetition of the Sacred Name as a way to concentration
on the Divine Essence, or as a form of meditation, or a step on the
path to Enlightenment, is practised in different forms of Buddhism.
'The Nembitsu literally means "to think of the Buddha", and
consists particularly in the recitation of the name of Amitabha
Buddha.'[3] After pointing out that there is a psychological similarity
between Nembitsu and the holding of a koan in Zen, Dr. Suzuki
further explains that there are

. . . two ways in which the Buddha-name can be invoked; that is, when
the name is announced, there are two attitudes on the part of the devotee
toward the object of his adoration. In one case, the invocation takes
place with the idea that *nomen est numen*, or as a sort of magical formula.
The name itself is regarded as having some mysterious power to work
wonders . . . It further enables the devotee to get whatever happiness
he desires . . . In the second case, the name is pronounced not necessarily
as indicative of things that are therein suggested, but in order to work
out a certain psychological process thus set up.[4]

---

[1] Anawarti and Gardet, op. cit., pp. 242–4 for full discussion of the physiological effects of these techniques. The origins of the *Dhikr* are dealt with at
length in Massignon, L., *Essai sur les origines du lexique technique de la mystique
musulmane*, Paris: J. Vrin, 2nd edn., 1954.

[2] See *Quran*, xviii, 24: xxxiii, 41: xxxix, 22: xliii, 36: lxiii, 9: *inter alia*.

[3] Suzuki, D. T., *Essays in Zen Buddhism* (2nd Series), London: Luzac &
Co., 1933, p. 115.   [4] Ibid., pp. 126–8.

It also appears from Scholem's discussion of Merkebah mysticism
that such a technique was used in the ritual of that form of Jewish
mysticism.

In cyclical rhythm the hymns succeed each other, and

within them the adjurations of God follow in a crescendo of glittering
and majestical attributes, each stressing and enforcing the sonorous
power of the word. The monotony of their rhythm . . . and the progres-
sively sonorous incantations induce in those who are praying a state of
mind bordering on ecstasy. An important part of this technique is the
recurrence of the key word of the numinous.[1]

Anawarti and Gardet point out that it was a technique of the
monks of the Near East in the fifth to seventh centuries A.D., with
the 'prayer of Jesus'.[2] Furthermore, the associated control and
regulation of breathing has its place in Yoga, Buddhism, and
Taoism.[3]

Within the general framework of belief outlined above, there is
much variation in performance of the *dhikr*. It ranges from the
quietism of the individual Sufi and certain of the Brotherhoods
such as the *Khalwatiya*, to the ecstatics and hysterical behaviour
characteristic of those which are most extremely 'popular'. The
form of the *dhikr*, the degree of movement, the use of music and
overt emotionalism vary correspondingly. In some Orders singing
and the playing of musical instruments such as the flute and drum,
the recitations of religious verse and dance in a section of the ritual
called the *sama'*, are highly important. Other groups such as the
Naqshabandiya, by contrast, even at one time frowned on the silent
communal *dhikr*.[4] Frequently the performance appears to have
become an end in itself, a vehicle for popular catharsis or emotional
indulgence rather than a means to the fulfilment of a specifically
religious intention as that is defined by the participants themselves
and by the Sheikhs. This tendency has been heavily attacked by

[1] Scholem, G., *Major Trends in Jewish Mysticism*, Jerusalem, 1941, p. 59.

[2] Anawarti and Gardet, op. cit., p. 190.

[3] Dumoulin, H., *A History of Zen Buddhism*, New York: Random House,
1963, p. 30. It is tempting, but I think, misleading, to draw a comparison here
between the *dhikr* of the Orders and the calling out or repeated murmurings of
the name of Jesus in the services of certain evangelical sects. Misleading because
although there is a similarity of intention and effect, the repetition is not the
raison d'être of the ritual, nor is it a *structured* group action.

[4] Molé, Marijan, 'La Danse extatique en Islam', in *Les Danses sacrées*,
Collection Sources Orientales, no. 6, Paris: Éditions du Seuil, 1963, p. 150.

the *'ulema'* who saw licence taking the place of orthodoxy and enthusiasm breaking the limits of obedience.[1]

All the Orders hold *hadrahs* (meetings) at regular or irregular intervals depending on custom, the decision of the Sheikh, or the active numerical strength of the group concerned.[2] Most of the main Brotherhoods meet at least once a week for a *hadrah* held either in a public mosque (with the permission of the Sheikh in charge of the mosque), or in the *zawiya* (local centre) of the district, usually after the evening prayer has been completed. The members sit around chatting or greeting friends until, at a signal from one of the officers of the Order, they arrange themselves in the positions prescribed for the *dhikr* just prior to the arrival of the Sheikh or whoever has been delegated to lead the ritual. The following is a description by a member of the *Hamidiya Shadhiliya* of the arrangement of the brothers as laid down for that Order (Diagram 1):[3]

When the knots of brothers arrange themselves, they sit in parallel (Arabic *'ufqiya*, literally 'horizontal') ranks, stretched out so that half the brothers in one half of the mosque face half the brothers in the other half of the mosque. It is ordered in this way so that two ranks of hymn-singers (Arabic *munshidin*, singular *munshid*) are in the centre of the meeting place facing each other. This facilitates the alternation of the hymns between them. There is an external rank surrounding the ranks of tightly packed brothers seated in straight lines, protecting the backs of those doing the *dhikr*.[4]

Each man is linked with the brother on either side of him by handclasping with the fingers interlaced.

[1] A hymn of the Bektashi Order gives some feeling of the attitudes of the Orders to the teachings of the *'ulema'*; 'Thou hast set a balance to weigh evil deeds; Thou hast purposed to cast me in the Fire. / A balance is suitable for one who would be a grocer; or one who would be a jeweller or a seller of perfume. / Thou art the All Knower; Thou Thyself knowest my condition; what need is there for weighing my acts?'. A poem of the same Order tartly comments on the asceticism frequently urged upon them: 'What you sow upon marble grows not'. Quoted in Birge, J. K., *The Bektashi Order of Dervishes*, London: Luzac & Co., 1937, p. 55.

[2] '*Hadrah*' means 'presence', and is used by the Sufis as a synonym of *hudur*, 'being in the presence of Allah'. *Shorter Encyclopedia of Islam*, p. 125. It is also taken to refer to the presence of the Sheikh during the meeting.

[3] The accounts which follow of the *Hamidiya Shadhiliya* and the *Demerdashiya Khalwatiya* are of the main *hadrahs* held in Cairo by the Head Sheikh. Those held under the local officials in the *zawiyas* are naturally somewhat different in that the *Sheikh as-Sigada* is not present and numbers are considerably smaller. Nevertheless the patterned outlined below is the paradigm for the Order in general.   [4] Saif, op. cit., p. 84.

It will be seen from Diagram 1 that the external surrounding rank forms an inward-facing square and that all the members are also facing inward. The significance of this was explained in various

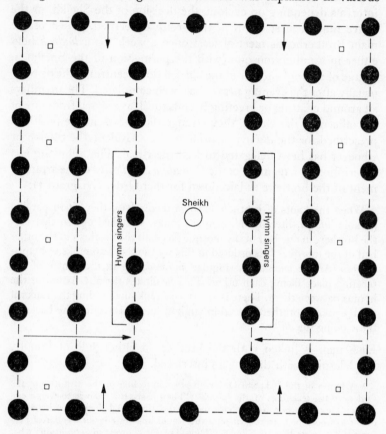

Arrows show direction faced by the lines of *muridin*
— — Indicates linked hands
☐ Indicates officials of the Order (they have in fact no fixed position
but walk around as necessary to control the movements)

DIAGRAM 1. The Dhikr of the Hamidiya Shadhiliya

ways by different informants who belonged to the Order. One stated that the outer ring was to prevent the *'afarit* (sing. *'ifrit*, evil spirits) from breaking through, and another added in an interesting juxtaposition, though with no identification of the two, that it was to 'keep out any stranger who might wish to enter'. The form can be seen symbolically as a spatial representation of the separation of the group from the world to which the outer ranks have their backs. To move into the square from outside is to move from the world into the community of brothers who are oriented to the Sheikh spatially, institutionally, and spiritually—the three levels which are symbolically so closely interlinked in the *dhikr*. The solidarity of the group thus finds expression in formal terms. The Order is 'directed inward' and inviolable by anyone of the outside world. This separation from those who are non-members is hinted at in Saif's remark quoted above (p. 263): 'There is an external rank surrounding . . . protecting the backs of those doing the *dhikr*', and is perceived to some degree by the brothers.

The Dhikr *of the* Demerdashiya

This aspect of spatial representation is a distinguishing factor among the Orders in general. An examination of the form and structural implications of the *dhikr* of the *Demerdashiya* branch of the *Khalwatiya* Order (Diagram 2) and comparison with that of the *Hamidiya Shadhiliya* (Diagram 1), already briefly touched on, demonstrate this clearly.

Among the *Demerdashiya* the outer square forms in the same way, looking inward and containing the mass of the brothers. There are, however, major differences in the position of the Sheikh and the *nuqaba'* (officers, or deputies of the Order), and in the placing of the other members. The Sheikh sits with the symbol of his authority, the *sigada* (carpet), set before him, apart from the others and facing them. Immediately in front of him is the rank of the *nuqaba'* of the Order who form as it were a barrier between him and the brothers. This is a reflection of the greater emphasis placed in the *Demerdashiya* on the hierarchy, obviously distinguished from the ordinary members by their position in the ritual.

These *nuqaba'* are twelve in number and ranked in strict seniority, the first facing the Sheikh and on his left. When one dies a new *naqib* is chosen by the Sheikh and the other *nuqaba'* and he enters at number twelve, those before him moving up a place. Thus, should number eight die or for some reason leave the Order, those below advance one in rank and a new, and therefore the most junior *naqib* is elected. As a result of this process of only filling vacancies in a small number and never creating them, entry into the élite is severely limited. It was from the *nuqaba'* that the present Sheikh was chosen when the previous Sheikh, who was of the Demerdash family, fled to Switzerland after the Revolution in

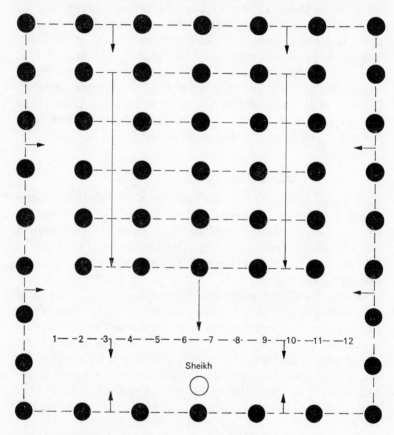

Arrows show direction faced by lines of *muridin*
— — Indicates linked hands
Officials (nuqabā') indicated by numbers 1–12

DIAGRAM 2. The Dhikr of the *Demerdashiya Khalwatiya*

1952. In this crisis, the leader, by virtue of the charisma of lineage which bestowed office, was replaced by one without such charisma, though from the hierarchy of the Order. He then became a link in the *silsilat al-baraka* (chain of grace) but could not, of course, claim a place in the *silsilat al-damm* (chain of blood) hitherto necessary to legitimate authority. The nature of the leadership underwent a change which has affected the pattern of succession in an important way.

It was explained to me that the choice might have fallen on any of the members. There is, however, no doubt that the one who became the head of the group was almost certain to come from the élite. For the Sheikh must be thought to be possessed of sufficient understanding and spiritual advancement to justify his elevation, and the fact that an individual is a *naqib* is of itself a mark of his proper superiority in these respects. Each of the *nuqaba'* is therefore now also potentially the Head of the Order, a factor increasing yet further his status.

This institutional and, *ipso facto*, religious status is expressed in the role of the *nuqaba'* in the performance of the *hadrah*. Their function is the exemplary leadership of the brothers in the different sections of the ritual. At certain points they alone carry out parti-cular actions. They, but not the *muridin* (sing. *murid*—ordinary members), stand for the recitation of the *la ilaha illa allah*, 'there is no God but Allah', which follows the initial recitation of a part of the Quran and the first *dhikr* of 'Allah'. The senior *naqib* chants the rubric of those (usually the Prophet Muhammad, the Saints, and the community of Muslims) for whom the opening chapter of the Quran (the *fatiha*) is to be recited at the conclusion of the *hadrah*.

They are further distinguished by their ritual dress. Though only two of the *nuqaba'* are in fact '*ulema*' of al-Azhar University, during the *dhikr* all adopt the clothing worn by that class of 'reli-gious specialists', the long outer coat or *quftan* and the turban or '*imma*. This marks them off from the *muridin* as particulary quali-fied in religion, and identifies them with the orthodox élite of Islam.

The Dhikr *of the* Hamidiya Shadhiliya

A glance at the spatial arrangement of the *Hamidiya Shadhiliya* for the *dhikr* (Diagram 1) shows the significant difference in the pattern of placing of the brothers. Whereas among the *Demerdashiya* the Sheikh is positioned very much 'at the head' of the members, set apart from them by the rank of the *nuqaba'* and with the symbol of his authority before him, the Sheikh of the *Hamidiya Shadhiliya* stands in the centre of the lines. He too is the direction point, but of a centripetally ordered group. He stands alone, but amid the brothers and not separated off from them. His position as institutional/religious axis of the Order is spatially expressed in his position, but with a significantly different symbolic stress from that of the Sheikh of the *Demerdashiya*. One should not overestimate the differences here. In broad general terms the role of the Sheikh is theoretically the same in all the Orders, whatever the distinctions may be in their ritual character. Nevertheless, subtle distinctions in emphasis are present and expressed in the physical form of the *dhikr*.

A major point of contrast lies in the position and function of the *nuqaba'*. Those of the *Hamidiya Shadhiliya* are usually referred to as *munazzimin* (organizers or arrangers), a term which is the key to their role in the *dhikr*. They occupy no fixed position in the group, form no rank between members and the Sheikh, and are not distinguished in any way by their dress. Nor do they perform any special ritual actions. Their duty is to make sure that those taking part keep in time with the others, that no one loses control of himself in the emotionally highly-charged atmosphere, and that those who join in the *dhikr* after it has been begun are taken through the outer square and properly placed in line. This latter reflects their role as channels of introduction to the Order. A man may not simply 'walk in', either to the ranks of the worshippers or membership of the Order; he must in both cases be led in by a *naqib*. At the end of the ritual they open a way through the outer rank by which the Sheikh leaves the *hadrah*, preceding the *muridin* back into the world. The stress is on their function as necessary helpers of the Sheikh, and they are not set apart in the ritual as an élite as are the *nuqaba'* of the *Demerdashiya*.

The Performance of the Dhikr

The details of the performance of the *dhikr* are in most cases laid down for an Order by the Sheikh or one of his predecessors. As the following account by a member of the *Hamidiya Shadhiliya* shows, within the general composition of the ritual there is allowed a certain very limited variation.

The Sheikh opens the *hadrah* by the recitation of *Hizb* (one of the sixty sections into which the Quran is divided). . . . Then he recites the phrase 'la ilaha illa Allah' (there is no god but God) and the rest of those making *dhikr* follow for a full period of time.

Then he stands with them reciting the name *Allah*, sometimes in a soft voice, then in a medium and then thirdly in a raised tone; between the course of recitation of the holy name, the *munshidin* (hymn singers) begin their task with the religious *qasidas* (odes) or sufi hymns or '*tawassulat*' (applications or petitions) to '*Al al-Beit* (the family of the Prophet, particularly his grandsons through Ali, Hassan and Hussein). The Sheikh claps to order the voices of those making the *dhikr*, walking between their lines, wakening the hearts of the brothers, inflaming their feelings and stirring their inner secret parts.

Until when they have finished their portion of the lights of the glorious name he transfers them to others. . . . *Huwa* (He), *Hayy* (the All Living), *Qaiyyum* (the All Sustaining). Until the Sheikh and they sit down and he recites something from the Quran following with the declaration of faith three times and sealed with the phrase '*Muhammad Rasul Allah*' (Muhammad is the Prophet of Allah). Then if he wishes, he appoints one of the hymn-singers to sing one of the odes or something other than it; then a section of the Quran; and when they finish they recite the declaration of faith once more and finish it with '*Muhammad Rasul Allah*'; then a recitation of the first *sura* of the Quran (the *fatiha*) a varying number of times, then the *hadrah* is completed with the *la ilaha illa Allah*.[1]

In order to compare the formal theory with the actual practice, I shall now describe in somewhat fuller detail a *dhikr* of the *Hamidiya Shadhiliya* typical of the many I attended. For the sake of clarity the different stages of the ritual have been numbered.

1. The first act of the *dhikr* is the quiet rhythmical recitation (seated) of the phrase *la ilaha illa Allah*, the witness that is the fundamental absolute of the Islam, of the oneness (*tawhid*) and unity of God. Together with the recognition that 'Muhammad is the Prophet of God', it constitutes the basic creed, acceptance of which marks one's identity as a Muslim. This first stage sets the boundary of the ritual, delimits a frame within the individual's experience, and directs the consciousness and an active intention away from the everyday world towards a transcendental end. The four-stressed phrase with its heavy dominant stress on the initial word, and the rocking movement of the brothers back and forth, in unison, begins the process of the regulation of the individual's physiological nature in the rhythm of body and breath.

[1] Saif, op. cit., pp. 84–5.

2. All then stand and chant the word 'Allah', beginning slowly with violent expulsions of breath on the last syllable and in increasing tempo to the quickening handclaps of the Sheikh who controls the speed throughout.

3. *Dhikr* of 'Allah' is begun again in a low tone with forward and backward movement of all the brothers in unison. At the same time the first hymn is sung by the *munshidin* in the centre of the ranks of members. The two facing rows of singers alternate the lines of poetry between them against the background of the chanted 'Allah'.

4. When the first hymn is over they begin a soft-breathed repetition of 'Allah' which becomes louder and more violent as the leader of the *munshidin* chants the *madad*. This word basically means 'assistance'. As part of the *dhikr* it is a supplication to the Saints for help. The singer calls on them in his plaintive solo chant: *Ya Sidna Hussein, Ya Sidi Salama*, and at particularly beloved names such as the last individual brothers call out also.[1]

5. This finally builds up into loud climactic shouts of 'Allah', to very fast time; shouts that blur into a torrent of indistinguishable sounds as the *madad* ends.

6. There follows the intoning of *Huwa*—'He', the supreme and only One (the word, in fact, is chanted as a long *Hu*, the last syllable, '*wa*', being unpronounced), accompanied by slow bowing movements from the waist. The second *nashid* is sung, counterpointed with the chanting of the brothers until the rhythm is changed to a swift, staccato explosive and heavy-breathed *Hu* repetition, and ever faster singing of the hymn to a loud climax of sound and violent movement.

7. The members then change to staccato rhythmical shouts of *Hayy* ('the All Living'), while the chief *munshid* again chants a *madad*. The tempo and movements increase to a climax.

8. *Hayy* is breathed softly while the third *nashid* is sung, again leading to a climax.

9. *Qaiyyum* ('the All Sustaining'), is chanted in quickening time.

10. The *Hadrah* proper ends with a recitation (seated) of part of the Quran and the singing of the creed, *la ilaha illa Allah*. Finally the opening chapter of the Quran is recited as a prayer for the community of Muslims and Saints, and the Sheikh leaves the

---

[1] The Hussein referred to is the Prophet's grandson whose shrine, supposed to contain the Saint's head, is in the mosque in Cairo named after him.

ranks of members. The ritual thus ends as it begins, with a reaffirma-
tion of the group's participation in the universal community of
Muslims.

The dominant symbol of the ritual is manifestly the Word, God's
own name for Himself, *Allah*; the dominant purpose the 'satura-
tion' of the self in the Name of the All Powerful Being who sent
down His revelation (*tanzil*) to the Prophet Muhammad. The
recitation is therefore God-given and God-ordained and to follow
the injunction *Wa' idhkuru Allaha dhikran kathiran la'allakum
tuflihun* (so remember Allah often that ye may prosper) is to obey
the direct Word of God. The Word being inherently sacred it
imparts sanctity to the ritual, rather than being sanctified by it.
There is thus a double and highly concentrated affective charge.
The 'condensation of energy' in Sapir's phrase,[1] the power of the
Word in the rhythmic proclamation of the transcendence of Allah,
is a key to the extraordinary emotional effervescence of the *dhikr*.

All the Names used come from the 'Throne Verse' (Quran,
Sura of the Cow, v. 256); a verse which is perhaps the most well
known among Muslims and according to tradition the most excellent in the Quran:

Allah, there is no God but He, the Living, the All Sustaining; slumber
affects Him not, nor sleep; to Him belongs whatever is in the Heavens
and whatever is in the Earth; who is there that will intercede before Him
except by permission? He knoweth what is before them and what is
behind them, and they comprehend not anything of His knowledge but
what He willeth; His Throne extendeth over the Heavens and the Earth;
to guard them wearieth Him not; He is the Exalted, the Mighty.[2]

The important characteristic of the Names of God used, *Hayy*
('the living'), *Huwa* ('He'), and *Qaiyyum* ('the Eternal', or 'All
Sustaining'), is that they are those Names which focus on the
transcendence and power of Allah. Put another way, they are
the most 'essential' of the Names. No plea is addressed to the
Almighty; there is no supplication, no imploring of His grace.
Indeed, this is explicitly rejected as being an inferior form of the
dhikr. It is thought that the greatest *dhikr* is of those Names which
are not connected with questions or requests.[3] For example, if one

---

[1] Sapir, E., 'Symbolism', *Encyclopedia of the Social Sciences*, old edn., vol.
14, p. 493.
[2] Bell, R., *The Quran Translated*, vol. 1, Edinburgh: 1937, pp. 36–7.
[3] Saif, op. cit., p. 102.

were to say *Ya Rahman* ('O Merciful One'), it would mean 'be merciful'; divine aid in human affairs would be sought, and this is not the proper purpose of the *dhikr*; the concentration is on the Absoluteness of God, on His Transcendent, Eternal Being, *not* His attributes such as those of Mercy and Compassion. No action by God is requested, or expected in, the *dhikr*. No material blessings will follow. From this point of view the *dhikr* is non-instrumental in character.

There is, however, another and highly important aspect of the *dhikr* of the *Hamidiya Shadhiliya* at which the rite takes on a dual nature. It will be recalled from the brief description of the different stages of the ceremony (pp. 165–6 above) that at two points, the third repetition of 'Allah' (stage 4) and the shouts of *Hayy* (stage 7) *madad* is chanted by the chief hymn-singer. He pleads for 'succour' and 'assistance', invoking the names of different well-known or much-beloved Saints. In the case of the *Hamidiya Shadhiliya*, the name of Sheikh Salama—*Ya Sidi Salama*—is the climax of this section. Worshippers call out with intense emotion *Ya Sidi, Ya Sidi Salama, madad*. However, while this prayer for help is being made, the *dhikr* of 'Allah' and *Hayy* is continued by the mass of the members. The prayer to the Saints is counterpointed with the reiteration of the All-Livingness and Supreme Oneness of Allah, and both are combined in the unity of the ritual. The *madad* is made within the over-all framework of the repetition of the name of God, and subordinated to it. The Saints take their place, as it were, but are not allowed to overshadow the Transcendent Being, nor is this aspect of the ritual dominant. The request for help does not form in any way the climax of the *dhikr* nor is it the *raison d'être* of the occasion. The 'Friends of God' are supplicated while the acknowledgement of the All Powerfulness and Absoluteness of God is made.[1]

The ritual then has a primary and a secondary direction during the *madad*. The primary is entirely other-worldly, having no reference to the social or personal condition of the worshippers here on earth, but being concerned only with the *dhikr* of the names of Allah. The secondary direction, on the other hand, is in

---

[1] In this way the Order manages to combine the two elements of appeal to the Saints and orthodoxy without incurring the criticism of the doctors of religion that it is pandering to the base superstitious beliefs of the masses or infringing on the cardinal point of the Oneness of Allah.

a generalized and non-specific form to this world and the mediating
powers of the Saints operating in it (one of whom in this case is
the founder of the Order, whose death was recent enough for him
to have been personally known to many of the senior and older
members of the Order). The ritual balances and unifies within itself
the polar tensions of these two elements.

As observed among the *Hamidiya Shadhiliya* the *dhikr* is marked
by a series of climaxes rather than by any one particular moment
which might be described as the central vital instant or section of
the entire ritual. The recitation of each Name is equally important,
and it follows therefore that there is a series of climactic moments
rather than a gradual building up to one. These climaxes are at
once physical, expressed in the increasing violence of the bodily
movements and the vocal crescendo; and emotional, intensified by
the other elements such as the hymns, and the changing rhythms.

The function and importance of this psycho-physiological stimulation and emotional effervescence is realized by the group, and
is explicitly stated by Saif in his biography of Salama. Speaking of
melody and harmony, he says that they show the deepest thoughts
of the soul and are therefore 'More eloquent than speech, faster to
the heart and more effective to the mind and the community of the
hearts'. He goes on 'It appears that articulated speech is in three
stages: the least is prose, the medial, poetry, and the highest singing
or melody' (p. 87). If the words are sung in a good chant, then
the meaning begins to move and come alive. The function, he
continues, is to sharpen the responses, to fire with enthusiasm those
making the *dhikr*, to wake their minds to the meanings made clear
by the music, and to be a veil between the one making the *dhikr* and
whatever might divert him from it (p. 88). The speed of the chanting and the crescendo is controlled by the Sheikh, who wakens
the hearts of the brothers, inflames their feelings, and stirs their
innermost secret parts (p. 88).

Among the *Hamidiya Shadhiliya* the strong inherent possibility
of hysterical behaviour is limited by the careful control exercised
by the Sheikh in the duration of the climactic moments. Care is
taken to avoid outbreaks of group or individual frenzy, which could
easily occur in the heightened tension of the different sections of
the *dhikr*, where a torrent of rhythmical sound and increasingly
violent movement occur. Emotion must be stimulated, and is a
vital adjunct of the ritual, but must not be allowed to spill over

into totally unregulated ecstatic behaviour. One of the main functions of the *nuqaba'* is to restrain any one of the worshippers who
loses, or appears about to lose, his self-control. This they usually
do simply by a gentle pressure on the arm, forcing the individual
to cease performing the particular section of the *dhikr* for long
enough for him to quieten. They thus act to inhibit or balance the
feeling of freedom, luxury, and expansiveness which is created by
the rhythmic and poetic qualities of the hymns and the chanting.
Their function is to regulate rather than to exhort, and to prevent
the group expression from becoming completely atomized in un-
predictable individual behaviour. They are agents of control, not
stimulators of excitement. Part of their role is to ensure that
permitted emotional expression does not become unqualified
licence, a problem which faces all religious groups who utilize a
high degree of physically expressed emotion.

What constitutes the approved patterns of behaviour in the
dhikr of course varies from Order to Order, and is one of the most
obvious marks of differentiation between them.

A brief description of a *dhikr* of the *Ahmediya Idrisiya* of Aswan
will serve to point a contrast with the *Hamidiya Shadhiliya*. The
former are a small Order founded by a local holy figure. The
zawiya is at the back of Aswan city proper on the edge of the worst
slum area. On the night that I attended, eighteen men, ranging in
age from seventeen to seventy, were present. They appeared no
richer than the decaying mud houses around us, and the Sheikh,
a tall bearded figure in dilapidated *gallabiya* and head scarf, said
that they were all without jobs. My guess would be that they were
also minimally if at all literate. We crowded into the tiny room
under its single unshaded light bulb and the men formed two lines
facing inward with the Sheikh in the middle of one of the lines. As
the *dhikr* quickly built up to deafening shouts, movements became
violent, neck sinews strained, eyes clenched shut, bodies thrust
back and forward in intoxication, sweat streamed from faces expressing a kind of ecstatic exhaustion.[1] One man drifted from his
line hopping dazedly in circles, now on one foot now the other,
now clockwise, now anti-clockwise, arms dangling limp, silently
turning. A rending scream of 'Allah!' rose out of the waves of

[1] I should mention that at the end of the *dhikr* none of the participants evinced
any sign of tiredness whatever either in breathing or manner, though the expenditure of energy to the eye of the exhausted observer appeared enormous.

sound as another of the brothers flung himself outstretched, face first into the wall. A moment, then again the howl of 'Allah!' and his body catapulted itself across the room smashing into the other wall, knocking his gently spinning friend in wild circles but with no sign of awareness of the impact by either. His shrieks and rushes went on unchecked while pandemonium broke out as men jumped up and down, bowed almost to the earth, and then threw their bodies back as though at the ceiling, shouting and moaning. For an hour and a half the tide of sound ebbed and flowed. Then, quite suddenly, it ceased.

This kind of ritualized emotionalism is by no means uncommon; it can be seen at any of the *mulid* celebrations. Observation suggests that at the most deprived levels of Egyptian society, as here in Aswan with a *lumpenproletariat* on the poverty-striken fringe of a materially otherwise expanding urban environment, this form of the *dhikr* would probably be typical. This particular group is at the lowest social level by any scale of economic, educational, and material criteria and is therefore denied most of the other avenues of expression and gratification open to those above them. Comparative evidence on religious groups would seem to indicate that the stimulation of emotionalist states characterizes those strata which are economically, politically, and perhaps even culturally marginal within the wider social system. The proportion this lower level actually constitutes of a population will not affect their position as the socially marginal, in the sense of being subject to, or rather the object of, severe restrictions on their access to the political and economic 'means of production'. Their situation is at once the most structured, or determined, in respect of the social system, and in existential terms the least structured and amenable to comprehension or control. Dominated by a forthcoming rather than a future, uncertain even of subsistence and liable to the blind workings of what is resignedly referred to all-embracingly as the *dunya* (the world), these men turn to the *dhikr* as to any narcotic.

The taking of narcotics, indeed, as is true of the *dhikr*, is usually with friends participating in a group (whether formally or informally constituted), a *collective* and not merely an individual action. At this level the main distinction between the two activities lies in that, when taking drugs, the actor induces a pleasurable physio-psychological state in relative passivity and through the medium of a specific substance; whereas in the *dhikr* he can 'work out' tensions, release emotions, and induce satisfaction by the explosive and violent movements of his own body. In either case he does so in the close and intimate context of the group.

At the other end of the scale are those Orders whose ritual is distinguished by a high degree of control of individual and collective emotional expression. Such a group is the *Demerdashiya Khalwatiya*, the formal nature of whose *dhikr* has already been touched on above. This Order is of the quietist type laying stress on individual asceticism and on the hierarchical nature of the organization, following the principles of religious understanding and learning. As has been previously pointed out, the *nuqaba'* play an exemplary and leadership role during the *dhikr*, in contrast to the far smaller degree of emphasis accorded them in the *Hamidiya Shadhiliya* and *a fortiori*, in the highly emotionalist groups where formal organization and the role of officials are at a minimum. Where the *Ahmediya Idrisiya* stress equality to the point that the Sheikh takes part as an ordinary worshipper, the *Demerdashiya* stress rank and status. Their ritual is (correspondingly) restrained in character. There are no hymns and no use of music to stimulate emotion. By far the greater portion of the ceremony is given over to group recitation of sections of the Quran and *dhikr* of *Allah* and *la ilaha illa Allah* performed with restrained rhythmic movements back and forth. There is no *madad*; no appeal to the saints. At no juncture are there any group crescendos of sound or movement. Rather emotion is at a constant level, and there are no climactic moments.

The only exception to this, and it is an important one, is the *halaqa*, in which the Sheikh joins a circle of the worshippers (some of whom are *nuqaba'* and some *muridin*) in the area just before the *sigada*. They then move in an anti-clockwise direction in time to his call of *Hu* (*Huwa*—He) at a rising crescendo echoed by those in the circle and to an increased tempo. The stress is otherwise entirely on the Word without additional stimuli of music, counterpointed rhythms, or the encouragement of violent motion. Excitement (*ihtizaz*) is at a minimum. The *dhikr* is addressed to absorption in the Names of God used, and to the Quranic Revelation. Opportunity for the physical expression of emotion is thus severely limited. The *nuqaba'* do not act as agents of control, since the nature of the ritual and the institutional norms of behaviour for it eliminate this necessity.

It is not the case, however, that this Order is composed only of those who possess a high degree of education or religious learning, or who are on the higher levels of economic and occupational status. While it is true that the *Khalwatiya* in general is the most 'intellectualist' of the Orders, this does not in any way preclude the membership of *muridin* drawn from the lowest status groups of the society. Whereas it is almost impossible to find men *above* these lowest levels participating in *dhikr* where extremes of ecstatic behaviour are tolerated, not to say actively encouraged, it is not at all rare to find the reverse. So that although the frenzy of the *Ahmediya* is the exclusive domain of the deprived, the restraint of the *Khalwatiya dhikr* can accommodate all levels. It is not the *degree* or *intensity* of emotion in the ritual which is the key factor here, for the recitation of the Quran itself in this setting is an intensely emotional experience, but rather the institutionalized manner of its expression.

In this range of behaviour the *dhikr* of the *Hamidiya Shadhiliya* may be roughly described as being the medial point, as indeed it may be in terms also of structure and belief—medial in the use of emotional stimuli, modes of permitted expression, and the degree of control exacted. While, as we have seen, there is the use of music and rhythmic movement, a plea to the Saints in the *madad* and a series of climaxes, all of which have no part in the ritual of the *Demerdashiya*, there is also a counterbalancing emphasis on organization and control of behaviour far beyond that exercised by the *Ahmediya* and similar groups.

The Sheikh, by clapping his hands in increasing tempo, builds up each of the series of climaxes to a high pitch, but stops abruptly before the danger of mass frenzy can be realized. At no time have I ever seen more than one or two individuals (the usual group at the major *dhikrs* of the *Hamidiya Shadhiliya* is about 700 to 1,000 strong) who have lost control of their actions. On the occasions that this occurs, when a man continues shouting wildly *Hayy! Hayy! Hayy!*, jumping violently up and down or making rapid movements after the Sheikh has stopped clapping, the *nuqaba'* swiftly restrain him. Where the condition is such that he has to be removed from the lines of worshippers, it is a matter for disapproval, manifested either in direct admonition, or in general expression of irritation and criticism. The member has violated the norms of behaviour in the *dhikr*, norms which carry the authority of the Sheikh who established them when he laid down the form and rules of the ritual. Such behaviour is therefore a kind of disobedience.[1]

At the same time, by the nature of the *dhikr*, this type of anarchic, individual, and *ipso facto* 'anti-group' action is always potentially present: the ritual unity of the group is always threatened. It is safeguarded by the Sheikh, the officials, and the norms of the Order which are in varying degrees internalized, but it is perpetually at risk. Whereas the *Ahmediya Idrisiya* approve of and encourage these outbursts, and the character of the *dhikr* of the *Demerdashiya* precludes them almost completely, the *Hamidiya Shadhiliya* must attempt to balance between the two. Their ritual therefore contains a high degree of internal polar tension: between freedom and control, between unrestrained emotional ecstasy and formal regulation, between the individual and the group experience which must be one, though the first always threatens the second. In a sense this tension reflects a wider motif in *tasawwuf* as a whole. For though Sufism places strong emphasis on the link of the individual with God (*al sila bain al muhibb wa 'l mahbub*—the link between the lover and the Loved), in the Orders, by definition, the individual is part of a communality that remains such by the maintenance of a structure that must in part control and limit. The nature of the expression of individual experience is determined by the group. The link is to the group as well as to God. It is this tension which is *par excellence* concentrated and transcended in the rite.

The group framework for the individual experience is associated with the emphasis on harmony and order which 'contains' the polar tensions; on communal, patterned, and equal participation in the *dhikr*. This emphasis is also, at a higher level of abstraction, expressive of the quality of the ideal mutual relations among the group as a whole, which are theoretically governed by precisely these principles. All movements in the different stages of the *dhikr*

---

[1] 'Il est bien connu que Djunaid avait un disciple qui était très excité dans le sama' au point qu'il en venait à troubler les autres derviches. Ils se plaignirent auprès du chaikh. Il lui dit: "Désormais, si tu t'excites dans le sama' je ne veux plus te parler." Abu Muhammad Djurairi dit: "Lors d'un sama', je l'observai: les lèvres serrées, il se taisait tandis que des gouttes de sueur sortaient de tous les pores de son corps, jusqu'à ce qu'il perdît connaissance, et restât sans connaissance pendant une journée.... On raconte qu'un novice poussa un cri dans le sama'. Son maître lui dit: 'Tais-toi.' Il posa sa tête sur ses genoux. On le regarda: il était mort."' Molé, op. cit., p. 187.

should be made in unison by the worshippers. They should move in the same rhythm following identically the crescendos built up by the hand-clapping of the Sheikh. They should move in the same appropriate manner back and forward, or side to side, with the whole body or just the head as the case may be. In chanting, not only should all be in time and at the proper level of sound, but the regulation of the breathing technique used for each section should be the same. The *nuqaba'* walk round the ranks correcting those who are out of rhythm and indicating by movements of the hand the right tempo for those who cannot hear the clapping of the Sheikh or are unable to follow it. As section of the *dhikr* succeeds section, all the actions of the members should be in consort so that there is unity of performance in every respect.

It will be noted further, from a glance at the spatial arrangement of the *dhikr* (Diagram 1 of the *Hamidiya Shadhiliya* and Diagram 2 of the *Demerdashiya Khalwatiya*), that it reflects the same concern with symmetry. The lines are all equal and parallel within the square that the whole forms. When members of the *Hamidiya Shadhiliya* join the *hadrah* after it has commenced, they are placed by the *nuqaba'* so that the lines remain the same length. The *muridin* are well aware that the performance does not always, or even often, come close to this ideal; the lines are unequal, movements are not made in precisely common time, the singing of the *munshidin* is not as firm as perhaps it might be. But they strive to realize the symmetrical arrangement of the paradigm just as they strive for the absolute harmony of sound, breath, and movement.

The Social Frame

The ritual itself is part of a sequence of events; it has, to put it simply, a before and after that are for most members integral to the occasion. The brothers make the evening prayer together before the *dhikr*, or sit in the mosque in small groups greeting friends, discussing general matters, or issues more specifically affecting the Order. After the *dhikr* many of them go into the various coffee houses for an hour or two, and on such occasions conversation is frequently about the Order, the Sheikh, any coming religious celebrations, and other members. Acquaintances are renewed or made, new members introduced; personal matters are discussed, as are events in contemporary Egypt. Such informal gatherings both bring about and reinforce a consensus of opinion over a broad range of issues and the sense of communality of the group. They ensure that many members are personally acquainted with one another. Furthermore, they are a most important 'indirect' sanction for behaviour in the Order. Any problems the individual has are likely to become known (their solution is one of the major functions of the Sheikh and the heads of the local *zawiyas*), but so will any personal lapses from what is regarded as proper behaviour, whether in some matter directly concerning the Order, or relating more immediately to the member's family circumstances, economic position, or personal habits. This interest in the activities and behaviour of the member on the part of the other members is legitimized by common brotherhood in the Order. Sympathetic advice in adversity has, as its other face, direct or indirect criticism of, or gossip about, the person's activities in any sphere. It is as a result of the *hadrahs*, whether the general *hadrahs* held in the mosques, or the smaller ones in the different *zawiyas* of the Order, that the members are brought together socially, and it is these ritual gatherings that are so important in the social cohesion of the group.

The regularity and frequency of the *hadrahs* in an Order as dynamic as the *Hamidiya Shadhiliya* ensures that the members are involved in an intense round of group activity. Participation, at any rate in that Order, is to a great extent compulsory, though perhaps 'preferred' would be a better way of expressing the pressure that is put on members to attend. Indeed, it is not going too far to take participation in the ritual as the crucial index of membership. Non-attendance is questioned by friends and ultimately by the Sheikh himself. If so-and-so has not been present, then the fact is remarked on by his closer friends and acquaintances in the Order, and any long period of absence from the *hadrah* without good reason would be taken as equivalent to lapsed membership.

The main general *hadrahs* of the *Hamidiya Shadhiliya* are held twice a week in Cairo, and there are additional regular meetings in the different *zawiyas* in the capital and throughout the country. Also important from the point of view of maintaining the network of primary relations, there is the *maglis* of the Sheikh and the *khalifas*, in which religious topics are discussed and the Sheikh's role as teacher is paramount. Furthermore, as already mentioned, 'visiting' is officially encouraged, and groups are always making journeys to hold a *dhikr* with brothers in near-by villages and towns. Afterwards they will gather in the house of one of the members for tea and refreshments and sing hymns, talk about the Order and its founder, and generally chat among themselves. In this way *zawiyas* establish relations one with another and set up a pattern of mutual hospitality that is of the greatest significance for the functioning of the Order.

The *dhikr* being thus the major activity of the Order, its regularity and the numbers attending are two of the complex of indices by which we can attempt to assess the strength of the internal dynamic of the *tariqa*. Such assessments require considerable caution, however, since Orders only function in the main as loosely organized networks of discrete local centres. The amount of social and ritual interaction of the members, the degree of cohesiveness and group solidarity, may therefore be very different from one area, one social environment, to another within the same Order. Consideration of such differences involves the taking into account of many factors: the nature of the community and the history of the group in that community; the relation of the Order to the social structure of the community; the precise nature of the link between the *zawiya* and the Sheikh who is the head of the entire Order and the local prestige and reputation of the Sheikh; the personality of the local head or *khalifa* of the Order and his structural position in the community; and the functions of the group at the local level.

I was once informed, for example, by two old Sheikhs of the *Mirghaniya* in Aswan that: 'Once there used to be seventeen *hadrahs* in one street and now you do not find one *hadrah* in seventeen streets.' The truth of their lament was confirmed by investigation and further questioning of other informants from which it appeared that activity was limited to *dhikrs* at times of the great religious feasts and weddings. Other groups of *Mirghaniya* in Cairo and Alexandria, however, were much more active, among other reasons because they served as adaptive institutions for members in the alien urban environment. As far as my information goes, the *Hamidiya Shadhiliya* is at present the only Order which is centrally controlled to a sufficient degree to be regarded as acting as one cohesive organization, rather than as the sort of attenuated network I have outlined above.

Criticism of the Dhikr *and the Challenge to the Orders*

Members of the Orders are aware of the many Quranic verses which provide a justification for the *dhikr*, and can furnish explanations of the ritual that are fully in accordance with orthodox thought and structured after the teachings of Sunni Islam. They offer, in other words, a description of what Lévi-Strauss refers to as the 'conscious model', which in the case of Islam is a complex, ordered system of belief based on the Divine Revelation of the Quran, the Sunna, and the consensus of the community. Despite these justifications, however, it is the practice of the *dhikr*, or more accurately, the way in which the *dhikr* is practised (the two have been popularly identified), which has been and is particularly the subject of attack by the scholar-jurists, members of other religious organizations such as the *Ansar as-Sunna* and the Muslim Brothers, and many who do not belong to the Orders. (It is not uncommon to see the movements and chanting of the *dhikr* of certain groups imitated and ridiculed by those watching.)

The members are accused of using a technique designed to free the individual from the sensual self to indulge the senses; of degrading the *dhikr* to the point where it becomes little more than an excuse for uninhibited emotionalism at the lowest level; of pandering to the basest instincts of the uneducated. The *Sheikh al Masha'ikh*, Head of all the *Tariqas* in Egypt, had particularly to defend the Orders against these charges, though adding at the same time that it was his aim to 'take the *dhikr* off the streets'.[1] The view of many outside the Orders is well shown by the following passage from a high-circulation illustrated magazine, *Al Musawwar*: 'But . . . does anything now remain of *tasawwuf* . . . other than the processions, the *dhikr* circles, the embroidered clothes, the flags and the coloured banners and scores of Orders and groups! The confused mumblings and the hysterical movements . . .'[2]

This wide-ranging attack aroused the anger of those members of the Orders who discussed it with me afterwards. They felt that they had been held up to ridicule and slandered by those who understood nothing of either Sufism or its followers. This anger reflected a considerable concern on their part, and there was also a distinct defensiveness in their reaction. It was realized that the

---

[1] *Al Musawwar*, 7 May 1965, p. 22.
[2] Ibid., p. 21.

article in fact exemplified a widespread conception of the character
of the *turuq* on the part of a broad spectrum of Egyptian society.
This anxiety centres particularly upon the *dhikr*. The members of
every Order whose *hadrahs* I have attended constantly pointed out
how superior their *dhikr* is to that of other groups. The latter are
represented as somehow degraded, or worthy but misguided, or
positively unorthodox, *whether in fact they are or not*. Allegations
are made about the nature of the ritual of such-and-such an Order:
that their movements are too wild and excessive, that they have
musical instruments and drums which are not permissible, that
they cannot bear comparison with the ritual activities of *our* group
which are closest to the ideal. Such notions are found even in those
groups which permit the greatest degree of uninhibited behaviour.
The *Ahmediya Idrisiya* Sheikh of Aswan, for example, compared
the formal simplicity of their *hadrah* with what he described as the
over-elaboration of the other Orders. Exaggerated or only partially
accurate ideas about behaviour at the different *dhikr* are therefore current among the Orders, as well as among non-members.
Misconceptions of the actions of the groups and distorted versions
of them based on incomplete knowledge, common perhaps in all
spheres of social action and often most strikingly in religion, are
general between Order and Order.

The fact that the *dhikr* is thus a focal point of criticism from
those who are opposed to the Sufi Orders for whatever reasons,
whether theological, or social and political, or indeed both, has led
to an increasing control over members' behaviour by some of the
Sheikhs, with the encouragement of the central organizations of the
Mashaikha of the *Turuq Sufiya*. The ritual must be defended, but
this cannot be done merely by the recitation of the appropriate
passage of Revelation. For the guardian of orthodoxy, the scholar-
jurist, can indicate the actual conduct of many who claim to be
following Quranic injunction, but take the Word of Allah as justification for unrestrained emotional transports that have no genuine
basis in religion. The hostility or contempt of outsiders can only be
counteracted by a higher degree of internal control of the *hadrahs*,
before such control is put in the hands of some external authority.
Care was taken by Salama in his Laws to ensure that the conduct
of the members should be beyond reproach.

Law 37. It is not permitted to use the tambourine, or the cymbals, or
stringed instruments or such like, or the drum or the one-headed hand

drum; nor may the pipes or the flute be used either in the *hadrah* or
in the *Mawkib* procession.

Law 41. It is forbidden to eat insects and cactus and glass and to strike
with the sword and pins [this refers to the practice of sticking long pins
through the cheeks or into other parts of the body. M. G.] and fire-
eating and what is like that; . . .[1]

This emphasis on the proper arrangement and manner of performance of the *dhikr* has been the subject of the scrupulous
attention of the Saint's successor. To the degree, in fact, that
reports are regularly submitted to the central office of the *tariqa* on
the *dhikrs* of all the different *zawiyas* set up throughout Egypt by
the Order. Those in Cairo, the major centre, are given a weekly
'inspection' by a special series of committees set up by Sheikh
Ibrahim for this purpose and composed of members of the hierarchy, whether *khulafa'* or *nuqaba'*. *Zawiyas* outside the capital
are visited less regularly, usually once a month, by similar delega-
tions, and there are, in addition, the irregular visits of different
officials who are in this or that area for whatever purpose. Each
committee takes with it a form, consisting of questions about the
zawiya and its activities, which must be completed and returned
to the *Mashaikhat as-Sigada* (central office of the Order). I give
the first seven items below (there are a total of sixteen, but only
the first seven refer directly to the *dhikr*):

1. The proper arrangement (*nizam*) of the *hadrah*.
2. The number of those in the *hadrah*.
3. The propriety (*adab*) of those in the *hadrah*.
4. The attention paid by the *zawiya* to the general *hadrahs* [i.e. those
held each week in mosques, rather than more informally in the *zawiya*
itself].
5. The remarks of the leader of the *hadrah* to the brothers.
6. The general conduct and behaviour of the leader in the *hadrahs*.[2]
7. The absolute correctness of the hymns [literally, 'poems' or 'odes'
—Arabic '*qasida*'].

The unusual degree of care taken over the arrangement of the
hadrahs ensures a general unity of performance in all the *zawiyas*,
however remote from Cairo they may be. The significance of these
regulations for the organization and control of the Order is gone

---

[1] This refers to practices at one time common, particularly in the *Rifa'i* Order.
[2] This subject is of particular concern to the Central Office.

into elsewhere. What we must remark here is that no other Order has paid such attention to the form of the ritual. Indeed, the *Hamidiya Shadhiliya* are known among the other Orders for the *nizam* (arrangement) of their *dhikr*, which is the subject of favourable comment, if not of direct emulation (there are some indications that officials of the old-established *Rifaʿiya* Order, which appears to have decreased considerably in recent years, are thinking about following the general pattern laid down by the Sheikhs Salama and Ibrahim, in an effort to revive their waning *tariqa*).

Perhaps the major result of this scrupulousness is what I can only describe loosely as the 'aesthetic tone' of the *dhikr* of the *Hamidiya Shadhiliya*, which is such as to give it a very broadly based appeal to Muslims of a wide range of occupational and educational status. The singing of the *munshidin* is strictly ordered. Though there are moments of an intense emotional 'charge' these climaxes are always controlled; no individual frenzy is tolerated, and anyone who is overcome, and does go into a kind of trance state, is removed from the lines and usually remonstrated with by the *nuqaba'*. A fine balance is held between the polarities of Freedom and Control so that the *dhikr* is neither over-reserved nor over-permissive. While the Saints are called upon for help, it is in the context always of the remembrance of the Name of God. Doctrinal and behavioural orthodoxy therefore enable the educated to take part without embarrassment in a ritual that at the same time gives a high degree of satisfaction to the illiterate.

Ritual and Experience

This discussion of the *dhikr* prompts reflection on the meaning and nature of the ritual within the framework of those beliefs and practices that are constituted as 'Islam' and for the communities of participants. It also directs us towards the problems of analysis posed by such a form of religious ritual. Anthropologists have concentrated their studies by and large on small-scale, technologically simple societies. Such societies are characterized by religious and cult systems peculiar to the given linguistic and/or ethnic grouping, and, while there is often a diffusion of symbols and beliefs across boundaries, the religious complex in its cognitive, ritual, and mythical dimensions is regarded by both observer and adherent as specific to that society. One speaks of Nupe religion, the religion of the Dinka, Nuer religion, Ndembu ritual, and so forth. Within these cultures moreover two types of ritual have been most the subject of analytical consideration: the *rites de passage*, classically defined by Arnold van Gennep, and *ceremonials*. The former category centres on changes in social positions and 'states', taking this last term in Turner's sense as referring to 'any type of stable or recurrent condition that is culturally recognised',[1] and the latter on those rituals whose primary intention is the confirmation in an office or status, whether jural, political, or religious. It appears to me that the *dhikr* cannot be comprehended under either of these categories and that we must rather consider it as part of a different class of ritual performances which are *sui generis*, and which I propose to call *liturgical* rituals.

Let us approach the question initially by way of negative definition. The *dhikr* is clearly not a ceremony of status confirmation, though ritual statuses are of course involved. Nor is it a rite of transition from one social state to another. What is especially important here is that whereas in rites of passage time and linear sequence are of the essence, and the 'from–to' movement is crucial, in liturgy time is non-linear and transformed into 'virtual time'. Whereas rituals of passage and ceremonial are deeply embedded in a matrix of social relations (of age sets, kin networks, and hunting groups, for example) and directed to social purposes of purification, initiation, social transition, or legitimation, liturgy is largely independent of socially defined processes of significance; it is least tied to a specific history and social life.

As is true of the two other categories, liturgy is communal or collective and taken as prescribed by an authoritative non-human power given to men through myth, traditions, or the annunciation of a revelation—'do this in remembrance of me', 'therefore remember God often that ye may prosper'. But participation in a ritual such as the *dhikr* further takes place on the basis of the individual's acceptance of a religious call that ideally transcends ascriptive statuses of ethnic or language groupings. It is thus characteristic of 'universal' religions such as Islam which encompass within an order of belief and religious institutions a wide variety of societies and modes of life. In these religions, in addition to the rites of

---

[1] Turner, V. W., 'Betwixt and Between: The Liminal Period', in *The Forest of Symbols: Aspects of Ndembu Ritual*, Ithaca: Cornell University Press (paperback edition), 1970, p. 94.

transition at birth, marriage, and death, there is a nucleus of imperative symbolic action, a ritual statement of what constitutes the primal identity of the congregations as, in this case, Muslims. Liturgy is performed by men in what are viewed as their primordial, 'total' identities set off from the identities and contingent situations of the everyday social world. These identities are part of what is taken to be the 'ground', or ultimate context of significance for the participants' *being* rather than their *behaviour*. The ritual unfolds inside a framework of an 'eternal', transcendental order at the greatest degree of independence from the on-going individual biographies of the actors, yet penetrating those biographies in repeated acts of re-creation.[1] This penetration inevitably bears on men's definition of, and action toward, those others who share in the ritual and those who do not, in given contexts where this 'total' identity is challenged or relevant; but this does not diminish the independent, non-contingent nature of liturgy. At the same time of course this independence is in the last resort relative. The form of a liturgy, and the meaning with which it is invested, will be of necessity subject to change, as the form and meaning of religion change within societies. The transfer of the altar from the east end of the church to the centre, the use of the vernacular instead of the esoteric language, and the flexibility of form of the *dhikr* demonstrate the variations that may be played on the liturgical theme. And the more radically religion is separated out from other spheres in life and its area of relevance diminished, as it is in advanced industrial society, the more liable liturgy will also be to change in meaning and structure.

The form of ritual in Islam which is quintessentially liturgical is the public prayer that takes place on Fridays and it is illuminating to contrast it with the *dhikr*. Both are part of the vocabulary of signs and modes through and by means of which the human and the divine are held to be in communication, and both in that aspect belong in the universe of the Revelation (*Quran*), prophetic inspiration (*wahy*), the truthful vision (*ru'ya*), sainthood (*wilaya*), *karama*, *baraka*, and the private prayer (the *du'a* where the verbal form is unprescribed, to be distinguished from the *salat* in which

---

[1] These identities are characterized by Alfred Schutz as 'motivational' as opposed to 'behavioural' types. See his paper 'Common Sense and Scientific Interpretation of Human Action', *Philosophy and Phenomenological Research*, vol. 14, no. 1, September 1953.

the language is formulaic and prescribed). The public prayer is fundamentally an acknowledgement, a restatement, and a communication: the first in the absolute submission, fear, and obedience, the '*remise totale*', as Fr. Louis Gardet has called it, dramatically symbolized in the prostration, head touching the earth; the second in as much as it renews the covenant of God with His community; the last in its 'direction' upward and outward to a power above and beyond. It crystallizes the individual's identity as '*abd*, servant and member of the Muslim *umma*.

When performing the *salat*, worshippers stand in parallel lines behind an Imam, who officially leads the prayers. But his office is one of very limited importance in Sunni Islam. In theory anyone may fulfil this function, though in fact it is usually carried out by the Sheikh in charge of the administration of the mosque. All face the *mihrab*, or niche, which indicates the direction (*qibla*) of the holy city of Mecca. At the termination of the prayer each man ritually greets his fellow to right and to left. It is impossible to imagine a simpler or more austere expression of worship and dependence, or a more complete symbolization of the irreducible core of Islam.

Contrast this with the spatial representation of the *dhikr*. There the brothers stand with hands linked in a *ramaz* (a sign) of fraternity and co-operation, facing in towards the Sheikh, not the *mihrab*. He is set apart as representing in his person through the chain of blessing (the *silsila* of *baraka*) the continuation of the Order through time; one to whom grace has passed, ultimately from God, through the Prophet, the founder, and the Sheikhs who followed him, and from whom it will pass to his successors. He contains the past, and is the promise of the future. He is the one to whom absolute obedience is sworn in the covenant (the '*ahd*) that each member must make on joining the Order. The *dhikr* thus presents, much more than the *salat*, a 'picture' of a communal group focusing on particular persons in line of succession from a certain holy figure. Relations between the participants are manifestly more specifically defined, and ties with the social world more particularistic. Furthermore, as the Orders lose their significance it becomes possible for men to see the *dhikr* as supererogatory rather than essential as the *turuq* themselves become so, as membership ceases to be taken for granted as part of the total identity of Muslims.

Yet it remains fundamentally liturgical in nature. Utterly

detached from the realm of the everyday and contingent, the *dhikr*
has no reference in its intention to the social world. In contrast
to the *salat* there is no prayer, no prostration, no gesture of
absolute submission or supplication. Rather it is directed inward,
not only in the obvious sense, to the person of the Sheikh, but
more profoundly to the state of being of the believer and the attainment of deep inner awareness of the link (the *sila*) between lover
and Beloved. *Salat* and *dhikr* might therefore be distinguished
respectively as liturgy of communication and liturgy of communion.

Interpretations in the exegetical literature of the *dhikr* are almost
as numerous as the Orders themselves. Its different forms yield
a multiplicity of meanings, many of which have their origins in
ancient themes of the representation in sacred dance of the movements of the cosmos and the oneness of the universe (a much
simplified version of which is the *halaqa* of the *Demerdashiya
Khalwatiya* referred to above).[1] What is important for our purposes
in these interpretations is not so much the schema advanced by the
Sufi masters as the way in which they highlight the transformation
of the performers into symbolic elements. In the example we have
considered there are no material symbolic objects, no special
vestments, no use of colour or images. It is the *muridin* who are
both ritual subjects or agents, and ritual objects. They become so
in the repetition of the most economical and condensed of symbols,
the word.[2] And it is not only the word *of* Divinity, but the *logos*, the
word that in a mysterious sense *is* Divinity. In this dimension it
can hardly properly be called a symbol at all since signifier and
what is signified are identified. But how is this identity experienced
and produced in the ritual for and by the participants?

Stravinsky has said that 'music is given to us with the sole
purpose of establishing an order in things, including, and particularly, the co-ordination between man and time'. This ordering
and co-ordination of men and time are central to the meaning of
the *dhikr*. The ritual pivots on the fusion in harmony of patterned
rhythms in sound and movement with the organic inner bodily

---

[1] The reader will find a guide to the extremely complex interpretations of
the *Mawlawiya* ritual (the celebrated 'dancing dervishes') in Molé, op. cit.,
pp. 246–8.

[2] S. J. Tambiah has provided a most interesting discussion of the significance
of the word as a source of power in 'The Magical Power of Words', *Man*, vol. 3,
no. 2, June 1968, pp. 175–208.

rhythms of the performers regulated through the prescribed forms of breathing control. The rhythm of ritual, like music, unfolds in a particular dimension of time, which, following Bergson, can be called the *durée*. 'In "pure duration" there is no "side-by-sideness", no mutual externality of parts, and no divisibility, but only a continuous flux, a stream of conscious states.'[1] It is the power of the ritual to bring about a total interpenetration of the symbolic and the organic in this pure duration which is so radically other than the chronological sequence of the everyday world.

As with a musical score, of course, the ritual can be 'read' both vertically and horizontally, and in inner and outer time. I have already described the *dhikr* as a set of succeeding stages that follow one another in outer time. But though convenient, if not unavoidable, this method of description, with its emphasis on a succession of parts is even more than usually obstructive for our understanding of the whole. For within the frame of ritual and symbolic performance culturally given and outer time are suspended, through the patterns of musical and rhythmical synchronization of the chanted word, breathing, and physical movement.[2]

Unlike the relation of an audience's participation to a composer's stream of consciousness, which is 'quasi-simultaneous', 'a derived form of the vivid present shared by the partners in a genuine face-to-face relation',[3] in the *dhikr* the participants are also the performers, re-creating the score and sharing the same symbolic actions, expressions, movements, words, space, and stream of time. Each individual is linked through the clasped hands with every other so that each experiences what might be termed a corporate, collective subjectivity. The 'transcendence' of the ritual is achieved on those occasions when all these dimensions merge into a state of consciousness which is felt as mysteriously yet completely 'coherent'.[4] It is this that the brothers attempt to express in their

[1] Alfred Schutz, 'The Constitution of Meaningful Lived Experience in the Constitutor's Own Stream of Consciousness', in *The Phenomenology of the Social World*, trans. by George Walsh and Frederick Lehnert, Evanston, Ill.: Northwestern University Press, 1967, p. 45.

[2] The physical movement is often violent and intense, leading to stress and hyperventilation.

[3] Alfred Schutz, 'Making Music Together', in *Collected Papers*, vol. 2, ed. and intro. by Arvid Brodersen, The Hague: Martinus Nijhoff, 1964, p. 171.

[4] Ritual shares with music also the mysterious ineffable quality which participants can never 'translate' into another medium without a sense of loss or distortion.

explanations of their innermost feelings during the *dhikr* (explanations which are structured in reflection by the terms of Sufi teaching). The lines were equal, they moved in unison, the singing was perfect, all these elements are part of an order in things that is 'lived-in' in pure duration and as a whole, in contrast to the noncoherent, partially ordered world of everyday life. When the most essential of the Names is chanted, *Hu* (He), indistinguishable from that other source and symbol of power and life which delivers it, the breath, men can experience for a rare moment the unity of the beyond and the within.

VII

CONCLUSION: THE ORDERS IN A CHANGING SOCIETY

SCHOLARS have described the position of the Orders in a traditional Egyptian society as one of paramount importance. According to Heyworth-Dunne, in the eighteenth and up to the early nineteenth century their influence was felt in almost every sphere of life.

> The relationship of eighteenth century *tasawwuf* to religion and to all classes of Muslim society cannot be underrated . . . Religious life was no longer governed by the simple tenets of Islam but rather by the various Sufi interpretations of religious law and texts . . . Ritual, prayer, mode of life and general behaviour were governed in the main by the rules of the Islamic faith but in detail by those of the *tariqa* . . .[1]

Gibb and Bowen also suggest that membership of the Orders was virtually synonymous with the profession of Islam.[2] They point to a symbiotic relation between the *turuq* and the *'ulema'*. In this view, the Orders preserved that perpetual spontaneous impulse, that concentration on the individual faith and practice, which breathes life into the necessary dogmatic framework of religion in its formal, institutional aspect. The brotherhoods served constantly to give life to the canon lawyers' interpretations and administration of the *Shari'a*, and to provide occasions for the expression of religious emotion, and for the affirmation of the personal link founded on love that joins the worshipper to God. As an integral part of Islam in Egypt the Saint complemented the legist.

This integration was bought at a price. Sufism had originally developed as part of a subtle, many-layered dialectic in Muslim history. In European religious history such a development of sectarian or *gemeinschaft* groups (such as the Friars) was closely

[1] Heyworth-Dunne, J., *Introduction to the History of Education in Modern Egypt*, p. 10.
[2] Gibb, H. A. R., and Bowen, H., *Islamic Society and the West*, vol. 1, Part II, p. 76.

associated with conditions of social conflict and protest, grounded in some major change in social life, and expressed in opposition to the Church, its agents, and its doctrines; the sects emerged as independent institutions, and if we follow the classical argument of Troeltsch, the dynamic of the dialectic was maintained and renewed in the beginnings of new challenges to what had become in their turn established groups. In North African Muslim societies the dialectical pulse kept beating in areas such as Morocco, where a city-based government could exercise only precarious and limited functions in a basically tribal and transhumant setting, and warrior and saint were constantly in tension. But Egypt has always been the most fundamentally homogeneous society of the Muslim world, dependent on the natural rhythms of the Nile and regulated by the dominance of strong, military-bureaucratic administrations. Everything has worked towards integration and centralized rule through government by corvée, conscription, taxation, and control of land and irrigation, made possible by the communications which the river valley offered.

The religion of the masses was thus absorbed into the form of the *tariqa* within which the unpredictability of holiness and the unstable manifestations of saintliness could be largely contained and rendered more tractable. Instead of new forms emerging, religious energy was harnessed and turned inward, away from true reformulation or rearticulation. The *'ulema'* thus dominated the relationship more than they knew, by the mere fact that the *turuq* were absorbed as the second term in this symbiotic system. The Sufi Orders thus became a profoundly conservative social and ideological force.

They wielded enormous influence. In education until the early nineteenth century they appear to have been in many ways the most significant medium of instruction in the doctrines and values of Islamic society, of an even wider significance indeed than the mosques, *madrasahs*, and *kuttabs*, where formal teaching was carried on.[1] The greater part of the literature popular among the learned was Sufi tracts in manuscript form.[2] The writings of the guilds also bore the stamp of *tasawwuf*.[3] In their wide-ranging links with these associations, to which the whole gainfully employed

---

[1] On the nature of traditional education in Egypt see Heyworth-Dunne, op. cit., *passim*.

[2] Ibid., pp. 10–11.   [3] Baer, G., *Egyptian Guilds in Modern Times*, p. 7.

town population (save the higher bureaucracy, the army and the *'ulema'*) belonged, they gave to labour a religious character.[1] The two chief socio-religious institutions were in this way closely knit together.

Their role was structurally that of mediator between military dynasty and people. In traditional Egyptian society there was an institutionalized disjunction between rulers and ruled. The *hukuma* (central government the Turkish officials of which were frequently non-Arabic-speaking) had power, in the sense of the capacity to control material resources and benefits and to compel obedience to political decree, enforce tax collection and so forth. But in so far as we may speak separately of leadership and authority, that rested with the Sheikhs. Or rather it rested with those individuals drawn from that stratum who, by the juggling of the opportunities open to them as 'men of the pen', by their abilities to attach themselves to or to use the *hukuma* in exchange for services rendered, or through local political or factional manipulations together with the prestige and influence of learning, could attempt to stabilize their positions instead of relying on the fickle circumstances of purely personal leadership. They founded family Orders, became the Sheikhs of the legal schools, acquired large estates or control over *waqf* (land endowed for religious purposes), and filled offices such as that held by the Bekri family of *Sheikh al Masha'ikh*.

Their double mediation between government and people, and between Muslims and Revelation, had its place in an agrarian society of small peasant villages scattered through the delta and valley of the great river. Until the nineteenth century it was a society in which, though dynasty succeeded dynasty in due time and season, time and seasons remained as cyclical and determinedly recurrent as they had always done (as did disease and plague epidemics). Material culture and modes of cultivation were unchanged, technology continued simple, social differentiation was minimal, and intellectual life in general ossified in the calcium of grammar and Quranic exegesis. The Orders were woven into this stable, indeed static, social world. Yet the picture I have sketched out in this book shows a very different role for the *turuq*, a 'separation from the common life', in a transformed Egypt.[2] How did this come about?

[1] Baer, G., *Egyptian Guilds in Modern Times*, p. 5.
[2] *Al Musawwar*, p. 21.

Demographic and Economic Factors

Taking the major demographic features of Egyptian society first, the most striking thing which emerges is the very high rate of urbanization over the past eighty years. In the first three-quarters of the nineteenth century this process had not been of great significance; for though Alexandria grew considerably, and Port Said and Zagazig were founded, other towns such as Rosetta and Damietta declined. By 1881 only 11·5 per cent of the population lived in towns with more than 20,000 persons.[1] But since then urbanization has gone on at ever-increasing speed. From 791,000 inhabitants in 1917, Cairo had grown to 1,312,000 in 1937, an increase of 66 per cent. In the same period the population of Alexandria rose from 445,000 to 686,000, an increase of 55 per cent, while over the country as a whole the rise was 25 per cent. In these two decades the population of the twenty largest towns went up by 54 per cent.[2] In the following ten years, from 1937 to 1947, the rural figures show an increase of only 11 per cent, but the urban data gives a rise of 44 per cent.[3] By 1960 over 40 per cent of the inhabitants of Cairo and Alexandria had moved in from the rural areas.[4] What lies behind these figures are two main streams of internal migration: from Upper to Lower Egypt (which has a higher average crop per inhabitant, and was less densely populated), and from the country to the towns, and particularly to the capital and Alexandria.[5] According to a French team's survey the great

---

[1] Baer, G., *Social Change in Egypt, 1800–1914*; in Holt, *Political and Social Change*, pp. 135–61.

[2] Issawi, C., *Egypt at Mid-Century*, London: O.U.P., 1954, p. 60.

[3] Safran, N., *Egypt in Search of Political Community*, Cambridge, Mass.: Harvard University Press, 1961, p. 182.

[4] Hansen and Marzouk, *Development and Economic Policy*, p. 31. Rough census figures for our period are as follows (from Hansen and Marzouk, pp. 22–3):

> In 1882 approximately 2·5 million
> 1897   6·8 ,,
> 1907   11·3 ,,
> 1917   12·8 ,,
> 1927   14·2 ,,
> 1937   15·9 ,,
> 1947   19·0 ,,
> 1960   26·1 ,,

[5] Issawi, *Egypt in Revolution*, Cambridge, Mass: Harvard University Press, pp. 83–4.

proportion of this urban population (around 60 per cent at the beginning of the 1960s) was either unclassifiable in occupational terms altogether (this category ranging from street vendors, soft drink sellers, etc., to the completely unemployed), or in unstable unemployment at an average income no higher than that of the mass of the rural population (servants, wage labourers, artisans, unskilled workers).[1]

Allied to these sweeping changes have been others equally far-reaching in the modes of production. We have drawn attention to the shift in the agricultural sector in the nineteenth century from subsistence farming to the production of cash crops, with its attendant linking of the peasant to the price mechanisms of the international markets. This went along with a change from basin to perennial in methods of irrigation,[2] and the break up of the villages as common fiscal units.[3] From this time also the patterns of consumption in the rural areas appear to have become far more closely connected to the external world. Colonial Egypt evolved as a 'pays au developpement unilateral, traitant avec les monopoles de pays industrialisés au developpement multilateral'.[4] Foreign commercial and banking interests and an indigenous landlord class developed the economic infrastructure, controlled transportation, investment, manufacture, and processing, and concentrated their resources on the dominant export crop, cotton.

Throughout this period there was a vast increase in the number of rural inhabitants that made up the *sans terre*. This class had expanded by 10–20 per cent at the end of the 1950s.[5] Of the total number employable in 1960 (approximately 10,000,000) only about a third had full-time occupations. This amorphous, un-differentiated mass has remained largely politically invisible; 'ces masses populaires apathiques ne participent en aucune manière à la vie générale du pays, ne désirent pas et ne croient pas faire leur histoire.'[6] Their existence has no stable economic or social base,

---

[1] Groupe de l'Étude de l'I.E.D.E.S., 'La société urbaine égyptienne', *Tiers-Monde*, vol. 2, no. 6, 1961, pp. 183–210.

[2] Berque, J., 'Dans le Delta du Nil', *Studia Islamica*, no. 4, 1955, pp. 91–109.

[3] Baer, G., 'The Dissolution of the Egyptian Village Community', *Die Welt des Islams*, vol. 6, 1959–61, pp. 56–70.

[4] Hussein, Mahmoud, *La Lutte de classes en Égypte*, Paris: Maspero, 1969, p. 22.

[5] I.E.D.E.S., 'Pression démographique et stratification sociale dans les campagnes Égyptiennes', *Tiers-Monde*, vol. 1, no. 3, 1960, pp. 319–20.

[6] Ibid., p. 325.

and those who move to the cities do not appear to do more than exchange one setting of their extreme poverty and deprivation for another (several of the brothers of the *Ahmadiya* of Aswan fall into this category).[1]

Very gradually the primary importance of agriculture in Egyptian society has declined, and its organization has undergone major alterations. From providing about half the total production of the country before World War II, it only contributed one quarter in 1962–3.[2] And by 1948 approximately half the farmers appear to have become members of co-operatives.[3] In terms of employment, this shift is reflected in the following figures: by 1960, 57 per cent of the total economically active population was in agriculture, 31·4 per cent in services, and 12 per cent in industry and construction.[4]

This last statistic, allied with the decline in agriculture and the higher rate of urban growth, is of considerable and increasing importance in modern Egypt. Baer suggests that by the end of the first decade of this century the core of a new working class had formed[5]. But it was not until the 1930s that any significant advance was made in this sector,[6] chiefly with the aid of foreign capital. At the present time, the extreme pressure of population on the land has made industrialization the first priority of the administration. We may therefore expect a marked rise in the proportion of the economically active engaged in industry and construction in both the immediate and the long-term future.

In the field of education, where we saw the Orders to have played a role important both for the traditional society at large and for the maintenance of their own influence, structural changes have been similarly fundamental. What was once the preserve of the small, literate, religious élite, has become almost completely secularized. Although by the end of the nineteenth century 'westernization' still affected the intellectual life of only the top layer of society, and the British gave education very limited support according to their own administrative needs,[7] the last fifty years have seen a rapid increase. A total school population of 324,000 in 1913, grew to 942,000 in 1933 and to 1,900,000 in 1951. Over the same three dates, secondary school enrolment (to be distinguished from

---

[1] See Hussein, op. cit., pp. 42–3.
[2] Hansen and Marzouk, op. cit., p. 12.   [3] O'Brien, op. cit., p. 49.
[4] Hansen and Marzouk, op. cit., p. 34.
[5] Baer, *Social Change in Egypt*, p. 156.
[6] O'Brien, op. cit., p. 14.   [7] Safran, op. cit., p. 55.

attendance) went up from 2,500 to 15,000, and then to 122,000. An almost non-existent university student body in 1913 was 41,000 by 1951.[1] Today the school population is around 4,000,000, while in 1961 the number of students at university was 53,000.[2] We should not allow an emphasis on quantity to obscure the failings of this expansion from the qualititative point of view, and the very varying standard of the schools. But the fact remains that the government is now within range of its goal of providing compulsory primary education for most of the school-age population,[3] while the old mosque–*madrasah*–*kuttab* system, and the *turuq* have ceased to be formal agencies of instruction.

The effects of these demographic, economic, and social changes, of the political and nationalist developments set in train during the British occupation, and of 'westernization' in general, have moulded contemporary Egypt. We now turn to the main consequences of these processes for the traditional society in which the Orders were of such paramount social significance.

The old forms of labour organization swiftly disappeared, apparently chiefly as a result of the changes in the commercial system and in the habits of consumption, the modernization of occupations and the administrative reorganization.[4] With their extinction the *turuq* lost their long-standing 'organic' links with the artisan and merchant strata. At the same time the quarters of the cities, too, appear to have notably declined as social units. Anouar 'Abdel Malek quotes a 1905 report by Lord Cromer, in which the proconsul comments on the swift diminution of the quarters as centres of small industry, and the sudden influx of western goods.[5] The often violent processes of urbanization, the vast increase in the population of the main cities, made the old organization by quarter largely obsolete.

Under Muhammed Ali the Sheikhs had already lost their importance as large landowners,[6] and were thus cut off from a major economic and power base and source of status. The government of the country itself was now under the direction of a colonial

---

[1] Issawi, *Egypt at Mid-Century*, p. 67.

[2] Mansfield, Peter, *Nasser's Egypt*, Harmondsworth: Penguin African Library, 1965, p. 120. [3] Ibid., p. 121.

[4] Baer, *Egyptian Guilds in Modern Times*, particularly pp. 138–44.

[5] 'Abdel Malek, Anouar, *Égypte: société militaire*, Paris: Éditions du Seuil, 1962, pp. 20–1.

[6] Baer, *History of Land Ownership in Modern Egypt*, p. 61.

regime, and the historical separation of the learned man from the state and its agencies made them ill-fitted to a political role. One begins to see that familiar phenomenon, the rapid shrinking of the wide field formerly embraced by the sacred as area by area of social life is taken over by new bureaucratic or economic organs; the interposition of a growingly complex series of sub-systems and organizations where once the 'ultimate' religious system pervaded; the defining more and more of what falls within the proper competence of the religious institutions, and the *de facto* separating-out of areas ruled explicitly by secular interests.

Politics, under the influence often of Western liberalism as much as of notions of pan-Islamic nationalism (which was of only limited currency and duration), came to play a completely different part in Egyptian society. The formation of the parties in the first two decades of this century linked large numbers, in however tenuous a way, with the processes of government, the nationalist struggle, and the new sources of power. These were largely located in what 'Abdel Malek terms the two wings of the Egyptian bourgeoisie; the Wafd party on the one hand, drawn mainly from the landed, intellectual, and commercial classes, and those who collaborated with foreign investors in industrial enterprises.[1]

At the opposite end of the scale we note too a new class entering into the realm of the political. In the revolution of 1919, groups of fellaheen went into action in whole regions, cutting communications, seizing the land they cultivated and even proclaiming short-lived republics. In the towns also there was a certain unity of purpose and action between the workers and the petit bourgeoisie.[2] Peasant disturbances, characterized by amorphous and sporadic violence, were nothing novel in Egypt. But here we see, though in an ill-developed and ephemeral form, attempts to mould political circumstances and to make a directed protest against specific social conditions.

The traditional order has thus been severely disrupted. The main trends of the society are away from the once dominant agricultural and rural spheres and towards the swift growth of

[1] 'Abdel Malek, op. cit., pp. 22–3. The author notes that no urban bourgeoisie of the European type emerged, but that even the industrial wing was rooted in the landed class, though closely linked with foreign capital. See also O'Brien, op. cit., p. 228, and Abdel Malek, op cit., p. 28.

[2] 'Abdel Malek, op. cit., p. 28.

towns by internal migration, and an expanding effort to indus-
trialize in response to intense demographic pressure. The economic
structure has become immensely complex and diversified, and
with it the patterns of stratification and groupings within the
society.

A relatively simple and defined traditional structure of 'class',
status, and power has been fragmented under the impact of this
process of rapid and fundamental change, and the swift currents
of social and geographical mobility. The distribution, allocation,
and achievement of power and authority is now on grounds other
than those of a century ago.

These developments, together with increasing social differentiation, have led to the erosion of the old unity of values based on
Divine Revelation. Though the ultimate moral authority of this
Revelation is not diminished, or necessarily of a lesser personal
significance to the individual believer, a whole series of secondary
values of sub-systems appropriate to the new groupings and strata
are pushed into the foreground of social life. It is no longer possible
to 'take for granted' the shared understandings of events, objects,
and facts in the common social environment, because that social
environment, that homogeneity of values, has been disrupted, and
with it the pre-suppositions of a shared set of symbols and
meanings of which the Orders were to so great an extent the
institutional and collective bearers. A formerly accepted complex
of significances, interpretations, and metaphors became, with the
breaking of the old continuities, moribund, the property of a
diminishing minority, where it had been the common cultural
heritage of all. The Brotherhoods came to constitute in their turn
only a sub-universe of meaning, within the religious system. For
with the multiplication of new perspectives, and the demographic,
economic, and political transformations, discrepancies between
the world view the *turuq* embodied, and the world as it was coming
to be, grew ever wider. Their vision increasingly reflected less and
less of the everyday life to which they had been so intimately
connected. The society was no longer able, in Alasdair MacIntyre's
phrase, 'to give expression to its common life in religious forms',
for the foundations of that common life were gone.[1]

[1] MacIntyre, Alasdair, *Secularization and Moral Change*, London: O.U.P.,
1967, p. 53.

Structure and Change

It is on the structural and moral elements of the *turuq* that the effects of these radical changes in the social setting in which they once fulfilled their comprehensive functions are most marked. We have seen the key organizational link to be the dyadic relation between the *murid* and the charismatic leader of the Order. If the latter is the founder, his claim to authority is usually based on a Divine command sent in a vision, and he is presented as having no freedom or choice in his call: as the humble instrument of God's will and the recipient of His honour he can only obey. The legitimation for his establishment of the *tariqa* is thus derived from the ultimate Power, and placed on a mystical plane beyond mere human question of challenge. If, however, the Sheikh is not the founder, then he takes legitimacy from his link with the Saint which may be (*a*) by descent, where that principle operates; (*b*) by the advice or order of his predecessor; or (*c*) by selection of the group guided by the accepted criteria for the fitting qualities necessary for the leadership. Once this choice has been made, he becomes the new link in the chain of grace.[1]

But we also showed that this connection of Sheikh to student is in the great majority of cases channelled through the medium of the *khalifa*, who controls the local *zawiya*. Authority is vested in him by the Sheikh, whose delegate he is, though again it appears that the status was often inherited in certain families, and the Sheikh's approval a secondary formality in the Egyptian instance. The *khalifa* therefore possesses in fact a considerable degree of autonomy, and occupies a key structural position (particularly as head of one of the major *zawiyas*). So although all the *turuq* are characterized by a hierarchy of ascending ranks ending in the *Sheikh as-Sigada*, and are thus in strictly formal terms highly centralized, the personality of the individual local deputy is crucial, and becomes ever more so as membership has ceased to be an integral part of social life. It is round this pivot of authority that fission is mostly likely to occur. This is particularly so where the Order is near to the organizational pole, and demands the 'total' allegiance of its followers. For the more powerful and effectively

[1] Throughout this section my debt to the writings of Max Weber on charismatic authority, particularly as contained in *The Theory of Social and Economic Organisation*, New York: Free Press of Glencoe, 1964, will be clear.

centralized the *tariqa* is, and the greater its importance in the wider society, the more crucial is the role of *khalifa* in the initiation of schism, especially at critical precipitating moments such as the succession to the head Sheikh.

Two further factors contribute to such divisions. There is first the difficulty of supervision of the *khulafa'* by the *Sigada*, which left them as virtually independent units. This problem has been greatly reduced, but not eliminated, by the development of modern means of communication. Even in the *Hamidiya Shadhiliya*, who have made the fullest use of these media in internal control, the collapse of the Alexandria *zawiya* because of the weakness of its head could not be avoided. The second factor is the more fundamental one that groups built on the charismatic impulse, unless it be institutionalized and rationalized to a quite exceptional degree, are inherently unstable. By definition, charisma is not subject to the normal processes and restraints of organization; its very nature is opposed, as Weber demonstrated, to rational and bureaucratic authority.

Schism has therefore been a common phenomenon in these religious movements, particularly in the organizational type, and it arises from this combination of structural principles. Thus we find both the challenge of the *wakil* to Ibrahim's authority and the rights to succession on the death of Salama, and the split in the *Tijaniya* Order in a struggle for the office of Sheikh, even after the founder had made his own selection.[1] So the more the group corresponds to this type, and the greater the control it seeks and the comprehensive loyalty it requires of adherents, the greater is the risk it runs of division over the allocation of authority statuses.

A certain constant potential of conflict is the price that its structure exacts. This conflict, seen from the sociological perspective, is an index of the continuing vitality of the *tariqa* and the high valuation placed on positions of power within it. The problem then for the group is to ensure that it is contained and does not lead to fragmentation of the organization. Hence, though for example competition between the *zawiyas* is encouraged in the prestige display and conspicuous consumption of the *mulid*, in other fields the *Hamidiya Shadhiliya* must endeavour to limit the possibilities of internal tension. This is done in part by the clear definition of roles and spheres of authority within the structure by

[1] Abun-Nasr, op. cit., p. 23.

the system of regulations (the Laws), and the whole apparatus of committees and reports; and in part too by the great stress on the Saint and his son, the present leader, for whom the officials merely serve, it is emphasized, as 'helpers' and 'organizers'.

But the *Hamidiya Shadhiliya* is the exception rather than the sociological rule. We have suggested that in general the Egyptian Orders have more nearly corresponded to the 'association' type. Which is to say that decentralization has predominated and the links of the *zawiyas* to the *Sigada* have remained tenuous. The Orders have rarely functioned as such, but rather as a series of loosely connected local centres. Over-all solidarity has existed at a low level, and the commitment of the *muridin* has tended to be of a limited and amorphous nature. Multiple membership has been common, and attachment to a given *tariqa* therefore of a highly non-exclusive kind. This in turn reduces the degree of internal conflict, but equally indicates the lack of a clear focus of solidarity and the well-nigh minimal definition of the group. There have been instances where specific demands have been made on members, but broadly speaking I believe the pattern I have outlined above to hold generally true.

In view of these structural characteristics, it is easy to understand the lack of positive adaptive response to the challenge which the changes of the nineteenth and early twentieth century presented. What political efforts were made were the work of individuals in the local setting, not of any of the Orders as such. Seyyid al Baghdadi, *khalifa* of the *Khalwatiya* in Sirs al Layyan, led the agitation for the Wafd in his village in 1919;[1] Sheikh 'Abd al Rahim al Demerdash Pasha (d. 1930), the *Sheikh as-Sigada* of the Order, was a noted member of the Umma party and served as a member in the first elected assemblies;[2] in Silwa the grandson of the Sheikh of the *tariqa* polled the same number of votes as the 'paternal cousin' candidate, on three previous occasions an overwhelming winner.[3]

While such personal activities were going forward, functions which were once the preserve of the Orders were taken over by other groups and agencies, either of the State (e.g. education), the

[1] Berque, *Histoire sociale*, p. 66.

[2] Adams, C. C., *Islam and Modernism in Egypt*, London: O.U.P., 1933, p. 209.

[3] Ammar, *Growing up in an Egyptian Village*, p. 47. We might add that in the elections for the Council of the Nation in 1957 only one Sheikh was chosen to serve among the 340 representatives. Malek, op. cit., p. 117.

intellectual and political élites, or recently founded voluntary associations and organizations. And instead of the active response to the critical diminution of social importance and the processes of change, there was only a gradual disintegration. The organizational unity of direction and control, the internal cohesion and the necessary dynamic, were missing.

Moreover the position of the leaders was undermined. The endowments that made some of the *turuq* wealthy and provided a power base for the Sheikhs in their control of that vital resource, land, were lost in Muhammed Ali's reforms or squandered by bad management. The Sheikhs had to take employment like their followers.[1] Nor were the Orders any longer a major source of status, authority, or even benefit in the society at large. As their significance diminished there were new avenues, of which the political parties were only one, through which men might seek these opportunities and in which power was increasingly located. The forces which once the Head of the *turuq* in Egypt could summon up in a day were now at the command of agents who derive their authority from sources other than the chain of blessing and the Divine vision.[2] The shared community of discourse, as MacIntyre puts it, which gives meaning to the notion of authority in morals (and other fields) was replaced;[3] particularly in the urban environment, different criteria began to be recognized for the purposes of action and the acquisition of prestige.

Social Ethics and Doctrines

The 'fit' of the *turuq* to the general structure of traditional Egyptian society extended to the realm of values and social ethic as well as status. This identification with the traditional order has now, in the midst of transition, become one of the groups' major weaknesses. As social differentiation has increased they have manifestly failed to reflect the breakdown of the old system, or to offer any

---

[1] Heyworth-Dunne, *Religious and Political Trends in Modern Egypt*, published by the author, Washington, 1950, pp. 34–5.

[2] 'In sum, they have the ability to assemble in a single day a powerful military regiment of at least seventy or eighty thousand men who are docile and loyal to them . . .' *Ottoman Egypt in the Eighteenth Century*; the *Nizamname-i-Misir* of Cezzar Ahmed Pasha, edited and translated from the original Turkish by Standford J. Shaw, Cambridge, Mass.: Harvard University Press, 1964, p. 23.

[3] MacIntyre, op. cit., pp. 53–4.

accommodation to the new strata in terms of attitudes to the world.

Indeed, in the majority of cases, in so far as there was a social ethic it was largely indistinguishable from other religious groups or from Muslim non-members. The diffuseness of the solidarity of the various Orders was in part the result of this lack of a distinctive ethical or doctrinal character which might give them definition and clear identity. They appeared to the Muslim reformers of the turn of the century, for example, to have become merely associations which perverted and reflected discredit on Islam:

But what was the effect of this (the increase in the influence of the Sheikhs of the Orders) on the Muslims? In part, the aims of true Sufism were transformed and nothing remained . . . save noises and movements which they call *dhikr* which every (genuine) Sufi keeps himself from; there is (in addition) the religious glorification of the tombs of the Sheikhs with the belief that they possess hidden power. . . . and this is contrary to the Book of God and the Sunna of His Prophet. . . .[1]

Before the sense of threat which the pervading influence of Westernization brought to the religious élite the *turuq* seemed at best irrelevant, at worst a ground for attack by outsiders against the true religion. To the fundamentalist puritan strain in some of the most important social organizations soon to emerge, moreover, these 'noises' and 'movements' of the ritual were particularly the subject of attack. For not only were they said to be un-Islamic and degrading to the faith, but they made it a mockery to non-Muslims. The *dhikr* appeared to have lost its true Sufi meaning and become no more than a quasi-institutionalized channel for frenzy. As such it lost its roots in the collective purposes of the time.

To the other emerging groups, and more specifically the whole range of the 'middle class', the Orders offered no interpretation of the world which had demonstrable significance for their social situation. The *turuq* may be thought of as existing in a continuous, cyclical time where the future is in one sense but a constant reliving of and returning to the past. This view, which is essentially non-progressive and non-linear, sees History (meaning the passing of events) as an excrescence, and looks to a permanent, static,

[1] *Al Manar*, vol. 7, 15 July 1904, pp. 331–2.

transcendent condition outside it. There is no question of alternatives, of other viable possibilities out of which what is to come
can be forged; only a withdrawal inward on the constant way after
the model of the Saint and in a religious community where the
great conservative force of consensus is one of the bases of the
society. For those classes actively concerned with the creation and
realization of possibilities in the future, with a different historical
consciousness, such a vision is empty of meaning. Where we find
even the fellaheen engaging in revolution, not mere unrest and
violence, but associated with a specific political programme, then
the scope of the change becomes clear.

There thus followed a considerable diminution in the social
function of the Orders at every level. And the diminution was
accompanied by an efflorescence of organizations which attracted
as members precisely those strata which the Orders might traditionally have claimed, and the new 'classes' they alienated. While
the *turuq* had no response to the political and social changes in the
society, these rising organizations presented at least some interpretation or structuring of the radically altered circumstances, and
fulfilled the functions appropriate to an urbanizing and industrializing environment. In the range of their activities, which was
extremely wide, and in their active ethical appeal to the membership, they answered those needs which the Orders seemed incapable of satisfying.[1] Heyworth-Dunne gives us the example of
the *Subkiya* movement which had its own mosque and head-
quarters in the Khiyamiya district of Cairo. It was composed
mainly of workmen, artisans, and small traders, particularly those in
government railways, tramways, printing, workshops, and public
services in general. They ran their own co-operative to deal with
petty trade within the group and the founder adapted certain social
institutions to raise the economic position of members.[2]

More well known than the *Subkiya* was the *Jami'at al Shubban al
Muslimin* (founded in 1927), which had as part of its oath the vow 'to
be active as a warrior (note the external reference given to the concept
of *jihad*, or holy struggle, which the Sufis had internalized) fighting
for the survival of the glory of Islam by restoring its religious law

---

[1] Heyworth-Dunne, *Religious and Political Trends*, pp. 90–1, gives a list of
135 such organizations which he classifies as (1) religious, (2) politico-religious,
(3) social, (4) co-operative, (5) vocational, (6) charitable.
[2] Ibid., p. 13.

and its supremacy'.[1] Henri Laoust says that they extended to Egyptian youth:

... les ressources d'un vast club littéraire, cultural et sportif. Elle a son Conseil d'Administration, ... son assemblée générale annuelle, un budget alimenté par les cotisations des membres et des donations, agit par l'intermédiaire de comités spécialisés, donne de fréquentes conférences, a ses hymnes et ... une revue mensuelle ...[2]

Most significant of all was the powerful organization of the Muslim Brotherhood. Its founder, Hassan al Banna, one of the most important popular leaders in modern Egyptian history, defined it in these terms: '. . . a Salafite movement, an orthodox way, a Sufi reality, a political body, an athletic group, a scientific and cultural society, an economic company and a social idea.'[3]

Once himself the member of an Order, and deeply influenced in his early career by *tasawwuf*, he considered the framework of a *tariqa* too limited for his mission, and so established a separate organization. Essentially an urban movement, the Brotherhood grew swiftly in the main cities, the areas of major social strain. By World War II, as a result of extremely active recruiting, there were approximately 500 branches all over the country[4] and this membership was further increased during the war, which in Egypt was a period of severe economic disturbance, inflation, and food shortage.[5] Its functions multiplied and ramified swiftly. It set up its own schools and health clinics, organized the Rover scouts for the youth (often in para-military style), and a secret army; it had its own newspapers, developed a co-operative system in the industrial, economic, and commercial fields, and made a concerted and highly controlled attempt to improve living standards.

---

[1] Ibid., p. 29, my emphasis.

[2] Laoust, H., 'Le Réformisme orthodoxe des "Salafiyya" et les caractères généraux de son orientation actuelle', *Revue des études musulmanes*, 1932, p. 180.

[3] Husseini, I. M., *The Muslim Brethren*, Khayat, Lebanon, 1956, p. 15. Translated from *Min Khutab Hassan al-Banna*, first series, Damascus, 1938, pp. 14–15.

[4] Heyworth-Dunne, *Religious and Political Trends*, p. 17.

[5] Safran, op. cit., p. 104. We should perhaps point out here that by no means all of the organizations founded during this period were religious in orientation. There were other channels for protest, action, and association. In 1945, for example, Wafdist intellectuals, nationalists, communists, and workers' syndicates started a new group, to which the Muslim Brothers were bitterly opposed, the National Committee of Workers and Students. See Malek, op. cit., p. 32.

All this it did in the name of Islam, but of an Islam in which the stress was very different from the passive retreatism of the Orders. The Brotherhood directed its followers to the working out of God's purpose *in* the world. It offered a vision of the future cast in religious terms. But though these terms derived their meaning and affective and symbolic connotations from the past, they were made to encompass the material world of the present. They were to guide positive social action on Islamic principles interpreted as a key to the reordering of a society dislocated by change. Individuals had status according to their efforts in the holy struggle, and not according to the uncertain new criteria which had appeared in the evolving pattern of social differentiation.

The lower middle and middle classes joined the movement by the thousand with those who had come sufficiently far under the influence of westernization to feel the old ethic to be called in question without an adequate substitute being put in its place. The *petite bourgeoisie* was caught '. . . à l'intersection de tous les processus du passé décadent et de l'avenir bloqué: elle incorpore et ressent doublement la crise de la transition';[1] and it lacked a means of exercising power to break out of its at once privileged and underprivileged position. To these classes Banna offered a programme which militantly asserted the relevance of the traditional beliefs and value system to their existence, and a dynamic reformulation of ultimate truths in the contemporary perspective.[2]

The success of the Muslim Brotherhood should warn us therefore against assuming that the currents of secularization run as deep as an examination of formal institutions might lead us to suppose; or that the normative and value changes to which attention has been drawn proceeded at equal pace among the different social strata. It should warn us also against the too-ready assumption that the decline of the Sufi Orders indicated a diminution in the significance of religion as a motive force in action; and against believing that such shifts in the economic structure as we have

---

[1] Hussein, op. cit., p. 41.

[2] Banna himself was murdered in 1949. In the revolution of 1952 the Brotherhood was the only political organization not to be banned by the military regime. The two forces fell out, however, and an attempt to assassinate the then Colonel Nasser in 1954 led to the dissolution by the government of the organization. In 1965, eleven years after this repression, another plot by underground groups of the Brethren to assassinate the President was uncovered and the leaders ultimately hanged. The most detailed study of Banna and his movement is by Richard P. Mitchell, *The Society of the Muslim Brothers*, London: O.U.P., 1969.

noted inevitably effected an immediate equivalent shift in the sphere of values and beliefs. Notions of what constitutes proper religious behaviour may change. But the history of modern Egypt shows how highly organized revitalizing movements based on Islamic principles could attract millions of members. To those undergoing the often confusing experiences of the colonial society they offered an integrating and transcendent meaning in terms drawing legitimacy from the ultimate order, but presented as having immediate relevance to the present spiritual and material realities at all levels. Such movements resolved, or pointed to the apparent resolution of, an increasingly obvious disjunction between the world order as it was and as it should be: they re-created the world in its old image and re-incorporated it into the divine system in a way which the *turuq* could no longer do.

The failure of the Orders must therefore be more precisely located in the general pattern of social change that I have sketched. It is not enough to talk of urbanization, population growth, the expansion of the *sans terre*, and the marginal classes, the diminution of the agricultural sphere and so forth. Such transformations, after all, might equally have led to a traditionalist retrenchment, even a revival of the *turuq*, perhaps, as the opium of an oppressed people in apathetic or sullen resistance, wishfully clinging to what was known and authoritative. Certainly these processes created, as Banna and others were quick to realize, new fields for organized action and new groups from which converts might be gained. That the Orders did not survive to provide a refuge is I think particularly because of the redefinition of the arena of politics in Egypt and of the relations and bases of power. This has already been pointed to in our discussion of the limitations on the exercise of Saintly authority and religious leadership. The great charismatic figures of twentieth-century Egypt, Mustafa Kamil, Saad Zaghlul, Hassan al Banna, and Gamal Abd el Nasser have all been men who could grasp the political realities at a national level in a society subject to colonial rule. Once the Sheikhs lost their structural opportunities for the performance of the mediating function they were left without a social *raison d'être*, or the means to assert their leadership. Neither they nor the Pan-Islamists comprehended the radically new meaning of politics, and they ceased to give authentic expression to men's collective and communal purposes.

The Hamidiya Shadhiliya

We return finally to the only one of the Sufi Orders which has not been rendered clearly redundant by the processes of social change in Egypt. That this has been the case is largely due to the regulations imposed upon it by its founder virtually at the moment of its foundation; to the highly centralized control, the definition, and distinct character thus given to it; and in part to its relative newness, which has meant that the original energy of the Saint's charismatic mission, now continued by his son, has not been dissipated.

Lacking the necessary information it is impossible to say what response the Order evoked in the period we have so briefly touched upon above. It seems a likely hypothesis that the Muslim Brotherhood were the most crucial factor in cutting off those groups from whom the *turuq* in general might have sought or expected members, and dealt the most serious blow to their recruitment and the authority of their leaders. At the same time, too, the proliferation of associations and avenues for leisure activities provided opportunities for emotional gratification beyond the frequently debased range of the *dhikr*. Certainly the *Hamidiya Shadhiliya* was in a sense in competition for members with the new groups. For it was, and is, primarily an urban phenomenon as they were. It seeks to provide those elements of mutual support and benefit, of psychological and material security in a fraternal circle built on co-operation and equality, that are most lacking in the urban environment; to fulfil the functions of ascriptive groupings which are more limited in the town setting than in the village and agrarian communities; and to furnish an intense communion solidarity which takes sufficient cognizance of the stream of contemporary mundane events to have relevance to the lives of its followers. But in the context of Egyptian Sufism it could not offer that range of activities which the Brethren and other organizations supplied, nor that profoundly *political* group programme in social affairs. It seems reasonable to suppose, therefore, only a slow growth of the *Hamidiya Shadhiliya* in the inter-war period and the succeeding decade.

Over the last eight or ten years, however, there has been a resurgence and, so informants told me, a marked increase in the number of adherents. The severe restriction by the regime of the political and social channels through which individuals might seek status and to play an active role in voluntary association with their like-minded fellows does open a new field to the Order. If it is alien to the ethic of work, sacrifice, and effort preached by the agencies of the government, it is not so turned inward as to neglect the positive valuation of labour in the world. The emphasis on orthodoxy, and the *Shari'a* and Sunna, the hierarchical system and controls, both preserve doctrinal integrity before the *'ulema'* and the devout, and show some adaptation to the transitional social differentiation while stressing a common equality as Muslims. It may yet appeal further to those who, as I have suggested, are uncommitted or in some way peripheral to the developing social order. It presents the known realities of the ultimate system as a basis for life to those who cannot fully accept, or find wanting, the new patterns of 'proximate' norms and values consciously inculcated by the sources of political authority or formed by the processes of change. The *tariqa* enunciates the eternal link of the human with the Divine, and tells of the worth of lives guided by the way of Sidi Salama. In a discontinuous world the *Hamidiya Shadhiliya* holds out to men an assurance of the continuity of the traditional Islamic communion in the brotherhood and encompassing warmth of the followers of the Saint.

APPENDIX

THE LAWS

WHAT follows is a complete translation of the second (and current) edition of the Laws. Where there are significant departures from the first edition they are noted at the appropriate point in the text. In all cases I have followed the division into sections of Salama.

I must record my debt to Dr. Abd el Hamid el Zein without whose patient help and guidance this translation could not have been made.

FIRST SECTION

The principles of the Tariq

1. The aim of the people of the *tariq* is to come to the intuitive knowledge (*ma'rifa*) of God and to obtain His approval and fulfil the duties of humble adoration and render the rights of divinity.[1]

2. Our way in Holy Law is built on the Quran and the Sunna and it is free from culpable heresy.

3. One of the principles of our way is the holy war of souls.

4. One of the principles of our way is humility, for it is the capital [wealth or resource] of the poor.

5. Surrender to the will of God is the distinguishing feature of our way.

6. Enduring harm purifies the essence of the *faqir* and clarifies his nature ['the needy'—that is, in relation to Allah].

7. The remembrance of God in the majority of occasions is the nourishment of hearts.

8. The recitation of the Quran brings one near God and light and mercy.

9. To learn the necessary manifest knowledge is an obligation on every *faqir* [this refers in particular to the prescripts of Holy Law].

10. Respect for Muslims and asking for their blessings is a guide to the satisfaction of God.

11. Sitting with the rich hardens the heart.

---

[1] We note that this establishes the clear distinction between the *'abd* (the worshipper) and the *rabb* (God) and thus opposes any notion of *fana'* or goal of union with the Almighty.

12. One of the principles is to leave pretence (*takalluf*—unnaturalness of manner).

13. One of the principles is friendly relations, mutual visiting, and love.

14. One of the principles is flawlessness of the heart and the excellence of thought about God and his worshippers.

15. Ordering with justice and prohibition of what is forbidden with courteousness and gentleness [softness—*lin*].

16. Helping the poor and being sympathetic to them materially and spiritually as far as possible.

17. The seeing by man into the inadequacy of himself.

18. No obedience to the created (men) in disobedience to the Creator.

19. It is necessary that a man be merciful to his brother; so he should not argue with him, nor quarrel with him, nor insult him, nor slander him behind his back, nor envy him, nor say he is a liar, nor harm him; and let him be kind to him and humble with him, and soft in speech and advise him with friendliness without humiliating him, so he may be a help to him against his *nafs*[1] and his *shaitan*[2] and not help them against him.

20. Holding to moderation and restraint with regard to what is in the hands of other people; if he offers them something he should not seek return except what comes to him as a gift out of satisfaction and freely without any asking.

21. It is necessary for each one who is attached to the *tariq* to be faithful to his religion; and not to speak of what he does not know; nor pass on any distorted *hadith* or what is like that; rather he must be certain of what he says lest he fall into what is *haram* [forbidden] and be held ignorant by the people.

22. It is necessary for the *faqir* to adorn himself with humility and dignity and avoid too much laughter and joking so that hearts should incline to him and thus people come near to the *tariq* or at least the *tariq* will be respected by them.

23. Suspicion of the *nafs* so that whatever it brings to you then you will suspect it so that the truth will be revealed to you.

24. Whosoever of the people of our *tariq* speaks of the truth must be supported by the Book (Quran) and the Sunna in his thinking.

---

[1] Here in the sense of the 'flesh' or lower nature. See *Encyclopedia of Islam* (old edition), vol. 3, Leiden, 1936, pp. 827–30.

[2] Devil; the power opposing God in men's hearts. See *Encyclopedia of Islam* (old edition), vol. 4, Leiden, 1934, pp. 286–7.

25. It is not permissible for anyone of our *tariq* to believe [*qawl* in the sense of believe and then speak about] in pantheism, or unity of the world with God (*ittihad*) or modality;[1] or that Truth is the same as creation or to say what Hallaj said.[2]

26. It is not permissible for anyone that he should be one of the people of *ibaha* [meaning the state of saying that the normal rules set by God do not apply to one because one has reached so high a stage of illumination; e.g. al Hallaj] so that he pretends to drop the commandments (of God) and allows the forbidden things (*muharamat*); for indeed this is *zandaqa* (usually translated as 'free thought') into which many have fallen and claim great saintship [sanctity or sainthood].

27. It is not permissible for anyone to use magic or anything similar to it for this cuts the relation with God.

28. It is not necessary for the Sheikh [here referring to all the *khulafa'* as well as the *Sheikh as-Sigada*] to be in control of the financial capital of the student to the extent that he orders him to sell what he owns and then takes (an amount) from its price; nor to (make him) transfer to him any of his possessions; as some without morals have done [i.e. other Sheikhs of other orders].

29. It is not necessary for him to order his student to what is harmful to himself; such as sleeping on the roof of the house in winter with one garment; or standing in water all night, or standing on a wall for the sake of the *dhikr*.

30. It is prohibited for men to behave like women or for women to behave like men.

31. It is prohibited to meet the *magadhib* (possessed), or to mix with them, or to walk with them, or to imitate them.

32. Long journeys are forbidden to the student without the permission of the Sheikh.

33. It is forbidden for one who causes something to deny that he is the cause [i.e. disclaim responsibility, *yatagarrad*. See Article 25]. [The Old Edition has 'except with the permission of his sheikh' added after 'cause'.]

34. Not permissible at all for one of our *tariq* to compose a prayer or *wird* (office) or task to be recited in the *hadrahs* to his students or others. [In the Old Edition 'except with our permission' is added after 'others'.]

---

[1] *giha*; I have been unable to find a satisfactory translation for this term.

[2] A celebrated Persian mystic writing in Arabic. Executed in A.D. 922 for heresy. The saying referred to is his famous claim: *Ana'l Haqq* ('I am Creative Truth'). See *Encyclopedia of Islam*, vol. 2, Leiden, 1927, pp. 239–40.

35. Not permissible to tell [*dhikr*] the *hadith* well known among the *Shadhiliya* as the *hadith as-Suq*[1] in a loud voice except by the permission of Sheikh of the *tariq*.

36. Every *khalifa* or higher than he who teaches his students names which are not Arabic or makes them enter the *khalwa* or orders them to pray the unlawful *awrad* or orders them to make *dhikr* with 10,000 names in every day and night; or orders them to make devotions which stop the eating of all things which were alive; or to make a fast for many months; or to use the *djinn* or anything like that; he is responsible for what he does and the consequence is on him; for the *tariq* is free from that.

37. Not permitted to use the tambourine, or the cymbals, or stringed instruments or anything like that or the drum or the one-headed hand drum; nor may the pipes or the flute be used either in the *hadrah* or in the procession.

38. It is prohibited to ride horses on people and other things; and this is known as the *dosa* [for a description of this now defunct custom see Lane, op. cit., pp. 456 and 474–6].

39. One must not take the side of the *nafs* for the assistance of the truth will leave whoever helps it.

40. One must not stand about speaking good or ill about people.

41. The eating of insects and cactus and glass, and beating with the sword, and pins and fire-eating and what is like that is forbidden; for this is trickery and the people of the *tariq* are above it.

42. It is permissible to visit the shrines of the *awliya'* (saints), not the living Sheikhs; and only he who has no doubt of his Sheikh and his *tariq* may visit them.

43. All who are affiliated to our *tariq* must not make it his profession to take his daily bread from it but he must find a job or occupation to get his sustenance from other than the *tariq*.

44. The student must not argue with the Sheikh nor ask from him a proof for what he orders him or makes him do for the Sheikhs are the trustees of God.

45. Whoever opposes his Sheikh has broken the *'ahd* and cut off from the Sheikh even though he sticks close to the Sheikh; and the door of *madad* (assistance) is closed to him.

46. Every student sees the Sheikh at his own valuation.[2]

---

[1] Traditionally said in a high voice walking in the streets and made up of a few pious words or prayers. Often consisted of shouting praises of the Prophet.

[2] i.e. All have different levels of understanding and will comprehend the Sheikh to different degrees.

47. Those who want *zuhur* (to make a fine worldly show) are the slaves of appearance; those who want the *khafa'* (hidden things) are the slaves of the *khafa'*; those who want God will be the slaves of God; and if He wants to reveal it [i.e. the hidden] He will do so, and if He wants, He will keep it secret.

SECOND SECTION

The men of the Tariq

48. Since the Sheikh has work which requires someone to help him, necessity has compelled that every man have a function which he must perform and the men of our *tariq* are those following:

> Nuqaba' and *munshidun* (hymn-singers) in all the *beits* (groups of *zawiyas*) related to the *Sigada*.
> The Khalifa
> Khalifa of the Khulafa' not in the *Beit as-Sigada*.[1]
> Khalifa of the Khulafa' in the *Beit as-Sigada* (central office).
> Na'ib of the *beit* not in the *Beit as-Sigada*.
> Na'ib of the *Beit as-Sigada* in the *balad* (town).
> Na'ib as-Sigada in the *markaz* (division of the governorate).
> Na'ib as-Sigada in the *muhafza* (governorate).
> Nuqaba' as-Sigada with the rank of *Khalifa of the Khulafa'*.
> Naqib of the Nuqaba' of the *Sigada*, and he is on the level of the Na'ibs of the *beits*.
> Wakil of the *Sigada*.

al Khalifa

49. When the *Sheikh as-Sigada* finds competence in one of his students from the *Beit as-Sigada* he makes him a *khalifa* and gives him the authorization.

50. It is necessary for the *khalifa* not to make the office inoperative; he must have students so that the *tariq* will spread and the people have benefit from it.

51. He must know a large section of the Holy Quran and know how to make the ritual ablutions and the ablutions with sand; and how to wash and pray and the regulations for fasting. He must have a sound belief in *tawhid* [the absolute unity of Allah] as has been mentioned in our book *Murshid al Murid*.

---

[1] In the Old Edition this office and the office listed immediately succeeding it were in reverse order. The change reflects the increasing importance of offices attached to the central office. The list is from lowest rank to highest.

52. When he has students he must hold a *hadrah* or *hadrahs* for the remembrance of God in a *zawiya* or *beit*.

53. He must discuss religion with his students and what will be of benefit in their way to God; he must teach them good behaviour in the *tariq* so that their souls will be refined and their hearts purified.

54. He must read the books of the Sufis and the explanation of the aphorisms of Sidi Ahmed ibn 'Ata' Allah and the *Ihya*' and our books which we have put in the *tariq* and what is like that.[1]

Khalifa of the Khulafa'

55. If the *khalifa* finds among his students who have taken instruction from him one who is fit for the *khilafa* (office of *khalifa*) then he must introduce him to the *Sigada*; and if the *Sigada* gives the authorization of the *khilafa* then the *khalifa* who introduced him to the *Sigada* becomes *khalifa of the khulafa*' providing that he makes at least five *khalifas*.[2]

56. The *khalifa of the khulafa*' must visit his *khulafa*' and he must not neglect them and he must advise them and guide them to what is good for them.

57. Photocopy of the official document of the new *khilafa*:

B'ism illah ar-Rahman ar-Rahim

The *Hamidiya Shadhiliya Tariqa*

Authorization of the *Khilafa*

Those signed below certify

that al Seyyid   son of   son of

born   *markaz/qism*[3]   *muhafza*

residing now

has been taught the *tariqa* of the *Hamidiya Shadhiliya* from

from   from   and we agree to give him the

authorization of the *khilafa* from the *tariqa* in

and the matter is put before the Sheikh of the *tariqa* to sanction what he considers

witnesses of the *faqir*   witnesses of the *faqir*

Date

N.B.   (the function of the two witnesses must be mentioned.)

---

[1] Of al-Ghazali (d. 1111). The most celebrated of Muslim mystics and theologians. His greatest work is that referred to here, the *Ihya*' *'ulum al-din*, 'The revival of the religious sciences', in four volumes. He represented '. . . obedience to the prescriptions of the *Shari'a* as a meaningful way of life.' W. Montgomery Watt, article on al Ghazali, in *Encyclopedia of Islam* (new edn.), vol. 2, Leiden, 1965, pp. 1038–41.

[2] This last phrase, 'providing that . . .' is not in the Old Edition.

[3] Division of governorate/district.

I, the *faqir*, received

The authorization of the *khilafa* from the *tariqa* of the *Hamidiya Shadhiliya* in that district

It carries the number   date   sanctioned by the *Sigada*

                                        the *faqir* [seeking the *khilafa*]

Date

        Details to be provided concerning the proposed khalifa.

Full name   Married or single   Age

Current Address

Occupation

Place of Work

Social status

Level of Education

Telephone number (if there is one): in the house   at work

Date on which he took the (oath to) *tariq*

Any other information

I certify that all the above details are correct and I undertake to inform the *Sigada* of any change in my address or my social position

(the above is then witnessed by two persons)

58. Every document which differs from this is to be considered void and unacceptable.[1]

Na'ibs of the beits other than the beit as-Sigada

59. When a great number of *khulafa'* and students gather to the *khalifa of the khulafa'* in the *beit as-Sigada*, whether they took the *tariq* from him or from his *khulafa'*, then it is permissible for the *Sigada* to give him the position of *na'ib of a beit* and this *beit* will be attached to him and called by his name.

60. When the *na'ib* of the *beit* or the *khulafa'* of the *beit* or their *khulafa'* give the *tariq* in any area to students, then they are followers to that *beit*.

61. It is necessary for the *na'ib* of the *beit* to undertake to visit his brothers at least twice a year so that he can look over their situation and guide them to what they need.

Na'ib of the beit as-Sigada

62. All those who take the *tariq* from us and every *khalifa* or *khalifa* of the *khulafa'* whom we appointed over those who have taken (the oath) from us and who have not been given the title of *na'ib* of a *beit*, will be followers of the *beit as-Sigada* and the *na'ib* of the *beit as-Sigada* will be a *na'ib* over them in the area in which he is residing.

---

[1] Neither law 57 nor law 58 is in the Old Edition.

63. It is incumbent on the *na'ib* of the *beit as-Sigada* that he should look after the conditions of this *beit* at all times.

Na'ibs of the Markaz

64. The *Sigada* may appoint *na'ibs* in every *markaz*.

65. The *na'ib* may be the *na'ib* over two *markaz* but there may not be two *na'ibs* in one *markaz*.

66. The *na'ib* of the *markaz* must be at least of the rank of *khalifa*.

67. The *na'ib of the markaz* must be liable for those who are attached to the *Sigada* in his *markaz* and he must visit them at least twice a year and must look after their conditions and their way of walking (in the way of the *tariq*) and their endeavour.

68. It is not permissible for the *na'ib of the markaz* to do anything except with the agreement of the *na'ibs* of the *beits* and the *na'ib* of the *muhafza* even when it is in accordance with the Law.

Na'ib al Muhafza

69. The *Sigada* can appoint a *na'ib* for itself in every *muhafza*.

70. The *na'ib* in the *muhafza* must be at least *khalifa* of the *khulafa'*.

71. The *na'ib* of the *muhafza* is liable for those who are attached to the *Sigada* and he must visit them once a year at least.

72. The *na'ib* of the *muhafza* may not do anything at all except with the agreement of the *na'ibs* of his circle even when it is in accordance with this law and he must inform the *Sigada* of what he does.

73. The *khulafa'* and the *khulafa'* of the *khulafa'* and the *na'ibs* at their different levels must send detailed reports to the *beit as-Sigada* on their activities and the activities of the brothers of their circles at least once every three months.

74. The *khulafa'* and the *khulafa'* of the *khulafa'* and the *na'ibs* at their different levels must fill in the following form and send it to *beit as-Sigada* and inform the latter about every change which will take place in the future; and the secretary of the *Sigada* is responsible for receiving these forms and he must write the information down in the register set aside for that.

B'ism illah ar-Rahman ar-Rahim
al tariqa al Hamidiya Shadhiliya

as-seyyid:

(greetings): it is our desire to secure the advancement of the *tariq* and to discover the conditions of our *ikhwan* (brothers). We hope that you will fill in the items in the attached form in order to facilitate the visit of a committee of the *ikhwan* of Cairo acting on our behalf to communicate with you, and co-operate with you in whatever you want them to discuss with you which will contribute to the advancement of the *tariq*. This information must return to us within ten days in detail from its date (of sending) because of its extreme importance. *as-Sallam* (greetings).

The *Khadim* of the *Fuqara'*

(the Servant of the needy)
Ibrahim Salama Radi

The Tariq Hamidiya Shadhiliya

Report of the brothers of the *tariq* in the district　　　　*markaz muhafza*　　　　　　to the *mashaikha* of the *sigada* of the *Hamidiya Shadhiliya* in Cairo presented by:

1. Name and address and nearest telephone to the responsible *khalifa* (*muqaddim al ikhwan*).
2. Names of the *khulafa'* in the district.
3. Nights of the weekly *hadrahs* and the time of their beginning and the places where they are held.
4. Nights of the meetings of the brothers and their times and places.
5. The visiting of the *ikhwan* to the neighbouring districts.
6. Was any disagreement or disharmony found between the *ikhwan* or the *ikhwan* of the district or the *ikhwan* of another district and what is it?
7. Number of the *ikhwan* in the district　　the average number of people who gather in the *hadrah* and the meeting separately.
8. The way of reaching the area (the communications from Cairo).
9. The way of reaching the place of the meeting of the *ikhwan* or to the *khalifa* of the district.
10. Do the brothers have a special *zawiya* (local centre) or mosque?
11. Important general notes on the advancement of the *tariq* in the area.

Date

Signature of the presenter of the report
Signature of two
of the brothers

Wakil as-Sigada (*the deputy of the Sheikh*)

75. When the *Sheikh as-Sigada* is present in a place the *wakil* has to take his orders from him and transfer them to whomsoever it is necessary that he should transfer them, if the *wakil* is present at that time. When the Sheikh considers that it is necessary to delegate someone for that because the *wakil* is absent or for any other reason then there is no objection to that.

76. It is necessary that the *wakil* be informed about everything which occurs in the affairs of the *tariq* such as the giving of the *khilafa* or the *niyaba* (office of *na'ib*) or a *mawkib* (procession) or *mulid* or anything else; he will know either by asking the Sheikh or the *nuqaba* or others or looking in the registers or papers or anything else.

77. It is permissible for the *wakil* to visit the *ikhwan* in every place without restriction and take care of them and advise and guide them with friendliness and he must inform *Sheikh as-Sigada* as to his opinion (as to what he sees).

78. If the *wakil* is present in a *mulid* or a tent or procession or *hadrah* or any meeting of the *tariq* he has precedence over all the *khulafa'* and *khulafa'* of the *khulafa'* and *na'ibs* and the *nuqaba' as-Sigada* and the *naqib* of the *nuqaba'* of the *Sigada*.

79. When the *Sheikh as-Sigada* is absent he will act as the Sheikh himself in all the affairs of the *tariq* except in the dismissal of a *khalifa* or anyone of higher rank or in giving *khilafa* or anything more than that or appointing *nuqaba'* of the *Sigada* or a *naqib* of the *nuqaba'*; or having any connection with the *mashaikha as-Sufiya* or the administrative authority in what harms the *tariq* and on condition that he will not go outside the bounds of this law in his conduct.[1]

80. It is permissible for the *wakil* to go to any area to end a dispute after informing the *Sheikh as-Sigada* and his judgement will not be executed except when it is in accordance with this law and after the final approval of the *Sheikh as-Sigada*.

81. If the *wakil* of the *Sigada* is present in the meetings of the *na'ibs* of the *beits* or the *marakiz* (districts) or the *muhafazat* (governorates) he will act as leader in the meeting; the *na'ib* will be one member and three persons will be joined to them by election.

82. If the Sheikh is absent and the *wakil* holds the meeting of the *Sigada* then he will act as the leader (chairman) and the members will be formed from the *naqib* of the *nuqaba'* and three of the *na'ibs* of the *beits* by election; the decision of the meeting will not be executed save with approval of the Sheikh.

83. The *Sigada* must have the following books (registers)

   1 Register of all outgoing material.
   1 Register of all ingoing material.
   1 Register of the *khulafa'* and the *khulafa' of the khulafa'* and the

---

[1] *Mashaikha as-Sufiya*—the central administration of all the Sufi Orders in Egypt, under the *Sheikh al Masha'ikh*, or Chief Shaikh of the Orders.

na'ibs and the *nuqaba'* of the *Sigada* and the *naqib* of the *nuqaba'* and the *wakil*.

1 Register of cases (matters of dispute) and the decision taken.

84. These books must be stamped with the stamp of the *Sheikh as-Sigada*.

The Nuqaba' of the Sigada

85. The *nuqaba'* are especially devoted to the *Sheikh as-Sigada* and they are not attached to any of its *beits*.

86. The *naqib* of the *Sigada* is equivalent to the *khalifa* of the *khulafa'* and he is of the same rank.

87. The *naqib of the nuqaba'* of the *Sigada* is equal to the *na'ibs* of the *beits* and he is below the rank of the *wakil* in the public receptions.

88. The *Sheikh as-Sigada* may delegate one of the *nuqaba'* of the *Sigada* or the *naqib* of its *nuqaba'* to render judgement in any dispute which occurs in any district but his judgement is not final save after the approval of the *Sigada*.

89. The *naqib* of the *nuqaba'* may not go on his own account to inspect a *khalifa* or any higher than that except with the permission of the *Sheikh as-Sigada*.

90. If the *nuqaba'* of the *Sigada* differ they take as a judge the *naqib* of its *nuqaba'*; if the dispute is not ended then it is submitted to the *wakil*, then to the *Sheikh* of the *Sigada*.

91. The *naqib* of the *nuqaba'* may not prevent anyone from being a *naqib* save by the order of the *Sheikh as-Sigada*.

92. The rank of *naqib* of the *Sigada* may not be given save by written authority or permission from *Sheikh as-Sigada*.

93. The *naqib* may not do anything without the consent of the *naqib* of the *nuqaba'*, unless the Sheikh orders the *naqib* to do something which cannot be delayed or for any other reason at the Sheikh's discretion.

94. If the *naqib* of the *nuqaba'* finds a deficiency in one of the *nuqaba'* then he must put the matter before the *wakil* and then the Sheikh.

95. The number of the *Nuqaba'* of the *Sigada* is according to necessity and need.

The Singers who are called the Munshidun (Hymn-singers)

96. The Singer is the man who brings water to the people.

97. The Singer must, when he sings, have purity of heart and be responsive to Allah; so that the song will come from his heart and he will have the light of approbation.

98. The *munshid* must remember many of the words of the Sufis especially the *qasidas* [poems or odes] to which we are accustomed in our *tariq*.

99. What he remembers of the *qasidas* must be absolutely correct from the point of view of the Arabic language and the metre; and he must not sing any words which are ungrammatical or broken in metre.

100. He must know the tunes of the *qasidas* and their performance perfectly so that if he sings them he will be in harmony with his brothers.

101. The head of the *munshidin* must be active and urge on the singers to improve the *qasidas* from the point of view of memory, language, and metre.

102. The head of the singers must be active in making up new ways of performance; and the rest of the singers must be the same.

103. Every singer who makes up a new performance must submit it to the head singer whom he follows. If the latter accepts it he will order the rest of the singers to use it.

104. Every *khalifa* or higher than he may have a head singer and one *khalifa* or higher than he may have more than one head singer in different *hadrahs*; for every *hadrah*, one head singer.

105. At the beginning of the singing the leader of the *munshidin* begins or he orders one of the *munshidin* to begin and then the rest of the *munshidin* will follow him; no one is allowed to precede him.

106. The leader of the *munshidin* must not consider anyone as a *munshid* except after the permission of the *khalifa* or whoever is higher than he to whom the leader of the *munshidin* is attached; if the *khalifa* or one higher than he confirms him, he becomes a *munshid*.

107. If the head of the *munshidin* finds one of the brothers worthy to practise the hymns, then there is no objection to his teaching him; and he will be with the *munshidin* for practice when they make the hymns; and if the head of the *munshidin* informs the *khalifa* or one higher than him whom he follows about this, then there is no objection to that. [The Arabic carries the sense of it being free, but better that the *khalifa* should be informed.] If this person is taught and confirmed by the *khalifa* or any one higher than him, he will become a *munshid*.

108. If the head of the *munshidin* finds that one of his singers is incapable then he must put the matter before the *khalifa* or whoever is higher than he to whom he is attached.

109. The head of the *munshidin* has to wait for a sign from the man who is holding the *hadrah*; if he makes the sign to begin he will begin and his brothers the *munshidin* follow him.

110. Every head singer has *munshidin* appointed by the sheikh [here meaning *khalifa*] whom he follows.

111. It is not permissible for a *munshid* to leave his head singer and go to another in our *tariq* except by the permission of the head *munshid* whom he follows.

112. Every *munshid* must memorize a tenth of the Quran in order to recite it at the end of the *hadrah* if the sheikh [here meaning *khalifa*] tells him to do so.

113. The *munshid* must understand as far as possible the meaning of the words of the Sufis which he sings.

114. It is permissible for there to be in one *hadrah* two or more head *munshids* for the hymns; each head with his group in a particular area (place) with the permission of the sheikh [here meaning *khalifa*] of the *hadrah*.

115. The *munshid* must have a good voice. So no one who has not a good voice may be in front for the hymns unless it is absolutely necessary.

116. If the *munshidin* were singing something in the *hadrah* and the one in charge of the *hadrah* signs to them to fall silent, then they fall silent. Or if he orders them to change the *qasida* they change it if it is necessary to do so.

117. The hymn singing of the *munshidin* must be in harmony with the stages of the *dhikr* so that it will not muddle those making the *dhikr* and confuse the arrangement of the *hadrah*.

118. It is necessary for the head singer that he should be prepared to sing in the *hadrah* by himself or otherwise to choose one of his followers and order him to do so; if he chooses two or more then that is better.

119. The *munshidin* must be coherently organized so that no individual or group will deviate from the others.

120. In the general *hadrahs* the head singer must stick to the special poems which we have set out in 'The *Hamidiyat*'.[1]

121. Every *munshid* stands in the rank of singing in the place appointed for him by the head *munshid*.

122. A *munshid* may not leave the *munshidin* and stand with those making the *dhikr* on his own initiative but must ask the permission of the head hymn singer and the sheikh of the *hadrah*.

123. The head hymn singer may not forbid one of the singers to sing for any reason except by the approval of the sheikh whom they follow.

---

[1] The Old Edition permitted the head singer to select and examine books for *qasidas* which he could then submit to the Sheikh for approval.

124. When a *munshid* is ill the head singer may order him to leave the singing until he is cured and the *munshid* may not leave the singing without the order of the head.

125. In every dispute which occurs between the *munshidin* the head singer will be the arbitrator; if they consent to his judgement it is settled, and if not they will put the matter before the sheikh to whom they are attached.

126. The hymns must be in accordance with the school of the Sufis without there being anything in it which may do harm to the *tariq*.

127. If *munshidin* who follow different sheikhs of our *tariqa* come to-gether in one *hadrah* then the oldest of them will lead; if they dispute then they return to the sheikh who holds the *hadrah* if he is sheikh for all of them; otherwise the sheikh of the *hadrah* must be satisfied with his own *munshidin* who follow him in that *hadrah*.

128. If there are a number of heads of singers in one *hadrah* it is per-missible for them to choose one of the heads to be the head of the singing in that *hadrah* and the others will be followers to him on that occasion.

129. The head singers must prefer over themselves other heads whom they find with them as visitors to be heads of the singing even if by a gesture in the *hadrah*; and if they decline then the head who is appointed for the *hadrah* may begin.

130. It is permissible for one chief *munshid* to divide his singers into two groups and to order one of the *munshidin* to begin the *inshad* with those who are with him and that may take place on certain occasions for a special reason.

131. It is permissible for the head of the *munshidin* if he finds that one or more have deviated from the *inshad* (singing) to tell him to go in harmony with his brothers or to keep quiet.

132. It is necessary for the chief *munshid* to appoint someone in his group to be his deputy if he is absent in which eventuality he will assume his place and function.

133. Every *khalifa* or one higher than he may make hymn singers or chief *munshidin* for himself without the permission of the *Sigada*. [This law shows the lack of significance attached to the position of *munshid* in structural terms.]

134. It is permissible for every *khalifa* or whoever is higher than he to have *nuqaba'*.

135. The sheikh [here the local sheikh, i.e. the *khalifa*] may order the *naqib* to call the brothers or one of them at any time.

136. The *nuqaba'* must know most of the places [literally *amkina* means the home, coffee shop frequented, etc.] of the brothers and their names.[1]

137. It is permissible that the *naqib* or *nuqaba'* should be in front of the brothers when they walk [e.g. in a procession].

138. It is permissible that the sheikh [here meaning the *khalifa*] should order the *naqib* or *nuqaba'* to deliver anything or give a message or anything else.

139. The *naqib*, even though his function is very important, is nevertheless the servant of the *tariq*, and he must be easy in his manner, gentle in his disposition, smiling before the brothers, and meet them with a welcoming manner. He must bring pleasure to them so that love for him will be in their hearts.

140. If the *naqib* of the *nuqaba'* finds any failing in one of the *nuqaba'* then he must bring the matter before the sheikh [here meaning the *khalifa*] whom he follows.

141. If the *nuqaba'* have a dispute they must take the *naqib* of the *nuqaba'* as the arbitrator; if the dispute ends (that is the end of it) and if not they will take the matter to the sheikh [here meaning the *khalifa*] whom they follow.

142. The *naqib* may not neglect the office he holds on his own initiative.

143. The *naqib* of the *nuqaba'* has no right to keep a *naqib* from the exercise of his office or to attempt this, except by the order of the sheikh [here meaning *khalifa*] to whom they are attached.

144. If a number of *nuqaba'* for sheikhs [i.e. *khalifas*] of our *tariqa* meet, they will all be equal. The sheikh of the *hadrah* must arrange the functions among them giving due consideration to those senior by age.

145. The sheikh [here meaning *khalifa*] may order anyone he wishes to assist the *nuqaba'*.

146. Every *naqib* must know the conditions of the *niqaba* [office of *naqib*] to which he is appointed.

147. The *naqib* of the *hadrah* who is a *naqib* of the *nuqaba'*, has to arrange the *hadrah* which the *khalifa*, whose follower he is, holds. He will be at the head of the brothers at the time of the holding of the *hadrah*. He must carry out what the brothers need at the time of the *dhikr* under the order of the Sheikh.

148. The *naqib* in charge of the shoes must deliver the shoes of the brothers and put them in organized rows so that the shoes of the brothers of every district will be in the same place.

---

[1] Laws 134, 135, and 136 are not in the Old Edition.

149. The *naqib* of the shoes must be obliging in his manners; he should receive the brothers with smiles and welcoming and in his rank there is blessing, light, and the grace of God.

150. The *naqib* of the shoes must take care not to change the shoes or exchange them or lose them.

151. The *naqib* of the shoes may not leave the shoes and go to another place without appointing another *naqib* who is well known to him.

152. The *naqib* of the food must wear clean clothes, be refined in his manners, and excellent in his habits so that he does not put his hand in his nose when he is serving or do anything which the brothers consider dirty.

153. The *naqib* of the food must invite the brothers to food in a proper manner and with civility without insult, and he must avoid offending them; and he must not prefer the rich to the poor for all are poor (needy) to God.

154. The *fuqara'* must wear clean clothes, even if they are cheap or torn. They must be well-mannered in eating and behave with restraint though not avoiding eating. They should eat politely without being greedy. For whoever is most polite and his clothes clean though they are torn, will precede the other who may have the better dress or be rich.

155. The sheikh [here meaning *khalifa*] may order some of the brothers to sit at one table and some to sit at another table and no one has the right to ask him why.

156. Whereas food with the brothers is a gift [*nafha*, i.e. a gift bringing *baraka*] from God so it is necessary for them, if they are invited, to accept promptly, even though it is only one piece of bread.

157. Whereas restraint is a moral characteristic of the *fuqara'* it is necessary for them, if one of them is not invited to food and the brothers deliberately leave him, not to feel offended by that.

158. It is necessary for the *naqib* of the food to invite first for food every *faqir* coming from afar and put him over those of the immediate locality. If he finds a surplus of food he should invite the people of the area or some of them according to the situation.

159. It is necessary for the *fuqara'*, if they find only a little food or food which is not perfect, that they should receive it with joy and pleasure and consider it a gift; and if one of them gets a small piece, he should make do with it and praise God with satisfaction of the soul.

160. Whoever invites the brothers must not overburden himself for them because that will make him feel that the brothers are a burden and he will not invite them often for that reason.

161. It is necessary for anyone who is eating that he should not blow his nose at the time of eating, and not cough, nor laugh loudly, nor sniff, nor belch except after turning away from the food. He must break the bread into small pieces and chew it for a long time and not despise the food.

162. The *fuqara'* should not lick their fingers while eating, nor pick their teeth.

163. It is better that they speak about the right-doers [*as-Salihun*] and those like them while eating.

164. If one finds something which the brothers find offensive he must not inform them but rather should keep (the fact) hidden from them lest it do them harm.

165. The owner of the food must be happy and joyful and not look gloomy or regard anyone scornfully.

166. If the brothers are many they must go to eat group by group.

167. None of the brothers may take with him any of the food served unless he is poor and the brothers gave him that food, or if he is travelling or going to an area and the brothers give him food which he may eat after that.

168. Every *khalifa* or whoever is higher than he may have *nuqaba'* and *naqib* without the permission of the *Sigada*. [This refers to local organizations.]

169. The *naqib* of water and drinking must wear clean clothes and he must not do anything which the brothers would find offensive.

170. The *naqib* of the water must supervise the cleanness of the pots and the water and other matters. He must smell the things which he brings and take one swallow before he distributes it among the brothers, so that he may know its taste. If it is good, he will distribute it, if it is not he will return it with civility.

171. He must wash the pots whenever necessary.

172. He must be ready for the demand of water from him at any time.

173. He must help the *naqib* of the food whenever he asks his help but he is not a follower of the *naqib* of the food [i.e. not a subordinate].

174. The *naqib* of the *nuqaba'* must observe the work of all the *nuqaba'* and he must guide them in what they are deficient and make clear to them what is difficult for them.

175. In the absence of one of the *nuqaba'* he may order another one to replace the absentee; and he may ask from the sheikh for someone to help the *nuqaba'*.

THIRD SECTION

The Hadrahs

176. The *hadrahs* of our *tariq* may be held either at night or in the day-time.

177. It is not permissible to hold a *hadrah* in an unsuitable place, such as places which are dirty and of bad reputation and so on.

178. No one may open the *hadrah* except the *khalifa* or anyone higher than he or one who has permission from the *khalifa* or anyone higher than him. The highest takes precedence over the lowest.

179. The *hadrah* is in the form of concentric circles or one circle inside which there are rows. It is permissible for a good reason that it may be all rows.

180. The *hadrah* begins with sitting as for the prayer. Then the one who is holding the *hadrah* must open it by reading the *wazifa shadhiliya*, or the *gawhara hamidiya shadhiliya*, or some part of one of them. After the reading the *dhikr* opens with *la ilaha illa Allah* [there is no God but Allah] in a sitting position. Then they stand and say the single name, *Allah*, in a loud voice. Then they say it in a medium voice and then again in a voice just higher than a whisper. They then say *Huwa*, then the name *Hayy* [the Living], then the name *Qaiyyum* [the All Sustaining]. The mentioning of the latter name must be little. Then they say the name *Allah* loudly. Then they sit in the position of prayer. Then they rest cross legged by order of the man holding the *hadrah*. Then one reads one tenth of the Quran. Then they say *la ilaha illa Allah* three times. And they end it once by *Muhammad rasul Allah* [Muhammad is the Prophet of Allah]. Then they sing the poem by order of the man holding the *hadrah*. Then they speak of what is relevant in their way to Allah. Then they say: 'O God, O Kind One (*latif*), we ask you for kindness in the face of what has been decreed; be kind to us O Kind One; God is kind to his worshippers, He sustains whom he wishes and he is the Strong, the Mighty.' Then 'O Kind One' ten times. Then the entire section again once. Then 'O God, O Kindly One with His creatures, O Knower of His Creatures, O Knowing One with His creatures, be kind with us O Kindly One, O Knower, O Knowing One', once as it is known. Then 'O Most Esteemed' seven times, then 'O Omnipotent One' eleven times; then 'O Victorious One' eleven times; then *la ilaha illa Allah Muhammad rasul Allah* once. Then the reciting of the *fatha* [opening chapter of the Quran], then *la ilaha illa Allah* three times, and they finish it with *Muhammad rasul Allah* once. Then they stand for the *musafaha* (mutual kissing of hands) which is with sniffing (of the hands) and kissing.

The singing of hymns during the *dhikr* is permissible providing it is suitable for every stage. If there are many hymn singers it is permissible to divide them into two groups, or more, each group in a place to counterpoint the singing.

181. It is permissible to cut short the *hadrah* by leaving some Names or the reading or singing or something like that because of necessity, or shortage of time, or for any other reason.

182. It is not permissible to go beyond what is prescribed for the *hadrah* by making *dhikr* of another Name or reading anything else.

183. It is permissible to give gifts (*nafha*) to the brothers in the *hadrah*, when they are sitting, with the permission of the man holding the *hadrah*; the one who is distributing the *nafha* may not take his *nafha* except when he is a *khalifa* or higher than he and as for others than him, they are given the *nafha* from the one holding the *hadrah*.

184. It is not permissible for those in the *hadrah* to look around or stare at anyone, or to make a lot of movement, or to transfer from his place to another or to speak. He has no right to leave the *hadrah* for any reason except with the permission of one of the *khulafa'* who is near to him and who is one of the organizers of the *hadrah*.

185. Whoever wishes to enter the *hadrah* or to return to it must ask permission from one of the *khulafa'* so that he may guide him to a place in which he may sit; except if the outer row is open, in which case he may sit in it if he wishes; but otherwise he asks permission of the *khalifa*.

186. Sometimes one may read something of the *mulid* [here meaning panegyrical round sung at the *mulid* of Muhammad] which is attached to us in the *hadrah* during the last sitting with the permission of whoever is holding the *hadrah*, if he does not consider the brothers to be bored.

187. It is not permissible during the *dhikr* or the hymns or the listening to the *mulid* for one to shout or repeat anything and one must not say *Allah* in a high voice while listening to the Quran as the masses do but must pay attention and listen to the Quran.

188. If seven come together in the *hadrah* it is permissible to stand for the *dhikr* and if not then the *hadrah* is held sitting.

189. It is not permissible to drink water directly after the *dhikr* except after half an hour at least.

190. It is permissible for the *khulafa'* to enter the *hadrah* for some reason such as giving something that has fallen from those making the *dhikr* or arranging the ranks or something like that.

191. The corrupted *dhikr* is strictly forbidden in the *hadrah* and anything else (like the *hadrah*); rather the *dhikr* must be in concordance with what is in the *Shari'a* and the one making the *dhikr* must take care

not to shorten the negative *la* (in the *shahada*) nor to lengthen the *ha* of *ilah*, nor to stretch out the hamza in *illa* nor the hamza in *Allah*.

192. It is strictly forbidden to mention non-Arabic names in the *hadrahs*; rather the *dhikr* must be of the Glorious Names of Allah as set down for the *hadrah* which have been mentioned before.

193. Neither women nor babies may be present in the *hadrahs*.

194. The singing of melodies is strictly forbidden in our *hadrahs* [meaning here secular songs].

195. The *dhikr* must be performed with gentility and dignity in the *hadrahs* and the *dhikr* of *la ilaha illa Allah* must be from left to right in the negation[1] and vice versa in the affirmation[2] and the other names are said facing to the front.

196. It is forbidden in the *hadrahs* of our *tariq* for men and boys and women to sit in the middle of the *dhikr* circle.

197. Dancing and swaying are completely prohibited in the *dhikr*.

198. The *Ikhwan* must intertwine their hands in the *dhikr*.

199. The one making the *dhikr* may not raise his feet from the ground during the *dhikr* unless he is overcome.

200. If the *hadrah* is under the control of one man and one higher than him from the same *beit* comes then the first joins the rank and gives over the *hadrah* to the new man and if the man who came is from another *beit* then he must be given the preference.

FOURTH SECTION

The Studies

201. The man who holds the *hadrah* begins the *mudhakirat* (the studies) either with advice to the brothers and guiding them and teaching them or by submitting an aphorism (*hikma*) or verse of Quran or *hadith* to be discussed by the brothers.

202. It is permissible for anyone who wishes to speak to do so on what-ever occurs to him after taking the permission from the man holding the *hadrah*.

203. Two may not speak at the same time.

204. Dissension must not occur in the *mudhakirat*, so that for example one calls his brother a liar, even indirectly; rather one must speak of what occurs to him without referring to any other brother.

205. No one will take part in the studies in a conceited manner with haughty language but rather must do so with gentleness and civility.

[1] The saying of *la ilaha*, 'there is *no* God'.　　[2] *illa Allah*, 'save *Allah*'.

206. It is not permissible for the *faqir* to insist on his opinion but rather he must be civil with his brothers.

207. If any one of his brothers or other than he makes him angry in the studies he must put up with his brother.

208. He must not speak a verse of Quran or *hadith* unless he remembers it perfectly so that he does not fall into an error.

209. The study must not be prolonged so that the students become bored.

210. One must not mention the sin or fault of his brother frankly but rather must allude (to it) and it is better that he treats it obliquely and does not mention one's brother's name.

211. All speech must be directed to the holder of the *hadrah* so that members do not talk among themselves.

212. All studies in (giving) confirmation (of religious truths) which involve confusion in the minds of some should not be carried out during the *hadrah*. [i.e. the deeper meanings of *tasawwuf* are beyond the general and should be left to the *maglis* of the Sheikh.]

213. There should be nothing like talking about one who is absent or any insulting in the *hadrah*.

214. If one of the brothers makes a mistake in his *mudhakra*, or his ignorance appears in it, the brothers must not reject his opinion or embarrass him but rather they must receive it well and teach him with kindness and civility.

FIFTH SECTION

al Munasifat (*the penalties*)

215. If one of the brothers falls into an error it is approved to treat him with equity.

216. Making a just judgement is a correction and a benefit and it is not the kind of judgement which is registered in books or which needs a special formal meeting, but rather it is given verbally.

217. Equity is a means of bringing the man closer to Allah, of refining his character, of purifying him from any fault into which he has fallen.

One must not judge his brother save in such a way as he could bear himself; he must not judge him to gain revenge, nor for vengeance but rather he makes the judgement for God and he intends by this to improve the condition of his brother out of mercy and compassion.

218. With regard to every man whom the brothers judge, the judgement should be according to his capacity (to bear it) and the seniority in the

higra [refers to seniority in time after taking the oath], and age and things such as that.

219. When the brothers judge their brother and he finds the judgement too much for him then he should ask his brothers for sympathy and they should take pity on their brother and lighten the judgement for him.

220. No one of our *tariq* may judge our student [i.e. a student of the *Sigada*] or any *khalifa* of the *khulafa'* or *na'ib* of the *beit as-Sigada* except in a *hadrah* of the *beit as-Sigada* held in any place.

221. No one may prescribe a penance for anyone who follows a *beit* other than his or prescribe anything except in the matter of the small penances like (the recitation of) 300 *dhikr* or what is like that.

SIXTH SECTION

The Awrad (daily office)

223. The *wird* of the *tariq* for the morning and the evening is as follows: 'I ask God's forgiveness' a hundred times. 'O God bless our lord Muhammad Your worshipper (*'abd*) and Prophet and Your messenger, the illiterate Prophet[1] and his family and companions and grant him salvation (saying *sallim* with that vocalization and not *sallam*) a hundred times. *La ilaha illa Allah* a hundred times, on the final time saying '*la ilaha illa Allah*, our lord Muhammed the messenger of *Allah*, may God bless him and his family and his companions and salutations' [using *sallam* with that vocalization, thus changing the sense from above] once.

224. One may make a *dhikr* of *la ilaha illa Allah* in the morning and the evening from one hundred to a thousand times and perform it between a hundred and a thousand.

225. Whoever does not recite his *wird* once must go over it twice (later) and if he repeats this up to seven times then he must present himself [i.e. put the matter] before the brothers.

226. One must read the *wazifa* of the *Shadhiliya* once every day and the *gawhara* of the *Hamidiya Shadhiliya* once on the day for which it is prescribed and so on; if one finds the memorizing difficult, or there is a strong necessity (stopping one performing it) then let him read as much as he can of one of them every day.[2]

227. Either one of the above may substitute for the other in the *hadrah*.

228. One may not go beyond this in the *awrad* over what has been

---

[1] The Prophet Muhammed is traditionally supposed to have been unable to read or write, and this is commonly adduced as proof of the miraculous nature of the Quran.

[2] These are two of the religious texts of the order.

mentioned except by the permission of the Sheikh. As for the increase between which and the *wird* proper there is a division providing it is of the same form then there is no objection. [i.e. supererogatory *awrad* may be read by the member if he so wishes.]

229. It is forbidden for the student to take a *wird* other than what is laid down in writing in this *Qanun* from anyone other than the Sheikh of the *Tariq*.

230. It is permissible to read the *Dala'il al Khairat* in a group or individually or (one may read) part of it. ['the signs of good deeds', one of the *awrad* of the *Hamidiya Shadhiliya*.]

231. It is permissible to read the *Burda* (a poem—*qasida*) of Busiri [the *Burda* is the cloak of Muhammed; when ill the poet was inspired by a dream of the Prophet who put his cloak over him and cured him] or part of it in a group or individually.

232. It is permissible to read the *Birr* [a religious text] of *al-Shadhili* in a group or individually in the morning.

233. It is permissible to read the *hizb* (office) of the 'freeing from melancholy' by us as a group or individually.

234. It is permissible to read the *hizb* of the *nasr* (victory) of *al-Shadhili*.

235. It is permissible to read the *hizb* of the sea of *Shadhili* after the afternoon prayer in a group or individually.

236. It is permissible to read the *rub'a* which is the Quran (read in) a group.

237. It is permissible to read the chapter *Ya Sin* [Sura 36 of the Quran] and *Tabarak* [Sura 67] morning and evening.

238. It is permissible to read the chapter *al Waqa'a* [Sura 56 of the Quran].

239. One may take for himself a *wird* from the Prayer [*salat*] and the Quran.

240. It is permissible to read the *awrad* of *al-Shadhili* such as the *hizb ash-shakwa* (the section of the complaint).

241. It is permissible to read *al masba'at*.

242. It is permissible to make the prayer of saying *subhan Allah* [glory be to God].

243. It is permissible to make the prayer of asking God for proper guidance.

244. It is permissible to make the prayer on the Prophet, may God bless and preserve him, in the form of *al-Shadhili* known as *an-Nur adh-Dhati* [the essential light].

245. One may not read the *ahzab* of other *turuq* or *awrad* other than the *awrad* which have been set above; such as the *wird as-Sahar* of Sidi Mustafa al Bakri or the prayers (*salawat*) of Sidi Ahmed ad-Dirdir or other than that, save by the permission of the Sheikh; the *munaqah* of Sidi Ahmed ibn 'Ata' Allah al-Isakandari[1] which is the end of the aphorisms of '*Ata*' and can substitute for the *wird as-Sahar*. And whoever wants to read this *munaqah* may do so.

246. Whoever wants to go on the way of the people (the Sufis) as the most distinguished have done and the Sheikh has seen in him the aptitude for that, he may order him to make a special *dhikr* which is suitable for him from the point of view of the Names and the number of times to be recited.

247. The Names of which he who goes on the way of arriving to God makes *dhikr* must not go beyond the Beautiful Names (the ninety-nine Names of God).

248. The stages of the *dhikr* are three. Firstly, the *dhikr*, *la ilaha illa Allah*. The second *Allah*, without the *ya* of invocation (termed by the grammarians *ya an-nida*, e.g. *Ya Allah—O Allah*). The third is His holy Name *Huwa* (He).

The first is in the denial of others (i.e. the assertion of the absolute Unity of God); the second is the assertion of the One of whom the *dhikr* is made. The third is the immersion in the One of whom the *dhikr* is made until the worshipper comes to the stage of *fana'* [the annihilation of self in God, one of the highest stages of the mystical path. See *Shorter Encyclopedia of Islam*, p. 98], then to union, then to witness of the distinction in the union, and its opposite, and the unity in multiplicity and *vice versa*, and the witness of the Truth with the assertion of Creation and the discharge of the prescriptions of the Holy Law. What is mentioned after these three names is only a detailing of the general concept of the *dhikr*.

249. Among the *Shadhiliya* seclusion lies in the unveiling [i.e. in insight into the *batin*, the internal reality beneath what is merely apparent]; their seclusion is their hearts so they will be with their hearts with God while with their bodies they are with the people. Every sheikh who orders his student to enter seclusion must beware of its dangers for in entering it there is a danger of which most of the people of the *tariq* are unaware. For much fasting and hunger and much sleeplessness and *dhikr* will lead to dullness of the brain and will create mental illness or disturbance in the mind. Or he [the student] will come by chance

---

[1] *Munaqah*, literally 'confidential discussion'. It is the last section of Ibn 'Ata' Allah's most famous work *al-Hikam al 'Ata'iya*, a collection of his mystical sayings.

upon a *sheitan* in his seclusion [or place of] who will harm him so that he will speak that which has no meaning. Or the devil will set forth something to him and some of the people will think that he has become a Saint of God. Or light may by chance come upon him or he will see an angel or a *wali* and he will not be able to bear what he sees and he will go out of his mind. All this requires a sheikh to have the medicine of the doctors, the religion of the prophets, and the politics of the kings. That sheikh must have been through that way and know it so that he may guide (people) to it. Then he who has no capacity for this should fear God from going ahead with that or ordering anyone to do it. For he will be in the wrong for himself and for the others.

250. As for every revealed occurrence, or dream vision, the student may not tell anyone of it except his sheikh who has taught him.

SEVENTH SECTION

The Processions

251. It is permissible to make processions for the brothers to walk in with the permission of the *na'ib* of the *beit* or of the *khalifa* of the *khulafa'* if there is no *na'ib* of the *beit* in the area. And it is permissible with the permission of the *na'ib* of the *Sigada* in the *markaz* or the governorate with the agreement of the *na'ibs* of the different *beits*.

252. Every new *khalifa* must walk at the head of the procession, he and those attached to him; and those senior (in length of membership) to him go after him and so on so long as all the *khalifas* and *khalifas* of the *khalifas* and *na'ibs* of the *beits* if one of them is present, agree on putting a group at the front for a proper purpose or holding them back.

253. If it happens that a group of *khulafa'* have been given the permission (to lead) at the same time then the youngest may lead in the procession; and the elder will follow him; every *khalifa* will follow in walking the *khalifa* of the *khulafa'* from whom he learnt [i.e. by whom he was recruited]. And every *khalifa* of the *khulafa'* or *na'ib* will follow those who are newer in his rank.

254. The *Beit as-Sigada* comes after every *beit* in the procession.

255. Riding is absolutely forbidden in the processions of our *tariqa*.

256. Walking in the procession must be perfect, with dignity and complete order. It must be free from what dishonours the *tariq* and its members.

257. One must ask permission of those in the government administration for the processions when necessary and for the day processions. Except if there is a *mulid* and the permission is general for the people of the *tariq*.

258. A group of the brothers must not be outside the procession unless for some service which they have been ordered to perform by those in charge of the procession.

259. The procession must be made up of two rows facing each other [i.e. when the Sheikh formally walks through it at the *mulid* of Salama].

260. It is permissible in the procession to give drinking water; and to sprinkle rose water; and to use incense.

EIGHTH SECTION

The Emblems (signs) of the Tariq

261. The emblem of the *tariq* is the white cloth; and the green band which goes across the chest and on which is written in white and yellow 'The *Tariqa* of the *Hamidiya Shadhiliya*'.

262. The flags are white and there is written on them in green the *shahada*. Under it in small letters *Madad ya Abu'l Hasan* [assistance O Abu Hasan, i.e. al Shadhili], and the name of the *tariq*. The flags may be green with these words written on them.

263. Every *beit* or area may have a sign on which is written the name of the *tariq* and the name of the house or the district and it is strictly forbidden to add any other expression except with the permission of the *Sigada*.

264. It is permissible that every *khalifa* or one of higher rank should have flags of the *tariq*.

265. The *na'ibs* wear the crescent if they so wish and this is good.

266. Everyone affiliated to the *tariq*, whether old or young, must wear on his chest a green band whose breadth is 15 centimetres with only the words 'The *tariqa* of the *Hamidiya Shadhiliya*' in white or yellow written on it.

267. The hymn singers wear on their chests a special sign which is obtained from the *beit as-Sigada*.

NINTH SECTION

The judgements which proceed from the tariq

268. Judgements in our *tariq* must proceed from a meeting made up as follows:

269. (*a*) *Maglis as-Sigada*: Made up of its Sheikh in his capacity as head and its deputy and the *naqib* of the *nuqaba'* and two *na'ibs* of the *na'ibs* of the *beits* whom the Sheikh elects and four in their capacity as members.

(*b*) *Maglis* of the *Na'ib* of the *Beit*: Made up of him in his capacity as head and four of the *khalifas* of the *khulafa'* by election in their capacity as members.

(*c*) *Maglis* of the *Na'ib* of the *Markaz*: Made up of him in his capacity as head and four of the *na'ibs* of the *beits* in the *markaz* by election in their capacity as members. And if there are not four of them then the rest from the *khalifas* of the *khulafa'* by election.

(*d*) *Maglis* of the *Na'ib* of the *Mudiriya*: Made up of the *na'ib* of the *mudiriya* in his capacity as head and the *na'ib* of the *markaz* and three of the *na'ibs* of the *beits* by election in their capacity as members.

270. Every *na'ib* of a *beit* or *markaz* or *mudiriya* or *muhafza* or the *Wakil* of the *Sigada* or *naqib* of the *nuqaba'* who has a case or a special problem which is before one of these *maglis* must not be a member of that meeting in which the problem will be discussed nor even any of his relatives nor any with an interest in that question.

271. The *khulafa'* and the *khulafa'* of the *khulafa'* have no *maglis* and if they want to execute any punishment they must inform the *na'ib* of the *beit*.

272. Every meeting of these four *maglis* is only held once a month on the first Saturday of the month if there is a necessity for it; and it is not public.

273. The voices of the members and the heads are equal in these meetings.

274. Every judgement which issues from one of these *maglis*, even if from that of the *beit as-Sigada*, the Sheikh may carry it out or not or order it to be reviewed. And he may elect other than those who discussed the question in the first place.

275. Every judgement to which the *Sheikh as-Sigada* agrees in writing is carried out.

276. Every meeting must have its minutes in which the subject is set forth in detail and what was done in regard to it. It must be registered in the register of the cases in every district where the meeting is held. It can only be registered with the approval of the *Sheikh as-Sigada* in writing on it.

277. Every district in which a meeting is held and a judgement issued from it, must inform the *Sigada* of that decision; it will not be authorized except with the latter's approval.

278. The judgements which are issued over the *muridin* are from their sheikhs, and included with them are the *nuqaba'* and the hymn singers; and they must be communicated to the *na'ibs* of the *beit* and it may be to those higher than them.

279. The judgements which are issued over the *khulafa'* are from the *khulafa'* of the *khulafa'* except the expulsion from the *tariq*.

280. The judgements which are issued on the *khulafa' al-khulafa'* are from the *maglis* of the *beit* composed of the *na'ibs* of the *beit* except expulsion from the *tariq*.

281. The judgements which are issued over the *na'ibs* of the *beit* are from the *maglis* of the *na'ib* of the *markaz* except the expulsion from the *tariq*.

282. The judgements which are issued over the *na'ibs* of the *markaz* are from the *maglis* of the *na'ib* of the *mudiriya* except expulsion from the *tariq*.

283. The judgements which are issued over the *na'ib* of the *mudiriya* or the *muhafaza* are only from the *Sigada*.

284. All the judgements which are over a *murid* or *khalifa* or higher than him may be appealed against to the *Sigada* for it to examine (the judgements).

285. In the case of the sins (*dhunub*) which are in the way of leaving the reading of the *wird* or being late for the *hadrah* once or several times the judgement is small with regard to the *munasafat* and does not require any meetings.

286. As for the greater matters such as going out from the *tariq* and not paying attention to it, or displaying disobedience, or harming some of the brothers, or doing something to their detriment, or committing any of the great sins,[1] advice must be given on this from the beginning; if one comes forward and demonstrates his repentance and then returns again he may be received (in again) with [together with] his punishment [discipline] such as being kept away [literally, stopped] (from the *tariq*) for some days or months or other than that—if he does not come forward and continues in his error he may be expelled forever and it is necessary in what is particularly concerned with the expulsion of the *khulafa'* that the matter be set forth in the *Sigada*.

287. Our assemblies (*maglis*) may give judgements according to the Sufi tradition whether of old or present times in those matters which are not stipulated for in this Law.

288. Every judgement which is not in accordance with this Law is void except the judgement of the *Sheikh as-Sigada*.

289. There are no fees for cases in our *tariq* of whatever kind in any assembly of our *tariq* but all the cases are heard gratis.

290. If a dispute arises between two *khalifas* or more of the *beit*

[1] See above, p. 104.

as-Sigada then the decision of the dispute is to the *na'ib* of the *beit as-Sigada* whom they follow.

291. If a dispute arises between two *khalifas* not of the *beit as-Sigada* then the decision in the dispute is to the *na'ib* of their *beit*.

292. If a dispute arises between two *khalifas*, one of whom is from the *beit as-Sigada* and the other of whom is from another *beit*, then the decision belongs to the two *na'ibs* of the two *beits*.

293. If a dispute arises between two *khalifas* both of whom are from *beits* other than the *beit as-Sigada*, then the decision is to the two *na'ibs* of the respective *beits*.

294. If there is a dispute between two *khalifas* of our *tariq* and it does not get settled by the two *na'ibs* of the respective *beits* then let it be taken up to whoever is higher than they until it comes to us; and the *khulafa'* of the *khulafa'* are like the *khalifa* in the settlement of dispute.

295. If a dispute arises between a *khalifa* or one higher than him and one of the *khulafa'* or *na'ibs* of a *tariq* other than ours, then let him who is of our *tariq* raise the matter before whoever is higher than he in our *tariq*; and if the dispute is not ended then let him raise it to whoever is higher until it comes to us.

296. If there occurs the expulsion of a *khalifa* or higher than him by order of the *Sigada* then he may not be received in a *hadrah* or a procession nor in the assembly of our *tariq*; it is not permissible to walk with him in a procession or a *hadrah*; if he has students and they leave him at that time then they are followers of the *Sigada* and it orders them with what it sees fit; if they follow him at the time of his expulsion then the judgement of expulsion is applicable to them; if among them there are *khulafa'* or higher the *Sigada* decides what it sees fit for those *khulafa'* or any higher.

297. It is not permissible for anyone other than the *Sheikh* of the *Sigada*, even its *Wakil*, to expel a *khalifa* in our *tariq*, or one higher than him particularly, for any reason whatever.

298. It is permissible for the *khalifa* or higher to expel his student but not one who is not his student; and a *khalifa* or higher than he may not be expelled except by the order of the *Sigada*.

299. It is not permissible for anyone other than the *Sheikh of the Sigada* to expel a student or a hymn singer or a *naqib* or *naqib* of the *nuqaba'* or *khalifa* or higher than him who belongs to the *beit as-Sigada*.

TENTH SECTION

General Rules

300. The position of *Wakil as-Sigada* is not inherited save when the *Sheikh as-Sigada* so recommends.[1]

301. The position of *naqib* of the *nuqaba'* of the *Sigada*, and its *nuqaba'* and the *na'ibs* of the *beits*, and of the *marakaz* and the *muhafazat* and the *khulafa'* of the *khulafa'* is not inherited.[2]

302. Every licence for the position of *khalifa* or *na'ib* must be given only by us and with our seal and signature; it is bestowed without any financial burden [*maganan*—literally, freely] and according to the form whose text we have given above.

303. The licence for the position of *khalifa* and *na'ib* may not be transferred to anyone.

304. It is not permissible for anyone to give the *tariq* to anyone unless he has the licence of *khalifa* or *na'ib* from the *Sigada*.

305. It is not permissible for a *khalifa* or higher than he to receive in the *hadrah* which he holds in any town, even if he is a follower of the *beit as-Sigada*, a student who has taken the *tariq* from a *khalifa* or higher than that in our *tariq*, except with the permission of the *khalifa* from whom he (originally) took the *tariq*; if necessity compels, the matter may be brought up before the *Sheikh as-Sigada*.

306. Any *khalifa* or higher than him may teach the *tariq* and take the oaths (of devotion to the *tariq*) [see Chapter III, pp. 83–7] from the people in any place and he may hold a *hadrah* or *hadrahs*.

307. It is permissible that there should be in any place a *khalifa* or *khalifas*, and *khalifas* of the *khulafa'* or *na'ibs* of the *beits*; and any one of them may hold a *hadrah* or *hadrahs*.

308. It is not permissible for a *khalifa* or higher than him to give the

---

[1] The Old Edition gives the following: 'The position of *wakil* of the *Sigada* is to be inherited among the sons of the *Sheikh* of the *Sigada* and their sons by seniority of age.'

[2] The Old Edition read here: 'The function of the *nuqaba'* of the *Sigada* and the *naqib* of the *nuqaba'* is inherited; after them their sons by seniority. If they have no descendants [*dhuriyya*] then the nearest patrilineal relatives if they are suitable. This is also the case for the *na'ibs* of a *beit* other than the *beit as-Sigada*.

The function of the *khalifa* of the *khulafa'* in any *beit* and of the *na'ibs* of the *beits* of the *Sigada* and of the *marakaz* and the *mudiriyat* [two divisions of the governorate] and the *muhafazat* [governorates] is not inherited, except whoever of them is the *na'ib* of a *beit* other than the *beit as-Sigada*; and the position of *naqib* of the *beit* attached to this latter is inherited as we have said before.'

tariq to anyone who has taken it from the Sheikh of the *tariq* or a *khalifa* or higher than he in the *tariq*.

309. A *khalifa* or higher than he may ask another *khalifa* or higher than he from our *tariq* to hold a *hadrah* with their brother [i.e. sharing] regularly or at a particular time.

310. A *khalifa* may not fail to appear at *hadrahs* in the *zawiyas* of the *beit* which follows him unless this *khalifa* has a *hadrah* or *hadrahs* [of his own and therefore cannot attend].

311. It is not permissible for a *khalifa* or higher than he to issue an order to one of his rank or higher; nor may he issue an order to anyone lower than him in rank unless that person is his follower; and he may not under any circumstances stop a *khalifa* [i.e. expel him or keep him from the *hadrahs*].

312. No one of our *tariq* is to mix the brothers of our *tariq* with the brother of another *tariq* in a *hadrah* or a procession or occasion.

313. No student of our *tariq* may go to the *hadrah* of another sheikh not of our *tariq* to attend his *hadrah* or to take guidance from him.

314. It is not permissible for the people of our *tariq* to take the *tariq* from one who is not one of the sheikhs of our *tariq*.

315. It is not permissible for a *khalifa* or higher than he to hold a *hadrah* with the brothers for a fee.

316. Everyone who is attached to us may not attach himself to a *tariq* other than ours.

317. It is not permissible for a *na'ib* of the *markaz* or the *muhafza* to appoint a deputy for himself save after the proper official measures (have been taken).

318. Everyone who has taken the *tariq* from the sheikhs of our *tariq* and then from us is our student and not the student of the person from whom he originally took the *tariq*.

319. If someone takes the *tariq* from a *khalifa* or higher than him in our *tariq*, and some of the people of the other *turuq* claim that he is their student in the Way then let the student be questioned. And if he says that he is their student then we have nothing to do with him.

320. It is permissible to set up a tent in a *mulid* or to gather for some elevated purpose.

321. It is permissible to make a *hadrah* at the tombs (of the Saints) avoiding what the Holy Law does not approve.

322. It is not permissible to make a procession or march except for the religious occasions or the occasions appointed by the *Sigada*.

323. It is permissible to meet the Sheikhs of the *turuq* other than ours; and to make prayers (*wasla*) and read the *fatiha* for the living and the dead if the man in charge of the *mawkib* sees fit.

324. It is not permissible for anyone of our *tariq* to enter a house without the permission of the owner especially in his absence on the pretext of being a sheikh; if the *Sigada* is certain of his contravention of this regulation it expels him from the *tariq*.

325. Every *na'ib* of a *beit* or of a *markaz* or of a *muhafza* must have registers of incoming and outgoing communications and the names of the followers of the *na'ib* and the cases and the judgements.

326. Every student, or *naqib* or *naqib* of the *nuqaba'* may ask permission of his sheikh [i.e. here his *khalifa*] to hold a *hadrah* in which he gathers those who love the *tariq*. And he unites their hearts. If his sheikh finds him suitable he gives him the permission; and if the sheikh orders some of the brothers of that student to attend that *hadrah* with him to help him in learning from what occurs in that *hadrah*, then this is good. And if the sheikh finds him suitable to be a *khalifa* he may bring him forward to the *Sigada* to make him a *khalifa*.

327. Communication with administrators in the *marakaz* and *muhafazat* is through the *na'ibs* of the *marakaz* and the *muhafaza t*if there are *na'ibs*, otherwise the *khalifa* or *khalifa* of the *khulafa'* or *na'ibs* of the *beits* may communicate with the administration in what is necessary concerning the *mulid* or meeting in any other matter. The *na'ib* of the *beit* comes first and after him the *khalifa* of the *khulafa'* and after him the *khalifa*.

The Covenant

This is an undertaking of a religious relationship like the undertaking of the *Ansar* [the believers of Medina who assisted the Prophet Muhammad after his flight from Mecca], may God be pleased with them, to protect the Prophet from what their children and their wives protected him.

And its form is as follows: The Sheikh orders the student who seeks to make the compact to make the ritual ablutions. Then the Sheikh sits as he would for the prayers and commands the *murid* to do likewise so that his knees touch those of the Sheikh. Then he makes a link with him, that is the Sheikh places his hand on the right hand of the student. Then the student looks into his eyes and repeats what the Sheikh says— as is contained in the text.

The *'ahd* is in two parts: the section of being blessed, which may be performed more than once, and the section of the mystical life which may not be taken again from another Sheikh. The Sheikh who gives this latter type must have many attributes. It is necessary that he should be of those who have mystical knowledge of God: and anyone who joins him (such a Sheikh) and then leaves him for another is like one who plays tricks. And it is fitting that the Sheikhs withdraw their hearts from him. Whoever is like that has indeed fallen from the eye of God. We take refuge in God from expulsion and deprivation. And whosoever fulfils the rights of his teacher with whom he has legitimate connection, God opens the eye of his intelligence and blesses him.

The beginning of Sufism is the curing of hearts, and the Sheikh is the doctor of souls and hearts. And the connection of the student to one as a Sheikh to whom there is no legitimate link [i.e. he is not fit to be a Sheikh] is like the sick man going to someone who is not a doctor; one who is not a doctor harms the patient. This is all in his mode of life in himself and in the stages (of mystical advancement). So why (join such a one) when the dawn of truth appears and revelation unfolds. For that Sheikh is the greatest harm, and in him there is the greatest danger. God helped us to the conduct of the way of His beloved in the guarding of the Book of God and the Sunna of His Prophet. Praise be to God by whose grace you accomplish righteous actions.[1]

There then follows the text translated in Chapter III, 'System and Sanction', pp. 95–7.

The Awrad of the Morning and Evening

[this section is not in the Old Edition]

As for the *wird* of the *tariq* in the morning and evening, it is as follows: I ask forgiveness from God the Most Great (a hundred times); O God bless our lord Muhammad Your Worshipper (*'abd*) and Your Prophet and Your Messenger, the illiterate Prophet, and on his family and his Companions (a hundred times) and its seal—*la ilaha illa Allah* —our lord Muhammad the Prophet of God, may God bless him and his family and his Companions.

(The Sheikh speaks the following and the brothers answer.)

Have you accepted what we have contracted with you and laid down as a condition for you?—We have accepted. And are you content with the *Faqir* [i.e. the Sheikh] as brother and guide in God?—We have accepted.

O God, verily I bear witness to you that I have accepted and received them all as brothers in God the Most High, and I have received all who have said 'we have received'. And whoever has said 'we have received' has become one of us—he has what we have [in rights] and our duties are incumbent on him also—and have you accepted?—(We have accepted—and we [i.e. the Sheikh] have accepted—and (recite) the *fatiha* on this (compact).

---

[1] This section was not in the Old Edition.

Far is your Lord, the Lord of Might, from what they ascribe to Him and peace be on those who were sent (by God) and praise be to God the Lord of the Worlds.

Say with me once *La ilaha illa Allah Muhammad Rasul Allah*.

329. For any law in this *Qanun* over which there is doubt in its comprehension, or which requires further detail or definition or (explanation of) meaning, this matter must be returned to the *Sigada* that the interpretation or completion may come from it. This will then be a supplement to this *Qanun*.

BIBLIOGRAPHY

I. SOCIOLOGY/ANTHROPOLOGY

ABD EL MALEK, A., *Égypte: société militaire*, Paris: Éditions du Seuil, 1962.

AMMAR, H., *Growing up in an Egyptian Village*, London: Routledge & Kegan Paul, 1954.

BERQUE, J., *Histoire sociale d'un village égyptien au xxème siècle*, Paris: Mouton, 1957.

—— 'Dans le delta du Nil', *Studia islamica*, vol. 4, 1955, pp. 91–109.

—— *French North Africa: The Maghreb between Two World Wars*, New York: Praeger, 1967.

EVANS-PRITCHARD, E. E., *The Sanusi of Cyrenaica*, Oxford: O.U.P., 1949.

GOFFMAN, E., *The Presentation of Self in Everyday Life*, New York: Doubleday, 1959.

GROUPE DE L'ÉTUDE DE L'I.E.D.E.S., 'Pression démographique et stratification sociale dans les campagnes égyptiennes', *Tiers-Monde*, vol. 1, no. 3, 1960, pp. 313–40.

—— 'La société urbaine égyptienne', *Tiers-Monde*, vol. 2, no. 6, 1961, pp. 183–210.

HUSSEIN, M., *La Lutte de classes en Égypte de 1945 à 1968*, Paris: Maspero, 1969.

LEWIS, I. M., 'Sufism in Somaliland: A study in tribal Islam', *Journal of the British School of Oriental and African Studies*, vol. 17, pp. 581–602 and vol. 18, pp. 145–60, 1955–6.

—— (ed.), *Islam in Tropical Africa*, London: O.U.P., 1966.

LUCKMANN, T., *The Invisible Religion*, New York: The Macmillan Co., 1967.

MACINTYRE, A., *Secularization and Moral Change*, London: O.U.P., 1967.

MANNHEIM, K., *Ideology and Utopia*, New York: first published 1936.

MERTON, R. K., *Social Structure and Function*, New York: Free Press of Glencoe, revised and enlarged edition, 1957.

—— 'The Role-Set: Problems in Sociological Theory', *British Journal of Sociology*, vol. 8, June 1957, no. 2, pp. 106–20.

PARSONS, T., *Structure and Process in Modern Societies*, New York: Free Press of Glencoe, 1960.

PETERS, E., 'The Proliferation of Segments in the Lineage of the Bedouin of Cyrenaica', *Journal of the Royal Anthropological Institute*, 90, 1, pp. 29–53.

POPE, L., *Millhands and Preachers*, New Haven: Yale University Press, 1942.

SAPIR, E., 'Language', *Encyclopaedia of the Social Sciences*, vol. 9, old edition, pp. 155–68, New York, 1933.

—— 'Symbolism', *Encyclopaedia of the Social Sciences*, vol. 14, old edition, pp. 492–5.

SCHUTZ, A., 'Common Sense and Scientific Interpretation of Human Action', *Philosophy and Phenomenological Research*, XIV, no. 1, Sept. 1953.

—— 'Making Music Together', in *Collected Papers*, vol. 2, ed., and with introduction by Arvid Brodersen, The Hague: Martinus Nijhoff, 1964.

—— 'The Constitution of Meaningful Lived Experience in the Constitutor's Own stream of Consciousness', in *The Phenomenology of the Social World*, trans. George Walsh and Frederick Lehnert, Evanston, Ill.: Northwestern University Press, 1967.

SOUTHALL, A., 'An operational theory of Role', *Human Relations*, vol. 12, no. 1, Feb. 1959, pp. 17–34.

SOUTHERN, R. W., *Western Society and the Church in the Middle Ages*, Harmondsworth: Penguin Books, 1970.

TAMBIAH, S. J., 'The Ideology of Merit and the Social Correlates of Buddhism in a Thai village', in Leach, E. R. (ed.), *Dialectic in Practical Religion*, Cambridge: C.U.P., 1968, pp. 41–121.

—— 'The Magical Power of Words', *Man*, N.S. vol. 3, no. 2, June 1968, pp. 175–208.

TROELTSCH, E., *Social Teachings of the Christian Churches*, London: Allen & Unwin, 1956.

TURNER, V. W., 'Betwixt and Between: The Liminal Period', in *The Forest of Symbols: Aspects of Ndembu Ritual*, Ithaca: Cornell University Press (paperback edition), 1970.

WEBER, M., *The Theory of Social and Economic Organisation*, New York: Free Press of Glencoe, 1964.

—— *From Max Weber: Essays in Sociology*, trans., ed., and with introduction by Gerth and Mills, New York: O.U.P., 1946.

WILSON, B. R., *Sects and Society*, Berkeley and Los Angeles: University of California Press, 1961.

—— *Religion in Secular Society*, A Sociological Comment, London: C. A. Watts & Co. Ltd., 1966.

—— 'An analysis of sect development', *American Sociological Review*, 24 Feb. 1959, pp. 3–15.

WOLFF, KURT H. (ed.), *The Sociology of George Simmel*, New York: Free Press of Glencoe, 1964.

2. ORIENTAL STUDIES

ABUN-NASR, J., *The Tijaniyya*, London: O.U.P., 1965.

ADAMS, C. C., *Islam and Modernism in Egypt*, London: O.U.P., 1933.

ANAWARTI, G. D., and GARDET, L., *La Mystique musulmane*, Paris: J. Vrin, 1961.

BAER, G., *History of Landownership in Modern Egypt*, London: O.U.P., 1963.

—— 'The Dissolution of the Egyptian Village Community', *Die Welt des Islams*, vol. 6, 1959–61, pp. 56–70.

—— 'Social Change in Egypt: 1800–1914', in Holt, P. M. (ed.), *Political and Social Change in Modern Egypt* London: O.U.P., 1968, pp. 135–46.

—— *Egyptian Guilds in Modern Times*, Jerusalem: The Israeli Oriental Society, 1964.

BANNERTH, E., 'The Khalwatiya', *MIDEO*, 8, 1964–6, pp. 1–75.

BIRGE, J. K., *The Bektashi Order of Dervishes*, Luzac & Co., 1937.

BROWN, J. P., *The Dervishes*, London: Trubner & Co., 1868.

BRUNEL, R., *Essai sur la confrérie religieuse des ʿAissaouia au Maroc*, Paris: Paul Geuthner, 1926.

CALVERLY, E. E., 'Nafs', *Encyclopaedia of Islam* (old edn.), vol. 3, Leiden: E. J. Brill, 1936, pp. 827–30.

DUMOULIN, H., *A History of Zen Buddhism*, New York: Pantheon, 1963.

GARDET, L., 'Dhikr', *Encyclopaedia of Islam*, (new edn.), vol. 2, Leiden: E. J. Brill, 1965, pp. 223–7.

GIBB, H. A. R., 'The Structure of Religious Thought in Islam', in *Studies on the Civilisation of Islam*, London: Routledge & Kegan Paul, 1962.

GIBB, H. A. R., and BOWEN, H., *Islamic Society and the West*. vol. 1, Part I and Part II, London: O.U.P., 1957.

GRUNEBAUM, G. E. VON, *Muhammedan Festivals*, New York: Schuman, 1951.

HANSEN, B., and MARZOUK, G. A., *Development and Economic Policy in the U.A.R. (Egypt)*, Amsterdam: North Holland Publishing Co., 1965.

HEYWORTH-DUNNE, J., *Introduction to the History of Education in Modern Egypt*, London: Luzac & Co., 1938.

—— *Religious and Political Trends in Modern Egypt*, Washington, D.C.: privately published, 1950.

HOLT, P. M., *Political and Social Change in Modern Egypt*, London: O.U.P., 1968.

HOURANI, A., *Arabic Thought in the Liberal Age*, London: O.U.P., 1962.

HUGHES, T. P., *A Dictionary of Islam*, London: W. H. Allen & Co., 1935.

HUSSEINI, I. M., *The Muslim Brethren*, Beirut: Khayats, 1956.

ISSAWI, C., *Egypt in Revolution*, London: O.U.P., 1963.

—— *Egypt at Mid-Century*, London: O.U.P., 1954.

IZUTSU, T., *The Structure of the Ethical Terms in the Koran*, Tokyo: Keio Institute, 1959.

—— *God and Man in the Koran*, Tokyo: Keio Institute, 1964.

LANE, E., *Manners and Customs of the Modern Egyptians*, Everyman Library, London: J. M. Dent & Sons, first issued 1908.

LAOUST, H., 'Le Reformisme orthodoxe des "Salafiyya" et les caractères généraux de son orientation actuelle', *Revue des Études musulmanes*, 1932, pp. 175–224.

LAPIDUS, I. M., *Muslim Cities in the Later Middle Ages*, Cambridge, Mass.: Harvard University Press, 1967.

LINGS, M., *A Moslem Saint of the Twentieth Century*, London: Allen & Unwin, 1961.

LUTFI AS-SAID, A., 'The Role of the *"ulema"* in Egypt in the Early Nineteenth Century', in Holt, *Political and Social Change*, pp. 264–80.

MACDONALD, D. B., *The Religious Attitude and Life in Islam*, Chicago, 1909 (reprinted by Khayats, Beirut, 1965).

MACDONALD, D. E., 'Hadra', *Shorter Encyclopaedia of Islam*, Leiden: E. J. Brill, 1953, p. 125.

MCPHERSON, J. W., *The Moulids of Egypt*, Cairo, 1941.

MANSFIELD, P., *Nasser's Egypt*, Harmondsworth: Penguin African Library, 1965.

MARTY, A., *Études sur l'Islam au Sénégal*, Tome 1, *Les Personnes*, Paris, 1917.

MASSIGNON, L., *Essai sur les origines du lexique technique de la mystique musulmane*, 2nd edn., Paris, 1954.

—— 'Tarika', *Encyclopaedia of Islam* (old edn.), vol. 4, Leiden: E. J. Brill, 1934, pp. 667–72.

MITCHELL, R. P., *The Society of the Muslim Brothers*, London: O.U.P., 1969.

MOLÉ, M., 'La danse extatique en Islam', in *Les danses sacrées*, Collections Sources Orientales, no. 6, Paris: Éditions du Seuil, 1963, pp. 147–280.

MONTEIL, V., *L'Islam noir*, Paris: Éditions du Seuil, 1964.

NASR, SEYYED HUSSEIN, *The Ideals and Realities of Islam*, New York: Praeger, 1967.

NICHOLSON, R. A., *Studies in Islamic Mysticism*, Cambridge: C.U.P., 1921.

O'BRIEN, P., *The Revolution in Egypt's Economic System*, London: O.U.P., 1966.

RAYMOND, A., 'Quartiers et mouvements populaires au Caire au xviiième siècle', in Holt, *Political and Social Change*, pp. 104–16.

SAFRAN, N., *Egypt in Search of Political Community*, Cambridge, Mass.: Harvard University Press, 1961.

SCHACHT, J., 'Shari'a', *Shorter Encyclopaedia of Islam*, Leiden: E. J. Brill, 1953, pp. 524–9.

SCHOLEM, G., *Major Trends in Jewish Mysticism*, Jerusalem, 1941.

SHAW, S. (ed. and trans.), *Ottoman Egypt in the Eighteenth Century; the Nizamname-i Misir of Cezzar Ahmed Pasha*, Cambridge, Mass.: Harvard University Press, 1964.

SUZUKI, D. T., *Essays in Zen Buddhism*, 2nd series, London: Luzac & Co., 1933.

TRITTON, A. S., 'Shaitan', *Encyclopaedia of Islam* (old edn.), vol. 4, Leiden: E. J. Brill, 1934, pp. 286–7.

3. ARABIC LANGUAGE BOOKS AND PERIODICALS

Al Manar, Vol. 7, Cairo: 1904.

Al Musawwar, 7 May 1965.

ALWAN, MUHAMMED MAHMUD, *at-Tasawwuf al Islami* [Islamic Mysticism], Cairo: 1958.

HUSAIN, TAHA, *Al Ayyam* [The Days], vols. 1 and 2, Cairo, 1958.

IBRAHIM SALAMA AR-RADI, *Murshid al Murid* [The Guidance of the Murid], Cairo, 1962.

SAIF AN-NASR, *as-Sira al Hamidiya* [The Biography of Sheikh Salama], Cairo, 1956.

SALAMA AR-RADI, *Qanun* [Laws], 2nd edn., Cairo, 1965.

INDEX